G000066428

TURNING THE KALEIDOSCOPE

PERSPECTIVES ON EUROPEAN JEWRY

TURNING THE KALEIDOSCOPE

PERSPECTIVES ON EUROPEAN JEWRY

Edited by
Sandra Lustig and Ian Leveson

Berghahn Books
New York • Oxford

First published in 2006 by

Berghahn Books

www.berghahnbooks.com

Library of Congress Cataloging-in-Publication Data

Turning the kaleidoscope : perspectives on European Jewry / edited by
Sandra H. Lustig and Ian Leveson.
   p. cm.
Includes bibliographical references and index.
ISBN 1-84545-076-0
   1. Jews--Europe--Identity. 2. Jews--Europe---History--20th century.
3. Jews--Europe--History--21st century. 4. Holocaust, Jewish
(1939-1945)--Influence. 5. Europe--Ethnic relations. I. Lustig,
Sandra H. II. Leveson, Ian.

DS135.B83T87 2006
305.892′404--dc22

                                                                2006040106

British Library Cataloguing in Publication Data

A catalogue record for this book is available from
the British Library.

Printed in the United States on acid-free paper

ISBN 1-84545-076-0 hardback

To my parents, Ernst Lustig (1921–1999) and Hanna R. Lustig, for raising me in a house full of books; to the memory of those who were murdered in the *Shoah*, and to those who lived through its horrors; and to the Jews of Europe, rebuilding Jewish life for ourselves and future generations.

Sandra Lustig

To the now almost vanished Dundee Jewish community where as a teenager I first learnt the meaning of collective Jewish responsibility, at least to assemble a minyan for Yom Kippur prayer, and to my father, Joseph Zvi ben Natan z"l (1923–1980) who inspired me to write and whose eloquence I still struggle to match.

Ian Leveson

Contents

Part III: The Jewish Space in Europe

ACKNOWLEDGEMENTS

A book like this one owes its very existence to many, many people. First and foremost, we would like to express our heartfelt gratitude to each and every one of the contributors. They gave most generously of their time to write. Without their hard work and dedication to this project, it would have remained a dream. In the course of editing this book, we have had the good fortune to get to know our contributors, a small network of Jewish thinkers across Europe. We are indebted to them for the opportunity to have worked with them on this project, and for all that we have learned in our discussions with them. Thank you all.

Some of the chapters began as papers presented at the conference *Galut 2000 – Towards a European Jewish Identity*, which was staged by Gesher – Forum for Diaspora Culture in Berlin on 5 and 6 December 1998. Several members of Gesher had been thinking about a conference on Diaspora issues for years, and these questions had been debated eagerly in Gesher again and again. When Nicola Galliner, Director of the *Jüdische Volkshochschule* (Adult Education Centre of the Jewish Community Berlin) offered us partial funding in the summer of 1998, we jumped at the idea and enthusiastically went to work, bringing together speakers from across Europe. The conference attracted approximately a hundred participants. It was made possible by additional support from *Partner für Berlin*, Barcomi's/Bravo/TriBeCa Foods as well as Star Bakery & Coffee. (*Galut 2000* was Gesher's largest project. The group is no longer active.)

Even though we could invite the speakers only at very short notice, they agreed to participate in the conference – without an honorarium, and some even contributed part or all of their travel expenses. The speakers at the conference whose papers have become parts of this book are Diana Pinto, Michael Galchinsky, Göran Rosenberg, and Y. Michal Bodemann. The other speakers, without whom the conference could not have taken place, were Robert Braun, Tom Freudenheim, Jacqueline Goldberg, Zinowy Kogan, Emmanuel Moses, and Bogna Pawlisz. In addition, Talin Bahçivanoğlu and Sevim Celebi shared their thoughts as discussants in a workshop on relations between minorities. Their Armenian and Turkish perspectives enriched the discussion immensely. Many thanks also to Axel Azzola.

Of course, gratitude is due to all those members of Gesher as well as others who were involved in making *Galut 2000* happen, both on stage and behind it, including Ewa Alfred, Michael Anthony, Hartmut Bomhoff, Michael Dollendorf, Michael Frajman (a co-initiator of the conference, who unfortunately died shortly before publication of this volume), Julia Friedrich, Eszter Gantner, Ronnie Golz, Gabriel Heimler, Sylvie Kajdi, Elisa Klapheck, Jonathan Laurence, Dr Thomas Müller, Judith Orland, and Richard Tarasofsky. Hartmut Bomhoff and Dr Thomas Müller deserve mention for their efforts to assist in the early phases of preparing the manuscript.

And of course, Marion Berghahn and her staff at Berghahn Books were wonderful to work with.

A word of thanks is also due to all those who helped keep our spirits up during the long process of editing this book. When we were searching for contributors for some of the papers, we spoke to a number of people who said, 'Now that's an interesting topic! I know nothing about it. And I can't think of anyone who's working in that field. But do let me know when the book comes out, because I want to read it!' Such conversations confirmed our suspicion that we were onto a field that deserves thought and has the potential to excite people, and they encouraged us to persevere and complete this book.

Lastly, we would like to thank all those people close to us for tolerating how we set our priorities during the many long months of putting this book together in our free time. Myra Leveson and Leslie Shaidnagle in particular housed and fed us while we retreated to Badenscallie, to Hanover, and to Schlanstedt to work on the manuscript. All in all, this book project turned out to be a larger hobby than we had anticipated, but in the end, we feel fortunate to have taken it on.

Sandra Lustig and Ian Leveson

INTRODUCTION

Sandra Lustig and Ian Leveson

Being Jewish, in Europe, in Diaspora, as a minority, today: these themes are at the centre of *Turning the Kaleidoscope – Perspectives on European Jewry*. The contributions to this book address, more particularly, the following questions. How can we delineate our collective Jewish identity while honouring the differences in the ways we live as Jews? What does living in Diaspora, and choosing to do so, mean for us? How do we perceive ourselves as European Jews, as distinct from Israeli or North American Jews? How has European Jewry developed since the rupture of the *Shoah*? How do we relate to our non-Jewish surroundings? How have we experienced living as part of a minority in different parts of Europe? Are our experiences comparable to those of other minorities? What does living in Europe, with its history of persecuting Jews, mean for us today, sixty years after the *Shoah*, whose after-effects we still experience, but which does not have the same central and defining position in our lives as it did and still does for our parents' and grandparents' generations? What are the effects on the European Diaspora of the collapse of the socialist regimes in Eastern Europe? What forms and significance does our relationship to Israel have? How has that relationship changed due to the Middle East conflict in recent years, and how has that conflict influenced the way Jews and others in Europe view and interact with each other? What effect does it have for those of us who are engaged in creative work, be it artistic, musical, writing, or research, that we live in Diaspora in Europe, in places where the *Shoah* was planned and executed, shattering so much of our Jewish heritage and culture? What consequences may all this have today and in the future?

Turning the Kaleidoscope – Perspectives on European Jewry is based on the premise that the history, current situation, and development of Jewry in Europe are distinctive enough to characterise European Jewry as a collective entity. This view is not at all commonplace; on the contrary. Especially from outside Europe, the continent is often seen as a place basically devoid of Jews; many assume that European Jews all emigrated or perished in the *Shoah*. However, the approximately two million Jews in

Europe today form a meaningful fraction of world Jewry, compared with five million in Israel, 5.5 million in the United States, and smaller Jewish populations elsewhere. In terms of Jewish culture, Europe is sometimes termed a void, overlooking the fact that Jews have been keeping Jewish culture alive here, even in the difficult years following the *Shoah*. At times, the Jewish view from outside Europe even seems to be that Europe is a place to be avoided because of its bloody history. This applies especially to countries like Germany and Austria because of their active roles in the *Shoah*. Europe thus seems to be alternately a blank space on the map, or a black hole. For example, the Institute of the World Jewish Congress published a special edition of *Gesher – Journal of Jewish Affairs* entitled 'The Jewish People at the Threshold of the New Millennium', which discusses various issues in Israel and the U.S., but does not even mention Europe as such, and only two articles out of the twenty-eight published in this edition are about individual European countries (Shafir 2001).

Such a negative stance towards Europe ignores the fact that Judaism is to a considerable extent a European religion; much of Judaism and Jewish culture was developed in Europe. Haskalah, Ladino, klezmer, Reform Judaism, Yiddish, Bundism, Hasidism, gefilte fish, and the Frankfurt School were all created in Europe. Indeed, two of the largest cultural groups of Jews – Sephardim and Ashkenazim – are both of European origin. Jewish culture blossomed in various places across Europe through the centuries: medieval Spain, nineteenth-century Salonika, and the great centres of learning in Germany, Poland, and Lithuania, to name just a few examples.

In fact, a substantial percentage of the world's Jewry actually is European or of European descent. Going back just a very few generations, many Jews have European ancestors. Of course, there was migration and emigration, and Jews left Europe for good reason. They took their European heritage with them, and handed down more or less of it to the following generations, in the form of language, forms of religious practice, humour, cuisine, ethics, artefacts, and so on. But Jews have continued to live in Europe; not all of them are gone. Some parts of Europe house the fractured remnants of a sometimes glorious Jewish past, still struggling more or less successfully to rebuild Jewish life. Other places in Europe were spared the destruction wrought in the *Shoah*, and Jewish life there could continue with less difficulty. And Jews have migrated across Europe and to and from other parts of the world.

The discussions in this book are founded on the premise that European Jewry can and indeed should form a third pillar of Jewry alongside the pillars of Israel and North America. For this, the combined Jewish population is large enough and shares a common European heritage and culture. Yet, if European Jewry is to form a third pillar of Jewry next to Israeli and North American Jewry, it will have to be a pillar of a different nature. Diversity is and must be the defining feature of European Jewry, to a far greater extent than elsewhere: after all, Europe itself is home to a host of different cultures, each rooted deep in time. The Jewries in each of those cultures embody unique combinations of Jewish culture and the culture around them. Diversity among Jews, too, can be found in even the smallest communities in Europe. (Five very different European Jewish communities are sketched out by the panellists in Chapter 6, the panel discussion 'Left Over – Living after the *Shoah*: (Re-)Building Jewish Life in Europe'.) Viewed close up, the diversity may seem so great that it obscures commonalities. But from a bird's-eye view, European Jews' Europeanness becomes visible (for instance, as discussed by *Clive A. Lawton*, especially in regard to forms of organising Jewish communities), and the quality of being European does set them apart from Jews in other places in the world. Therefore, Europe should be regarded as a meaningful entity for Jewry. The contributors to this book explore what that might entail.

Of course, Israel's Jewish population is diverse, too, but Israel is a largely Jewish society, unlike any society in Europe. In North America there are many places with substantial numbers of Jews, and there are no fewer than nine cities with a Jewish population greater than all of Germany's, which is Europe's fifth largest, at more than a hundred thousand. With large numbers of Jews present, like-minded Jews can form and run congregations and other organisations of their own that can coexist with each other (on better or worse terms). In places with fewer Jews, like most places in Europe, that is far more difficult, if not impossible. Both in Israel and in North America there are unifying cultures: Jews may be Reform or Orthodox, for example, but they are all Israelis or Canadians or U.S. Americans. In Europe they may be Conservative and French, or Orthodox and Greek, or secular and Russian, and so on, and many more combinations do exist. In Israel, Jews speak Hebrew as their everyday language; in North America they speak English (or French, in Francophone Canada). But in Europe a unifying language is lacking. Neither Hebrew nor Ladino nor Yiddish are commonly spoken. English is often the lingua franca, but for most it is a foreign language, and many Europeans do not speak English fluently. Even simple communication between Jews in Europe is not easy.

Since the early 1990s, Judaism and Jewishness seem to have become fashionable, with a plethora of books, conferences, films, TV series, festivals, and other events on some sort of Jewish theme. This has given rise to another misperception of the state of Jewry in Europe, namely that Jewish life is blossoming, that the tense relations between Jews and non-Jews in the aftermath of the *Shoah* have relaxed into a state of mutual goodwill, and that anti-Semitism has been overcome. Unfortunately, this view is too rosy. The third section of this book, 'The Jewish Space in Europe', is devoted to the complex relations between Jewry and our non-Jewish surroundings in Europe today. Despite the attention paid to Jewish themes, there has been little discussion about the state and future of Jewry in Europe as a whole. What discussion there is appears to have been confined largely to strategic thinking by the official bodies representing Jewry (e.g. anon. 1997). A few books with chapters on current-day Jewish communities in different places in Europe (Tye 2001; Ungar-Klein 2000)[1] or with a more anecdotal, journalistic approach (Kurlansky 1995) do exist, but there is nothing comprehensive. The editors of this volume have identified just three books concerned with Jewry in Europe today: *Jewish Identities in the New Europe* (Webber 1994), which is based on a conference in 1992, *Jewish Centers and Peripheries: Europe between America and Israel Fifty Years After World War II* (Troen 1999), and *New Jewish Identities. Contemporary Europe and Beyond* (Gitelman, Kosmin, and Kovács 2003).

The themes of diversity and change over time captured in the title of this book are currents that run through European Jewry in the past as well as the present, and we believe they will continue to do so in the future. But how to describe these themes succinctly? 'Hodgepodge' is just a jumble and lacks the positive connotations we believe are essential, and 'mishmash' is definitely too negative. 'Mosaic mosaic' may be catchy, but conveys a static image, one set in stone. 'Patchwork' might fit, yet much of the stitching has come apart, and some of the pieces have been worn thin, while others are woven strong. Furthermore, Europe is certainly no 'melting pot'. The kaleidoscope metaphor conveys a positive, colourful, ever-changing image, as the pieces inside move, mirror, and bounce off each other, representing the diversity of European Jews' customs, traditions, languages, and so on, as well as the variety of their interactions. One might even discuss whether the force that makes the kaleidoscope turn is a deity, or the actions of human beings, or simply the passing of time. Judaism allows room for all these interpretations.

The kaleidoscope metaphor applies to this book as well, in several ways. A kaleidoscope of topics is discussed, most of them with a pan-European view of a particular issue. The chapters are organised in three sections, as follows.

Overarching Questions are asked in the first section and set the stage for the discussions that follow. Diana Pinto explores 'A New Role for Jews in Europe: Challenges and Responsibilities'; Clive Lawton takes up Jews' models of community organisation in Europe in comparison with those in Israel and North America; Michael Galchinsky examines 'Concepts of Diaspora and Galut'; Lars Dencik investigates '"Homo Zappiens": A European-Jewish Way of Life in the Era of Globalisation'; and Göran Rosenberg discusses 'Israel and Diaspora: From Solution to Problem'.

Inner-Jewish Concerns: Rebuilding and Continuity are the subject of the second section. The first chapter in this section documents a panel discussion held at the Bet Debora conference in 2001 on the theme 'Left Over – Living after the *Shoah*: (Re-)building Jewish Life in Europe', chaired and edited by Sandra Lustig. It is followed by Elisa Klapheck and Lara Dämmig illuminating how they came to initiate the Bet Debora conferences which bring together women rabbis, cantors, Jewish scholars, and activists from across Europe, and what the conferences have achieved. Finally, Y. Michal Bodemann poses the question, 'A Jewish Cultural Renascence in Germany?'

The Jewish Space in Europe examines the relationships between Jewry and our non-Jewish environment. This section takes the form of a debate between Diana Pinto and the editors of this volume. Pinto's chapter 'The Jewish Space in Europe' inspired Ian Leveson and Sandra Lustig to develop their thoughts in their co-authored chapter 'Caught Between Civil Society and the Cultural Market: Jewry and the Jewish Space in Europe'. Sandra Lustig separately analyses a single dispute to illuminate for an English-language audience the intricacies of the relationships between Jews and non-Jews in Germany in '"The Germans Will Never Forgive the Jews for Auschwitz". When Things Go Wrong in the Jewish Space: the Case of the Walser-Bubis Debate'.

The authors, too, form a kaleidoscope of sorts. With one exception (Michael Galchinsky) they live in Europe, but in many different countries. Indeed, many of them have lived in more than one country, something not at all unusual for current-day Jews in Europe. And their parents and grandparents are often from different countries yet again. The countries where the authors (and discussion panellists) live or have lived include Sweden, Hungary, France, England, Germany, Denmark, Italy, Scotland, Switzerland, the Netherlands, Norway, Ireland, and Austria, as well as Israel, Canada, and the United States. Including their parents' former countries of residence, this extensive, but presumably incomplete, list expands to include Slovakia, Poland, Russia, and Argentina.

The authors' disciplinary backgrounds cover a broad spectrum, including sociology, intellectual history, urban planning, social psychology, economic geography, rabbinic training, public policy, and library science. Just as varied are their current professional occupations: research, administration, writing, environmental policy consulting, academic teaching, journalism, and network services management. Accordingly, this book features a kaleidoscope of writing styles and forms, ranging from essays to polemics, fully referenced academic papers, and a panel discussion. The authors were asked to pitch their pieces to a generally educated reader who is not a specialist in the contributor's field. Their individual styles also reflect different intellectual traditions and ways of thinking typical of the various cultures of Europe, as well as their diverse academic backgrounds.

The authors live their Judaism in a variety of ways, in a religious sense, but also in terms of dealing with Jewish issues professionally. Some work for Jewish organisations. Some are activists outside the mainstream Jewish establishment, and some write on Jewish themes from time to time. Accordingly, the authors view Jewish issues in Europe from various perspectives and in diverse contexts. All share a passionate concern for

Jewry and Judaism today and in the future, and all enjoy lively discussion about this issue.

Of course, *Turning the Kaleidoscope* cannot claim to cover the entire spectrum of views and issues concerning Jewry in Europe, nor is that the goal of this book. Rather, it seeks to open up new avenues of thought about the many questions relating to European perspectives on Jewry and to spark discussion and debate. The editors hope that others will be inspired to write on European Jewry, and that more and more voices will be heard. Only if we know more about each other as Jews in Europe, and only if we understand the diverse situations in which Jews live and their multitude of opinions and ways of thinking, can we begin to strengthen Jewry as a European entity.

Some themes could be touched on only briefly in this volume, and others had to be omitted entirely. Both Israel-Diaspora relations and gender issues could fill volumes on their own, for example. While neither spirituality nor religion per se are discussed, several authors did link their thoughts to these themes: Michael Galchinsky goes into traditional understanding and meanings of Diaspora and galut. In 'Debora's Disciples', Lara Dämmig and Elisa Klapheck show how, in exploring new and old forms of practising Judaism, they rediscovered parts of Jewish heritage they had been unaware of before. Anti-Semitism, too, is discussed only briefly. Ian Leveson and Sandra Lustig touch on some aspects of anti-Semitism in 'Caught Between Civil Society and the Cultural Market: Jewry and the Jewish Space in Europe', and Sandra Lustig dissects an instance of intellectual anti-Semitism in '"The Germans Will Never Forgive the Jews for Auschwitz". When Things Go Wrong in the Jewish Space: the Case of the Walser-Bubis Debate'. Unfortunately anti-Semitism has come to be of more immediate concern to Jews in Europe, too, since the second Intifada began in 2000 and also since the terrorist attacks of 11 September 2001. Analyses of the forms that present-day anti-Semitism takes (including Islamicist anti-Semitism, which is growing in Europe) and of different ways Jews and society at large might respond to it would be worth more detailed discussion as well as effective action. While Lars Dencik does touch on these issues in his chapter, further in-depth work is necessary.

Whether or not Jews constitute a minority in the European context is ambiguous. In terms of numbers, Jews are clearly a minority and, in most places in Europe, a very small one at that. In terms of belonging or not belonging to the majority, and of being singled out for discrimination or not, the situation is more complicated. Since the Enlightenment, many Jews have chosen the strategy of trying to blend in with the majority and to take full part in society as citizens who happen to be of a particular religion. That strategy is beginning to be questioned, for instance in a position paper by the Institute for Jewish Policy Research in London, which suggests that Jews should define themselves as an ethnic group in a multicultural society, that is, that they give up the position of being invisible in terms of difference or of being part of the privileged majority (Institute for Jewish Policy Research 2000, recommendation 1). Sweden, for example, has granted Swedish Jews the status as one of five national minorities (see Chapter 4). It would be interesting to survey across Europe how Jews feel about being considered a minority – officially or unofficially – and what effects this might have on their self-identification and identification by others, as well as on Jewish life, for example, through financing and management of Jewish institutions.

Another issue not discussed in this book is whether the Jews can or should be considered a small nation, comparable to the historically resilient nations like the Scots or the Basques, for the simple reason that the editors were unable to find a contributor for this subject. Unfortunately, this volume omits analysis of Central and Eastern Europe and chapters by authors living in the postsocialist societies there, though panellist Andrea Pető does speak about Hungary in Chapter 6. Likewise, countries with very small Jewish populations are largely unrepresented, although their perspectives would also be necessary to gain a more comprehensive image of Jewry in Europe today.

A comprehensive sociological survey of European Jewry since 1945 would have been a valuable addition, but too voluminous to be handled in a single chapter. The editors hope that others will undertake such research and publish the results. To date, there is no publication that systematically examines not only the numbers of Jews in various places across Europe since 1945 and their migrations, but also how the Jews integrated into their new environments, their ways of practising Judaism, their concerns relating to a multitude of Jewish issues, and the changing nature of Jewish organisations over time in various places.[2]

Clearly, European Jewry will be a rewarding subject for research for years to come. We encourage others to fill the gaps that *Turning the Kaleido-scope* has made apparent.

European Jews and Jewry

The development of Jewry and Judaism in Europe since 1945 is the story of the salvaging of remnants of a destroyed civilisation, the rebuilding of institutional structures which collapsed when their members fled or were murdered. (When we write of 'rebuilding' or 'recovering' Jewish life and Jewish institutions in this introduction, we do *not* mean to imply that what was destroyed in the *Shoah* is to be replicated. What was destroyed is gone. What is rebuilt draws on what was destroyed, but is not the same. It is something new and should be appropriate to today's circumstances.) But it is also an informal story of families, of survivors and their children dealing individually and collectively with the trauma of losing relatives, friends, home towns, and homelands, and of their experiences and emotions. While post-war Europe was able to revive fairly quickly (at least in the West), Jewish life recovered much more slowly because of the extent and nature of its destruction. Therefore, Jewish history follows different time patterns and scales than that of the European population at large. Of particular relevance to Jews have been the attempts by successive generations to deal with the *Shoah*, the founding and 'coming of age' of the state of Israel, and the changes in the composition of Jewry in Western Europe because of the new Diasporas which have moved here from various and diverse places.

Since 1945, the most immediate concern for European Jewry has been to rebuild or re-found families and communities shattered by the *Shoah*. In the first post-war decades, survivors, especially those who remained in Europe, were predominantly concerned with rebuilding their lives. This rebuilding process is a defining feature of those Jewish Diasporas in Europe which were affected by the *Shoah*, and it is far from complete. The task of rebuilding not just religious life, but Jewry in its entirety, including centres of learning and teaching, intellectual life, and non-religious traditions and organisations will remain a task for generations to come. Many aspects of rebuilding Jewish religious, community, and secular life were covered in the panel discussion 'Left Over – Living after the Shoah: (Re-)Building Jewish Life in Europe' (Chapter 6). Speaking about their experiences in five different places and types of communities, the panellists addressed a number of questions, including: what were their experiences in initiating new communities or founding groups, how might one confront myths, and how might Jewish schools actually endanger the development of homegrown Jewish leadership?

Indeed, the debates we are reopening in terms of European Jews and Jewry have a long history, despite having been silenced for a time by the *Shoah*. Following the Enlightenment and Emancipation, Jewry confronted the dilemmas of combining life outside the kehillah with the laws of the Torah. Jewry later also confronted the issues of modernism, socialism, and nationalism. The results of these confrontations were the development of various movements – including the religious Reform and *Haskalah* movements, Modern and Neo-Orthodoxy, Zionism and Bundism, as well as assimilation, if not conversion to Christianity – and vigourous discussions between their respective adherents. Today we must incorporate into those debates the experiences of the *Shoah*, as well as those of the period since then, and we must attempt to bridge the rupture that the *Shoah* caused in the discussions themselves.

Six decades have passed since the *Shoah*, and two generations have been born. As representatives of the 'second generation', our concern has been to establish ourselves and, after deciding to stay here in Europe, to start to think, together with the 'third generation', about what sort of Jewish life we wish to see here now and in the future. Since the Iron Curtain was drawn back, the generation that experienced the Second World War and the *Shoah* as young adults or at least as teenagers has handed over power to a generation without personal experience of that time. This generational transfer, common to the political and religious communities, introduces a new quality into the debates (about the *Shoah* and other issues), both within the Jewish community and between it and the non-Jewish world. Essentially, the *Shoah* does not have the same central place in our lives that it did for our parents' and grandparents' generations; nonetheless, it has a stronger influence on us than on coming generations, because of our closer personal contact with our parents and grandparents.

In the decades following the establishment of the state of Israel, European Jewry devoted attention and resources to supporting the fledgling state. In the aftermath of the *Shoah*, the future of Jewry in Europe was unclear, and the image of 'living with packed suitcases' was not an exaggeration. This was particularly true in Germany, where the prevailing view was that it was wrong to stay in the land of the perpetrators, and indeed most Jews left for Israel or other countries. A generation of post-war Jews grew up focusing on *aliyah*. Their creative energies were lost for the European Jewish communities (see Chapters 1, 5, and 8).

Half a century later, in the 1990s, and with the Oslo peace process looking promising, Israel had become securely established, had a mature independent economy, and its status had become more or less recognised by the surrounding countries, making it seem less reliant on support from the Diaspora. It was stated frequently that the suitcases were now unpacked, both in the literal and the figurative senses, whether or not that was true. European Jews' concentration on Israel decreased (see Chapter 5). Slowly, the Diaspora communities in Europe, no longer eclipsed by Israel, began coming into their own and shifted their priorities towards their own development (anon. 1997). Things have changed again since the second Intifada began in 2000. There again seems to be more of a view that Israel needs support from the Diaspora. Yet it seems less and less a viable option for most Jews to make *aliyah*, given the serious security situation and the resulting faltering economy. With this in mind, strengthening Jewish life in the European Diaspora is apt to remain a priority for European Jewry.

The difficulties of reconstructing Jewish communities have been most dramatic in Eastern Europe. Not only were the numbers of Jews lost there much greater than in Western Europe, but during the era of state socialism that followed the *Shoah*, religious activity was made difficult. The consequence was a deeper breach of the connection with the vibrant Jewish culture of the past, a theme developed in more depth by Diana Pinto in Chapter 1. The collapse of the state socialist regimes in Central and Eastern Europe has provided Jews there with opportunities to live more openly as Jews and to (re)create Jewish communities and institutions that have not existed since the *Shoah*. The challenge of rebuilding poses questions of Jewish identity in new ways, and many Jews in Central and Eastern Europe are only now discovering their Jewish backgrounds and developing their Jewish identities. For most of the Jews living there today, this is a very new situation.

The former Soviet Union is a somewhat different case. While the very large Jewish population in the former Pale of Settlement, which was largely overrun by German troops in the Second World War, shared a history of destruction with Eastern Europe, Jews in the rest of the Soviet Union did not suffer the annihilation of the *Shoah*. In addition, the difficulties which the Soviet system made for the continuation of Jewish religious life, particularly under Stalin, lasted a generation longer than in other parts of Eastern Europe. Even today, the situation of Jews in the Commonwealth of Independent States remains difficult.

One of the major challenges in those parts of Europe affected by the *Shoah*, and particularly in Eastern Europe, has been finding the expertise and teaching support needed to reestablish Jewish traditions, especially in the variety which would be necessary to ensure that the previous cultural and religious diversity is reflected in what is being rebuilt. Given the lack of professionals trained in many of these European traditions and the paucity of training facilities in Europe, rabbis and cantors from North America and Israel have assisted Europe's Jews with reconstruction, and they have brought their non-European traditions with them. One might ask whether the help offered by agencies based in the U.S. or Israel is always appropriate in meeting local needs. Outside agencies would be in the best position to succeed if they respected the local situation and offered help tailored to it. A partnership model may be appropriate here, where the individuals and organisations offering support are also prepared to learn from the communities that they assist. In any case, simply transposing concepts, forms of Jewish life, ready-made solutions, or even conflicts between Jewish religious movements from one country to another, whether within Europe, or from the U.S. or Israel to European countries, may not be adequate to nurture the development of (possibly new) local traditions.

Today it is virtually impossible to identify a specific mode of being a European Jew, much less a specifically European Judaism. Both 'European' and 'Jewish' are categories that display rich variety. Thus diversity constitutes a defining characteristic of European Jewry. Consider, for example, the Bulgarians, the Irish, the French, and the Finns – all European nationalities; Hanseatic, Mediterranean, state socialist, Celtic – all European cultures; as well as the Hungarian *Neolog*, the secular, the Liberal, and the Haredi – all Jewish religious convictions; Mizrachim, Sephardim, Ashkenazim – all Jewish cultural groups. Where such categories intersect, the kaleidoscope of Jewish Europeans and European Jews appears.

There are the old established Sephardi communities in the Netherlands and Britain, constituted by direct descendants of the Spanish and Portuguese Sephardim. There are the remnants of the Western Ashkenazi communities still present in Germany, France, and Italy. In Britain and France, there are the descendants of the Eastern Ashkenazi who came at the end of the nineteenth century. There are the vestiges, following the *Shoah*, of the Ashkenazi communities of German-occupied Europe, either still in Central and Eastern Europe or further west, where Displaced Persons or their descendants settled. Among the more recent arrivals are the large north African Sephardic community in France, the Jews from the former Soviet Union who have arrived in Germany in the last ten years – be they observant Uzbeki Mizrachim or assimilated secular Moscovites – the Israelis, many of whom live also in Germany, and others such as Polish Jews who left Poland in the mid-1950s and late 1960s, as well as Iranians who moved to Europe following the Iranian Revolution. In addition, there are those refugees to other parts of the world who returned to Europe.

These communities defy easy categorisation as well. For example, some have a strong and living Jewish tradition, while others have lost their connections to it or were weakened by the *Shoah* to such an extent that their tradition has died out. Some were affected directly by the *Shoah*, while others were not. The communities' forms of religious practice vary, as do the ramifications of such practice, for example, with regard to the roles of women in the Jewish community. (Incidentally, the Hasidic movement is neither the norm nor do its adherents constitute the majority for any of the communities mentioned here.) Some of these communities lived under state socialist regimes while others did not. Some lived in the developing world, while others experienced industrialisation generations ago. The importance and tradition of secular education varies for the different communities as well.

That diversity is a defining feature of European Jewry is nothing new. Before the *Shoah*, the majority of the world's Jews lived in Europe and had developed clear-cut and lively traditions with many local variations. The adherents of many of these traditions were killed in the *Shoah*, leaving individual survivors who could neither reconstruct those traditions as a whole on their own, nor hand them on to the next generation in a living form. In many places in Europe, the Jewish population is so small that in any given town or city there are only enough Jews to support at most a single minyan, for example, rather than both a Liberal and an Orthodox one. In places where the Jewish population is large enough to support a diversity of communities, each of those communities is made up of fairly like-minded Jews. But where there are fewer Jews, people with greater differences in their practice of Judaism have to join forces to create a Jewish community at all. One consequence of this is that some Jews do not feel that they can belong to the local Jewish community as it represents an interpretation of Judaism that is not theirs.

It is not uncommon for Jews in Europe not to be community members. In the Netherlands, for example, just 27 percent of the country's forty-five thousand Jews are community members (Kruyer, in Chapter 6). Sociologist Y. Michal Bodemann estimates that in Berlin alone, there are about ten thousand Jews or people of partly Jewish origin who are not community members, compared with more than eleven thousand members of the Jewish Community. It is estimated that 'membership in the Jewish Community is merely a third of what it would be if all those eligible for membership in the Stockholm area were to join' (Narrowe 1999: 181). In countries like Hungary, where 90 percent of the Jewish community describes itself as non-religious (Petö, in Chapter 6), the numbers of community members are apt to represent just a small minority of the total number of Jews. The reasons for not joining the local Jewish community may vary, for example: a self-identification as being Jewish, but not in the religious sense; the absence of a rabbi of one's own persuasion; a dislike of the politics within the Jewish community; a fear of having one's name on a list of Jews, in case Jews are persecuted again; or the cost of membership, which may be fairly high. Yet Jews who decide not to join a Jewish community do not necessarily lack interest in Jewish life, in having Jewish friends, or in undertaking Jewish religious or cultural activities. If there were more Jewish activities independent of the Jewish communities, these Jews may become more involved than they are now. Apparently, with a substantial fraction of Jews choosing not to be members of the Jewish communities, the communities are failing to meet the needs of these people. Maybe the communities need to change to meet those needs; perhaps those Jews are happy not to be affiliated with an official Jewish community, but would nonetheless like to be part of Jewish life.

Many of Europe's Jewish communities face a common issue: continuity. This is partly an issue of sheer numbers: the birth rate is often far lower than the death rate in communities small and large. Especially those countries with a small Jewish population cannot 'provide' marriage partners for all those Jews wishing to marry Jews, and in close-knit communities, people may be reluctant to marry someone they met in kindergarten. Here, too, diversity complicates things. Not only are the numbers of potential partners small, but singles who live their Judaism in very different ways, for example, as secular Jews and as devout Jews, are unlikely to make good matches. This is one reason why intermarriage is a common phenomenon. Bernard Wasserstein considers the demographic development of post-war Jewry in Europe to be so threatening that he titled his book on the subject *Vanishing Diaspora* (Wasserstein 1996). Because of high rates of intermarriage, there are many children with one Jewish parent, and Wasserstein asserts that most of them do not and will not consider themselves Jewish. In the past, emigration from Eastern Europe to Western Europe buoyed the numbers of Jews there, but he doubts that that will occur at meaningful rates in the future. He concludes that European Jewry is 'fading away' (p. 290), that this is 'the last act of more than a millennium of Jewish life in Eastern Europe' (p. 283) and 'the end of an authentic Jewish culture in Europe' (p. 284).

That the number of Jews living in Europe today is much, much lower than before the *Shoah* cannot be disputed, and that their numbers are dropping appears to be a reality as well. But continuity is not just a matter of numbers. It is also a question of keeping Jews interested in Judaism – or engaging their interest in the first place. It is a matter of the Jewish communities and other Jewish organisations recognising the realities of today's Jews' lives and adapting to their needs. Jewry cannot afford to close out Jews; we need each and every Jewish person if Jewry is to prosper. Jewish organisations should consider whether their programmes to reach out to unaffiliated Jews – insofar as such efforts exist at all – are attractive to their target group. A particularly contentious issue in this context is intermarriage, especially in those parts of Europe where inter-marriage tends to mean that *Shoah* victims' descendants marry *Shoah* perpetrators' descendents. Compared to the situation in the U.S., for example, where many Jewish families were not directly affected by the *Shoah* and many non-Jewish families have no connection to it whatsoever, this situation can make intermarriage much more contentious for the families and communities on both sides. At the same time, some Jews feel they have no alternative to intermarriage, given the paucity of Jewish potential marriage partners. Furthermore, whether or not a person is Jewish is but one criterion among many – albeit an important one – when choosing a partner. Love certainly can flower across religious, ethnic, and/or cultural boundaries; intermarried couples need to find ways to deal with the issues that arise. How the Jewish communities respond is critical for Jewish continuity. Are the non-Jewish spouses required to convert? Are they welcomed into the Jewish community in some way, whether or not they convert? Are their children welcomed? Or are they not recognised as proper Jews and discriminated against for that reason? Even when the mother is Jewish and the children are thus halachically Jewish, the answers to these questions are not at all clear. These are tricky issues for everyone involved, and if they are not handled very carefully, they will result in some Jews feeling alienated and even turning away from involvement in things Jewish. That cannot be the desired result.

Finally, at issue in Europe today is not only continuity of population or continuity of Judaism as a whole, but continuity of the kaleidoscope of European Jewish traditions. When conceiving efforts to maintain continuity, for example Jewish education for children, youth, and adults, it is essential to keep in mind the large variety of traditions of the Jews in most places.

At present there seems to be a lack of awareness among ordinary Jews, that is, Jews who do not hold any official position, about their representation at the European level. Of course, pan-European Jewish representative bodies do exist, for example the European Council of Jewish Communities (ECJC) and the European Jewish Congress (EJC), a branch of the World Jewish Congress. Yet it is not widely known what they do. Indeed, many Jews are unaware of even the most basic information about them, if they have ever heard of them at all. The ECJC's mission is to support social development in Jewish communities across Europe, and the EJC is the representative body of Europe's Jews. One reason for the lack of awareness on the part of ordinary Jews is that they vote only for the representatives at the level of their own community. In Germany, for example, it is then the community representatives who elect their representatives to the Zentralrat der Juden in Deutschland (Central Council of Jews in Germany), and the Zentralrat, in turn, elects representatives to the EJC. Only if a community's representative to the Zentralrat reports on matters discussed by that body are community members even informed of what their representatives at the national level do, since the Zentralrat's meetings are closed to the public, as are the minutes of its meetings and even their agendas (Klapheck 2002). The activities of the European bodies seem even more remote. Elazar describes them as 'weak to moderately functioning pan-European leagues' (Elazar 1999: 424). Also, they represent only those Jews who are community members.

Given that the official representative bodies appear not be linked well to the Jewish populations that they represent, they cannot perform the function of helping to forge connections between ordinary Jews across Europe. Perhaps they do not see that as their responsibility. It seems to have taken until 1997 for the two biggest Western European Jewish communities, those in France and the U.K., to realise that there was a European perspective waiting for them, despite the fact that twenty years had passed since the U.K. had joined the European Communities (anon. 1997 and untitled article on the first encounter of French and British Jews. *JPR News*. Institute for Jewish Policy Research. [Summer 1998]). Yet such linkages between Jews in different countries in Europe are desirable, even essential, for furthering Jewish life in all its varied manifestations. If that is an agreed goal, then networking among Jews should become a focus of activity for rebuilding Jewish life in Europe. The international contacts that have been developed in post-war Europe are the formal ones of national organisations, not the informal ones of business, friendship, marriage, or mutual interest. Such less formal networks, however, are the ones that would create meaningful contact between ordinary Jews. Finally, the existence of informal networks would be a way of encouraging those Jews who are not members of Jewish communities to be more involved in Jewish life. One example of a place where Jewish people could potentially form a network is the Bet Debora conferences, where ordinary Jewish women as well as Jewish professionals used the opportunity to meet and connect (see Chapters 6 and 7). Another example is the Limmud[3] conferences in Britain: the annual five-day conference is open to all Jews, and about two thousand of them participate in literally hundreds of workshops, lectures, and so on, on a wealth of topics, and meet and network with other Jews and Jewish organisations. There are also smaller Limmud meetings in various parts of the country.

Relationships between Jewry and the Non-Jewish Environment

Not only are there many Jewish Diasporas in Europe with few links between them, but there are also many different non-Jewish environments in which Jews live. European countries' cultures, histories, and general attitudes towards Jews, as well as languages, customs, etc., vary, as do Jews' relationships with those non-Jewish environments. In the early years following the *Shoah*, and when the state of Israel was still fighting for its existence, many European Jews focused on Israel and paid less attention to the non-Jewish environments surrounding them. Now that the attention of European Jews has shifted back towards Europe, their relationships with the cultures around them have become more important.

'Judaism survived for millennia precisely because it grew organically by confronting the challenges of the outside world', writes Diana Pinto in Chapter 9. Interactions with the non-Jewish environment are no less important today, and the fact that many of the chapters in this book discuss these interactions underlines this statement. Only a minority of the authors (Clive Lawton, Michael Galchinsky, and Lara Dämmig and Elisa Klapheck) deal entirely with issues internal to Judaism and Jewry. Two of the most important facets of these interactions today are anti-Semitism and the Jewish Space.

Unfortunately anti-Semitism still taints the relationship between Jewry and its non-Jewish environment in many places. There was state-sponsored or state-tolerated anti-Semitism in Poland and the USSR in the post-war decades. Albeit less virulent anti-Semitism existed in many of the other state socialist regimes in Central and Eastern European countries as well. Today there is open and politically organised anti-Semitism in Russia. In Western Europe there is less open anti-Semitism, although it has been increasing again since the second Intifada began in 2000 and the terrorist attacks on 11 September 2001. This new wave of anti-Semitism has not stopped short of physical attacks on Jews and firebombing of Jewish buildings. In particular, the rise in such attacks in France has been covered in the media. In addition, less violent forms of anti-Semitism have continued to exist.

There has also been a resurgence of nationalism leading to the re-establishment of extreme right-wing parties as serious and permanent features on the political scene (see Chapter 4). The level of potential support for these views lies between about 15 and 25 percent in a number of European countries, for example, Austria, Belgium, France, Germany, Hungary, Italy, Russia, Slovakia, and the Balkan countries. Although not all of those who hold such views actually vote for right-wing extremist parties, the numbers of votes cast for them have reached these levels in some elections. In some intellectual circles, far-right ideology, of which anti-Semitism – overt or not – is a part, has become respectable (again). These developments indicate that there are, unfortunately, severe obstacles to the realisation of such ideas as tolerant democratic pluralism, openness of European societies, and the acknowledgement of multiple cultural identities. While it would be incorrect to say that European societies are permeated by anti-Semitism, it does exist, and it causes tensions in the relationships between Jewry and non-Jews.

A section of this book is devoted to the facet of Jewry's relationship to its non-Jewish environment which has been called 'the Jewish Space'. The Jewish Space is thought to be a fairly recent phenomenon. The term refers to the cultural space in society, open to Jews and Gentiles, where events with Jewish themes – in the widest sense, far transcending the religious – occur. It may be thought of as a row of booths in the multicultural marketplace. Finding niches in that marketplace, or at least positions on how to deal with it, is a challenge to Jewry in Europe today. But the Jewish Space is also where non-Jews acknowledge Jewish history and thought as part of their own European legacy and identity. This seems to indicate a change in the role accorded to Jews and implies that Jewish culture is considered more important than before. 'The Jewish Space in Europe … [exists] in a context of Jewish and non-Jewish tension, inter-penetration, dialogue, conflict and even symbiosis', writes Diana Pinto in Chapter 9. Each of these forms of interaction individually is complex, and in the Jewish Space they may occur simultaneously and overlap. Of course, the emergence of the Jewish Space is only the latest episode in the long-running series of multifarious relations between Jews and Gentiles.

Germany as a Special Case

Germany is, of course, a special case, and we examine it here to illuminate how the issues discussed above play out in this particularly complex setting. We analyse the two facets introduced above in order to provide some background for the chapters in this volume which touch on Germany (Chapter 8 as well as the section on 'The Jewish Space in Europe').

It is important to remember that Jewry in Germany today differs markedly from German Jewry before 1933. Gone is the distinctive pre-war German Jewry, the Jewry which developed the Reform movement, and which to a large extent consisted of assimilated Jews who identified themselves as both definitely Jewish and definitely German (Mendes-Flohr 1999). Only a few of those Jews and their descendants live in Germany today. Most of the Jews in post-war Germany were Displaced Persons from throughout Eastern Europe who brought their Orthodoxy and their very different cultural backgrounds with them. They and their descendants constituted the majority of the thirty thousand members of Germany's Jewish communities through the 1980s. Thanks to the arrival of tens of thousands of Jews from the former Soviet Union, who have largely lost ties to religious practice and tradition, Jewish community membership has jumped to more than one hundred thousand today (within a total population of eighty-two million in Germany).[4] There is probably an increase in the number of Jews who are not affiliated with the *Einheitsgemeinden*, but the numbers are not known. The Jewish population in Germany is now the fifth largest in Europe, following France (whose Jewish population numbers six hundred thousand), Russia (five hundred fifty thousand), the Ukraine (four hundred thousand), and the United Kingdom (three hundred thousand).[5] This large immigration has made cohesion among Jewry in Germany even more difficult than before, especially with language difficulties now added to all the other existing issues.

Anti-Semitism.   Beginning in 1933, German Jewry was killed or forced into emigration – by Germans. The '*Ostjuden*', who did not have German citizenship, were summarily expelled. The after-effects of the *Shoah* linger in Germany, on both the Jewish and the non-Jewish sides, and they explain the tensions which we discuss below.

The relationship between non-Jewish Germans and Jews is complicated by psychological difficulties on both sides, and every generation puts a new twist on it. On the non-Jewish side are often feelings of guilt, the trauma of their own losses, distrust, lingering – and frequently sub-conscious – anti-Semitism (more on this below), and denial of any difficulties existing at all – but also a genuine desire by some to make amends. All this occurs in a situation of extreme unfamiliarity with Jews and Judaism: most Germans born since the Second World War have never spoken to a Jew and know next to nothing about Judaism. As a result they receive their mental images of Jews either filtered through the media and history textbooks, or unfiltered from teachers and family sources who lived through the Nazi era. Predominant themes are the *Shoah*, Woody Allen's film characters, images of the ultra-Orthodox, and clichés about Israel. Germany as a nation and many Germans as individuals have difficulties with their own national identity – and the issues have changed again with the unification of the country. Germany and the Germans are at times still regarded with suspicion by other European states and peoples, not just by Jews, and some Germans resent having to face this. Most Jews in Germany have to deal with the trauma of the *Shoah* in their own lives or the lives of their families, with feelings including grief, resentment, defiance, vengefulness (as a taboo),[6] fears, sadness, and numbness. Like it or not, since they live among a population that includes the perpetrators and their descendants, as classmates, co-workers, neighbours, and so on, they must develop ways of coping with the situation on a day-to-day basis.

What complicates the issue further is that many German Gentiles seem to have – unknowingly – redefined anti-Semitism as denoting only the murder of Jews in concentration camps. Anyone who did not personally murder a Jew in the *Shoah* is not considered an anti-Semite by this unspoken, but widely used, redefinition.[7] Most people in Germany agree that anti-Semitism is unacceptable, even evil. But since most people do not consider themselves evil, they do not believe they are anti-Semitic, even if they hold views that clearly are anti-Semitic. They would feel insulted to be called anti-Semitic, responding as though they had been wrongly accused of murder.

Thus redefined, anti-Semitism (as murder) remains unacceptable. However, statements using negative stereotypes of Jews are not considered anti-Semitic (since they are not acts of murder), and thus seem permissible. Such statements are frequently uttered in code, using innuendo and allusion, rather than explicitly. This is because people feel they have the right to make anti-Jewish comments, even though they do not consider them anti-Semitic themselves, but fear or resent being called anti-Semitic by others, especially Jews, if they make openly anti-Semitic statements. For instance, Rudolf Augstein, editor of *Der Spiegel* until his death in 2002, used the term 'New York lawyers' in a commentary (Augstein 1998) to refer to the fact that these lawyers – representing Jewish *Shoah*-related claims against Swiss banks – were Jewish. He also wrote of the 'New York press' and 'sharks in lawyers' clothing' to explain why German Gentiles would not dare to openly oppose building the Memorial for the Murdered Jews of Europe in Berlin, and used a number of other anti-Semitic patterns of argument such as blaming Jews for anti-Semitism.[8] Other instances in which coded language was used to convey a sometimes anti-Semitic subtext include the *Historikerstreit* (the Historians' Debate in the late 1980s about whether the *Shoah* was unique in history), the more than ten years of debate about the Memorial for the Murdered Jews of Europe in Berlin, Martin Walser's speech when accepting the Peace Prize of the German Booksellers' Society in 1998, and the ensuing controversy with Ignatz Bubis, which triggered a broader debate (see Chapter 11). Of course, anti-Semitism is also evident in regard to specific concrete issues such as the long resistance to actually paying compensation for forced labourers in the Nazi era, even though most of those who survived forced labour are not Jewish. These examples underline that anti-Semitism is present not just among neo-Fascist thugs, but also among parts of the intellectual, political, media, and business elites, as well as mainstream society.

The difficulties that many Germans have with Jews take on many forms. In contrast to the anti-Semitism described above, for some German Gentiles, anything and everything Jewish is a taboo. They feel uncomfortable about saying anything at all about Jews, and may even avoid using the word 'Jew'. They are reluctant to question anything related to Jewry or Israel for fear of being labelled anti-Semitic, regardless of the basis or justification for their comments. While bending over backwards in an attempt not to offend Jews, they may take an extraordinary interest in things Jewish and, as philo-Semites, place Jews on a pedestal to view them as a moral authority due to their suffering throughout history. At the same time, they may resent – consciously or not – that (in their view) Jews are on that moral pedestal. With this in mind, many Jews become cautious when confronted with philo-Semitism. They view it as suspect, shallow, possibly dishonest, and therefore not to be taken at face value, even if it is only an expression of tension in the company of Jews.

Jews in Germany, particularly those who have been here for decades, are highly sensitive to these issues, as if, crossing a frozen lake, they can never know how thick the ice is under their feet. One can never know when anti-Semitism might suddenly pop up in everyday situations or when people one thought were not anti-Semitic unexpectedly express such sentiment.[9] All this notwithstanding, it is necessary to underline the fact that there certainly are German Gentiles whose attitudes and behaviour reflect sensitivity towards Jews.

The Jewish Space in Germany.   The Jewish Space in Germany has grown very large, encouraged by government support and media attention. A multitude of events draw substantial audiences, but the 'dialectics of dialogue' (*Pinto*) are perturbed because of the awkwardness between Jews and Gentiles. Jews tend to be fairly sceptical about the roles that some Gentiles take on in the Jewish Space in Germany. Despite the population increase by virtue of immigrants from the former Soviet Union, the number of Jews in the Jewish Space in Germany is small, not least because the new immigrants tend to be less involved. The preponderance of Gentiles at Jewish events can be overwhelming at times. Gentiles who assume that synagogue attendance is a legitimate activity for anyone may on occasion outnumber Jewish worshippers in a synagogue. Jews may feel that regular attendance as 'tourists' on the part of Gentiles at a synagogue is neither legitimate, nor that religious services are part of the Jewish Space. (For a more detailed discussion of these issues see Chapter 10.)

Jews in Germany have reason to ask about the motivations of Gentiles who enter the Jewish Space. 'Jews will confront "others" [in the Jewish Space] whose religious mindcast still shapes European culture and whose institutions played a role in the *Shoah'*, writes Diana Pinto. She makes this statement in the European context, and it holds true all the more in Germany. Questions may arise about those who seek to take leadership roles, for example as rabbis, shortly after conversion. There is also an issue concerning uncertainty about who might be trying to pass as Jewish. Unfortunately a handful of Gentiles try to concoct a false Jewish identity for themselves, for psychological reasons of their own, or to gain other, possibly political, advantages. This may result in very destructive behaviour directed – consciously or not – against Jews. Jews in Germany have little interest in bearing the brunt of such behaviour. They feel that some Gentiles in the Jewish Space may be using Jews to deal with problems of their own. Especially those Jews who have experienced such behaviour themselves, in particular at a more personal level, become reluctant to participate in Jewish-Gentile activities: they simply feel that protecting themselves must take priority over promoting Jewish-Gentile relations until they can be certain that participating in them will not result in their being hurt. As a consequence, the number of Jews participating actively in the Jewish Space may dwindle, and the potential for dialogue may be reduced. A further result is that the Jewish Space may have little Jewish involvement.

Jewry in Germany faces some of the same challenges faced by Jewry in the rest of Europe: rebuilding, diversity, continuity. Another issue particularly poignant in Germany is dealing on a day-to-day basis with the aftermath of the *Shoah*, including the sometimes uncanny fascination with the Jewish Space on the part of non-Jews. The structure of Jewish communities plays a pivotal role, and their development in the coming years will be of critical importance.

Turning the Kaleidoscope – European Perspectives for Jewry

European Jewry today bears little resemblance to what it was before the *Shoah*. With just a few exceptions, it is still in a state of recovery from the destruction wrought in the *Shoah* and/or the suppression by the state socialist regimes in Central and Eastern Europe. Rebuilding Jewish life in all its variety and vitality, and with all its religious and secular institutions, will remain a major task for some generations to come. The rebuilding of Jewish communities and institutions in Central and Eastern Europe will change the orientation of Jewry in Europe from Western European to pan-European, whereby the enlargement of the European Union may foster this process.

Diversity is the defining characteristic of European Jewry. The great variety of Jews scattered across Europe indeed forms a kaleidoscope, with the colourful glass chips inside representing the varied traditions of religious practice, culture, place of origin, and so on, tumbling and forming ever new patterns over time as the kaleidoscope turns. How this diversity will develop in coming decades is an open question. Continuity of Jewish life is a common concern as much in larger communities as in small ones; it is also a prerequisite for productive exchange with the non-Jewish world. European Jewry also needs to develop the self-confidence necessary to take its rightful place alongside other Europeans, whether they belong to large nations or smaller minorities, in determining Europe's future. European Jewry is just beginning to explore its collective European dimension.

It may come to pass that Jewish traditions coalesce in Europe while they stand separate in the U.S. and Israel. European Jewry's future may involve crossover between Jewish traditions which remain distinct in the U.S. and Israel. This might happen if Jews of different traditions decide that Jewish continuity depends on their uniting to ensure their existence into the next generation. Alternatively, the traditions may remain distinct, with networks between like-minded communities across Europe providing mutual support for small communities. For the often tiny populations of Jews with a particular tradition in any one place, connection to like-minded Jews elsewhere in Europe is of vital importance. Yet the small communities, for whom networks are most important, each need a critical mass of active members (especially in the absence of paid staff) to sustain themselves individually, to join in piecing together networks, and to maintain their participation in them. A third possibility is that neither of these two scenarios will come about. Then, outside Europe's major Jewish population centres, the few Jews left will be unable to maintain self-sustaining Jewish communities.

Continuity of Jewry in Europe is thus also a question of the development of the institutional structure of organised Jewry. How to effect development in Jewish institutions in such a way that they adapt to the totality of Jews' needs, interests, and traditions is a major challenge for the coming years. Fighting against anti-Semitism is the one thing all Jews seem to agree on – at least in principle. But Jews need to harmonise their efforts far beyond this lowest common denominator – we have much more on our common agenda, like it or not. European Jewry may well diverge from the established coordinates of the Jewish world (on less or more friendly terms), finding its own path, kaleidoscopically turning further to generate new patterns. Some kernels will remain distinct as they tumble, some will be mirrored, and others will be overlaid, creating new patterns. It is up to us to keep the kaleidoscope turning.

Notes

The authors wish to express their gratitude to Dr Steven Less for his painstaking editing of this introduction as well as Toby Axelrod and Dr Jael Geis for their thoughtful comments on earlier versions of it.

1. Four of the seven communities Tye portrays are in Europe: Düsseldorf, Dnepropetrovsk, Dublin, and Paris.
2. Although Gitelman et al. (2003) gather in one volume a number of fascinating surveys of developments in social organisation and attitudes in European Jewish populations, a single volume cannot cover this entire field of research.
3. www.limmud.org.
4. The number of immigrants from the former Soviet Union who held Soviet passports with the nationality 'Jewish' and who entered Germany between 1989 and mid-2000 totals about 127,000 (letter dated 11 July 2000, Bundesministerium des Innern). Between 1990 and 2002, 83,603 of them joined Jewish communities in Germany. It is unknown how many have left Germany for other countries. Without this immigration, membership of Germany's Jewish communities would have dropped from 29,089 in 1990 to 14,732 in 2002. Between 1990 and 2002, the number of births in all the communities represented in the Zentralrat varied between 99 and 151 per year, while the number of deaths per year rose from 431 in 1990 to 1,000 in 2002, reflecting the age distribution where 35 percent are over sixty years of age. Deaths outnumbered births 8,758 to 1,641 for the 1990 to 2002 period. (All other figures from Zentrale Wohlfahrtsstelle der Juden in Deutschland e.V. 2003.)
5. Source: http://www.virtual.co.il/communities/wjcbook/chartmap.htm (World Jewish Congress web site), as of June 2000.
6. Profound insights into this issue for the years immediately following 1945 are provided in Geis (1998).
7. We are indebted to Salomea Genin for formulating this thought so clearly.
8. For an analysis of the historical development of the connections between anti-Semitism and anti-Americanism in Germany, see Diner 1992 (in English translation: Diner 1996).
9. A frequent trigger for anti-Semitic remarks is commenting on current events in the Middle East.

Bibliography

Anon. 1997. 'From Prague '95 to Strasbourg '97: Strengthening Jewish Life in Europe'. *JPR News* (winter).

Augstein, Rudolf. 1998. 'Wir sind alle verletzbar' ['We are all vulnerable']. *Der Spiegel* 49/30 November 1998: 32–3.

Diner, Dan. 1992. *Verkehrte Welten. Antiamerikanismus in Deutschland.* Frankfurt am Main, Eichborn.

Diner, Dan. 1996. *America in the Eyes of the Germans: an Essay on Anti-Americanism.* Princeton, NJ, Markus Wiener.

Elazar, Daniel J. 1999. 'Conclusion: Building a European Jewish Future'. In *Jewish Centers and Peripheries. Europe between America and Israel Fifty Years After World War II*, ed. S. I. Troen. New Brunswick/London, Transaction Publishers: 419–33.

Geis, Jael. 1998. '"Ja, man muß seinen Feinden verzeihen, aber nicht früher, als bis sie gehenkt werden." Gedanken zur Rache für die Vernichtung der europäischen Juden im unmittelbaren Nachkriegsdeutschland' ['"Yes, one must forgive one's enemies, but not before they are hanged." Thoughts on revenge for the annihilation of the European Jews in immediate post-war Germany'.] In *Menora – Jahrbuch für deutsch-jüdische Geschichte 1998*. Bodenheim, Philo-Verlagsgesellschaft: 155–80.

Geis, Jael. 2000. *Übrig Sein–leben 'danach'. Juden deutscher Herkunft in der britischen und amerikanischen Zone Deutschlands 1945–1949* [*Left Over–Living After the Shoah–Jews of German Descent in the British and American Zones in Germany 1945–1949*]. Berlin, Philo-Verlagsgesellschaft.

Gitelman, Zvi, Barry Kosmin, and András Kovács, eds. 2003. *New Jewish Identities. Contemporary Europe and Beyond*. Budapest, Central European University Press.

Institute for Jewish Policy Research. 2000. *A Community of Communities, Report of the Commission on Representation of the Interests of the British Jewish Community*. London, Institute for Jewish Policy Research.

Klapheck, Elisa. 2002. 'Mehr Demokratie wagen! Ein Kommentar zur Struktur nationaler und internationaler jüdischer Organe' ['Daring to Have More Democracy! A Comment on the Structure of National and International Jewish Bodies']. *Jüdisches Berlin* 1 (2002): 11.

Kurlansky, Mark. 1995. *A Chosen Few. The Resurrection of European Jewry*. Reading, MA, Addison-Wesley.

Mendes-Flohr, Paul. 1999. *German Jews. A Dual Identity*. New Haven/London, Yale University Press.

Narrowe, Morton H. 1999. 'From Mosaics to Jews: The Rejection of an Unsuccessful Pattern'. In *Jewish Centers and Peripheries. Europe between America and Israel Fifty Years After World War II.*, ed. S. Ilan Troen. New Brunswick/London, Transaction Publishers: 181–207.

Shafir, Shlomo, ed. 2001. *Gesher – Journal of Jewish Affairs. The Jewish People at the Threshold of the New Millennium*. Institute of the World Jewish Congress.

Troen, S. Ilan, ed. 1999. *Jewish Centers and Peripheries: Europe between America and Israel Fifty Years After World War II*. New Brunswick/London, Transaction Publishers.

Tye, Larry. 2001. *Home Lands. Portraits of the New Jewish Diaspora*. New York, Henry Holt.

Ungar-Klein, Brigitte, ed. 2000. *Jüdische Gemeinden in Europa: zwischen Aufbruch und Kontinuität* [*Jewish Communities in Europe: Between New Directions and Continuity*]. Vienna, Picus.

Wasserstein, Bernard. 1996. *Vanishing Diaspora. The Jews in Europe since 1945*. Cambridge, MA, Harvard University Press.

Webber, Jonathan, ed. 1994. *Jewish Identities in the New Europe*. London, Littman Library of Jewish Civilization.

Zentrale Wohlfahrtsstelle der Juden in Deutschland e.V. [Central Welfare Office of the Jews in Germany]. 2003. *Mitgliederstatistik der einzelnen Jüdischen Gemeinden und Landesverbände in Deutschland per 1. Januar 2003* [*Statistics of the members of the individual Jewish Communities and Länder Associations in Germany as of 1 January 2003*]. Frankfurt am Main, Zentrale Wohlfahrtsstelle der Juden in Deutschland e.V.

PART I:
OVERARCHING QUESTIONS

Chapter 1

A New Role for Jews in Europe: Challenges and Responsibilities

Diana Pinto

Never in Europe's millennial history have Jews on this continent lived in such individual and collective freedom and well-being as today. More than fifty years after the *Shoah* and at the close of this most terrible of centuries, Jews in Europe stand at the crossroads, just as Europe itself does. They must come to terms with their own conflicting emotions in order to rethink their role and future in a radically transformed continent. From Portugal to Russia, from Norway to Greece, Jews now belong along with their fellow European citizens to a geographic space which is no longer torn asunder by the ideological East-West divide, and which accepts in its vast majority, and for the first time in the East as well, the values of human rights and pluralist democracy. Jewish life has become not only plausible but even welcome in what were once the God-forsaken lands of history. The continent which witnessed the destruction of two-thirds of European Jewry a mere fifty-five years ago, and the Communist strangling of Jewish identity, has become today a continent where Jews must come to terms with their own collective 'success story' (in the West) and rebirth (in the East). To speak of the new Jewish Europe is therefore to speak about a future-oriented concept based on European and Jewish belonging, and on renewed religious vitality, community life and cultural blossoming in a continent defined by democratic pluralism. For post-war Jews, whose collective existence was essentially defined by two anguished struggles, combating anti-Semitism and supporting the state of Israel, this opening of new, above all positive, European vistas is not only destabilising: it is quite simply daunting. Yet this Jewish coming to terms with 'Europe' must take place because Jews are here to stay, and must therefore define their own sense of belonging to ensure a rich and creative presence inside a pluralist

Europe. Only in such a manner can Jews in Europe contribute positively and meaningfully to world Judaism, and to Israel's own tormented crisis of identity, while remaining faithful to the values of democratic pluralism, human rights, tolerance, and the respect of others which have lain at the heart of Jewish existence in the Diaspora.

First however, a word of warning. The very notion of a new Jewish Europe, of a possible future European Jewish identity, still borders on heresy for many Jews in America and Israel and also for many in Western Europe. In this view, European Jewry died at Auschwitz, and in the process Europe became the equivalent of post-expulsion Spain, a closed chapter with respect to Jewish life. Whatever Jews may still be left in Europe today are seen at best as a struggling remnant if not as a 'Vanishing Diaspora' (Wasserstein 1996), their ranks far too thin, their religious and cultural identity far too weak to generate any meaningful Jewish presence. To speak of a new Jewish Europe is both wrong and dangerous, according to the opponents of the concept. It implies not having learned any lessons from the continent's past while refusing to recognise the centrality of Israel and refusing to accept that Jews should be above all 'Jews' whose lay national or regional identity is quite secondary. The sceptics will add that 'Europe' itself is a loosely defined term, that 'Europeans' are hard to find, and that anyway, historically 'Europe' was the code word referring to Greek, Roman, and subsequently Christian roots. It has nothing to do with Judaism. Furthermore, how can one speak of 'European Jews' when Jews are already badly fragmented in their different Jewish, not to mention national, identities?

Behind such criticisms lies a seldom mentioned implicit assumption, that Europe is no place for Jews, its deepest cultural fabric contaminated by a long entrenched anti-Semitic poison, its deepest political reflexes permeated by xenophobia. To announce or even to encourage Jewish life in Europe is therefore tantamount to existential folly.

It is impossible to posit a new Jewish Europe without taking these objections into account. One must recognise, however, that European nations and their intellectual elites, with the exception of isolated cases such as former Yugoslavia, are not, unlike in the 1930s, the promoters of these poisoned values. But the essential point lies elsewhere. It is impossible to deny or to be blind to the signs of Jewish renewal which are sprouting East and West in a continent which is experiencing its own cultural comeback. It is this spontaneous Jewish reawakening, combined with a parallel strengthening of open democracy, that furnishes the best answer to the sceptics. Europe and 'its' Jews will be reborn together or not at all. This time, Jews will not only be the traditional passive 'litmus test' of a truly open and tolerant Europe, but are also called upon to be one of its principal motors. For Jewish life will not only continue in Europe but it will take on a new centrality. To speak of a Jewish future in Europe is therefore to evoke a series of challenges and responsibilities uniquely pertinent to this continent, but also existentially central to Jews around the world, including Israel. A discussion of the challenges and the various types of responsibilities follows below.

The Challenges

The new Jewish Europe is emerging from a set of four unprecedented historical circumstances which have come to the fore since the late 1980s:

1. The fall of the Berlin Wall, marking the end of the Cold War divide and inaugurating the opening up of the European continent to the values of democratic pluralism and human rights.

2. The intensification of Christian-Jewish dialogue culminating in the Vatican recognition of the State of Israel and in the acknowledgement of the role of the Churches in the anti-Semitism that led to the *Shoah*.

3. The political and cultural transformation of the *Shoah* itself from a source of private Jewish grief to the motor of new national and European self-understanding, with its correlate, the creation of an ever more vibrant, future-oriented Jewish Space.

4. Finally, Israel's coming of age as a fully responsible international actor at a time when democratic pluralism and human rights have become the twin pillars of a positive European identity and the cornerstone of Jewish life in Europe.

The fall of the Berlin Wall on 9 November 1989 marked the end of the post-war era. It provided a glimpse of the potential for a new free pan-Europe without ideological cleavages, and marked the beginning of a new Jewish Europe. At first, it was assumed by most Jews around the world that the open borders throughout Eastern Europe and subsequently the former Soviet Union would yield only one outcome: the mass departure of Europe's 'captive Jews' for Israel, thus bringing to a close another chapter of the continent's tragic history. Many Jews did in fact leave, but a significant number, contrary to prevalent expectations, not only chose to remain, but have since demonstrated a clear intention of resuming an active Jewish life in their respective homelands.

These new 'voluntary Jews', who have freely chosen to stay in former Communist lands undergoing a transition towards democracy, are now interacting with new types of Western European Jews. For Jews through-out Western Europe are themselves the product of an unprecedented post-*Shoah* mixing of different ethnic Jewish pasts, be they old Ashkenazi German, Yiddish from Eastern Europe, or North African Sephardic. Furthermore, the old pre-*Shoah* national patriotisms and their subtle 'pecking orders' (which made British, French or Italian Jews so proud of their national 'belonging' and so condescending towards the *Ostjuden* 'masses') have lost their divisive power. When one adds the sizeable number of former Soviet Jews who have recently settled in reunited Germany, it becomes clear that the Jewish Europe unfolding before our eyes is a new cultural and historical creation. The traditional militant Zionist as well as the anti-Zionist, revolutionary Communist identities which marked pre-*Shoah* Jewry in Europe, have now lost their historical relevance. The new Jewish Europe is thus very much the child of the democratic revolutions of 1989, for it could gain symbolic and even political reality only through the active presence of Jews from Eastern Europe and the former Soviet Union. The geographic scope of such a new Jewish Europe is more important than the relative numerical weakness of some of its constituent parts.

Second, the Vatican's recognition of the State of Israel marked a turning point in the long and often tense path of Christian-Jewish reconciliation begun with Vatican II in the early 1960s and carried out also by the Protestant churches of Europe. The symbolic and very real implications of this theological transformation have not always been understood in Jewish circles, which have tended to interpret these changes as simply the long overdue righting of a historical wrong, but a righting bereft of any significance for the future. Most Jews have not realised the Copernican revolution inherent in this changed Christian attitude which now considers Judaism not only as a positive, living, ongoing religion endowed with its own internal validity, but also as one empowered to shed light and teachings on a post-Holocaust Christianity. Understandably wary of Christianity's millennial history of 'co-optation' of Jewish themes, Jewish converts, and Jewish memories, Jews today still contemplate the most recent papal pronouncements and canonisations with scepticism and even rage, without grasping the extent to which the Church has sought to integrate Jewish 'otherness' into its own teachings. The most important historical cornerstone of European anti-Semitism, Christianity, has not only turned its back on anti-Semitism, it has finally acknowledged the negative role played by the hierarchies of the Churches in the unfolding of the *Shoah*, the Protestant Churches addressing this issue before the Catholic one. Polish, German, and most recently French bishops have made public declarations of contrition whose impact will be far-reaching. Religion, irrespective of the actual number of regular worshippers, still carries a crucial moral and symbolic charge. Combined with the lay democratic emphasis placed on human rights and pluralism, it is palpably transforming the political and cultural environment in which Jewish life is evolving in Europe. The result is that Christians now think of Jews increasingly as their 'older brothers' and of Judaism as a faith with a universal message. The challenge for Jews, and European Jews in particular, is immense, for they must project themselves positively and creatively as opposed to defensively in a newly open and pluralist agora of spirituality. Jewish-Christian relations will depend henceforth as much on Jewish openness as on Christian repentance.

Third, the *Shoah* in all its uniqueness is finally penetrating Europe's self-consciousness and becoming the filter through which a new reading of European identities is being fashioned. Relegated to the realm of private Jewish grief in the immediate post-war period, or buried beneath the universalist rhetoric of anti-fascist resistance or anti-capitalist logic, the *Shoah* has at last come into its own. How and by whom Jews were rounded up and sent to their deaths, what legacy they left behind, what happened to their belongings and to the survivors who returned, have become so many key references in evaluating (not just for the Jews but for all citizens) each European country's wartime behaviour and collaboration. The result is a most salutary 'greying' of Europe, one which is replacing the previous classifications of countries as 'resistant' (France), 'neutral' (Switzerland), or 'victims' (Austria) with respect to the Nazis. The *Shoah* has in effect 'come home' deep inside each national reality, and in so doing the Jewish experience and memory are becoming constitutive elements of Europe's own emerging historical identity. Such a profound transformation lies at the heart of the emerging new Jewish Europe, at a time when a 'my country, right or wrong' type of nationalism is losing its appeal in the context of a pan-European framework.

In part propelled by the spate of fiftieth anniversary commemorations which began in 1983 with the remembrance of Hitler's attaining power, Jewish references have increasingly occupied centre stage in Europe's cultural and political debates. The building of memorials and museums to commemorate both the *Shoah* and the previous Jewish heritage it nearly destroyed have generated passionate reactions further fuelled by the publication of books and the production of films, and the appearance, whether in print or on tape, of the last survivor accounts. What had lain dormant in European culture for the greater part of the post-war period was finally free to explode in full light. The *Shoah*, however, has only been the negative starting point for a far wider fashion for 'things Jewish', ranging from Jewish recipes and jokes to the far more important interest in Jewish traditions, life, philosophy, and culture, and above all religion itself.

The Jewish Space (see Chapter 9) is in constant expansion, for it is not populated only by Jews, but touches all others as well. Because identity themes dominate our *zeitgeist,* the Jewish experience in Europe in this century in all of its creativity and tragedy, and also in its post-war reconstruction, lies at the very heart of our current search. Factoring in the *Shoah*, but also a wider Jewish reference, to varied national histories, but above all into Europe's own identity, marks a conceptual revolution of sorts. The very parameters of cultural and political debates are being transformed in the process.

It is crucial to stress, however, that such a space without living Jews in Europe would be little more than a museum or an archaeological site for historical research. Living Jews instead will transform it into a setting for cross-fertilisation and symbiosis. Nowhere will this be more true than in Germany, where the Jewish search for identity is intertwined with the country's coming to grips with its own past. But the same holds true elsewhere in Europe, both East and West, in places such as Scandinavia, where the Jewish presence was always essentially homeopathic, or in Eastern Europe, where the presence/absence was massive. From an internal Jewish point of view, the Jewish Space will also greatly facilitate the consolidation of community life across Europe by acting as an amplifier and even as a bridge with the surrounding culture, particularly when the communities are small.

Fourth, Israel's coming of age as an independent and normalised international actor coincides with Europe's own increasing commitment to democratic pluralism and human rights against all racisms and xenophobias. Both factors are forging a new European Jewish sensibility. The visceral protective links which bound Jews in the Diaspora to Israel are becoming frayed, in part because the democratic and pluralist values which Jews in Europe cherish and expect their respective nation-states to uphold are being assailed by the ultra-orthodox Zionist right and the nationalist camp within Israel. At the same time, the anti-Zionism of the European Left and of the Soviet bloc has given way to a far more empirical peace-oriented approach based on historical reconciliation and democratic values. As a result of Israel's having come into its own internationally, Jewish life in Europe is no longer centrally defined by the Jewish state, but is slowly developing its own internal dynamic and its own priorities. Many European Jews now define their mission vis-à-vis Israel as that of supporting the peace process and maintaining links with the Palestinians rather than simply supporting Israel 'right or wrong'. They are also increasingly considering themselves as vital democratic and cultural 'anchors' for their Israeli counterparts who are threatened inside Israel itself. The time may even come when Diaspora Jewry turns out to be the equivalent of flying buttresses for Israeli democracy.

Jews across Europe must therefore confront these new challenges and take on new responsibilities because the Europe in which they live bears little relation not only to that of the pre-war period, but also to the confined, taboo-ridden continent of the post-war period, in the West hiding its traumas in the comforting siren-song of economic reconstruction and growth. Theirs will be a central role in a continent which, because it is at last able to confront its past, can at last address its future.

The Responsibilities

Jewish responsibilities inside a new Europe are the outcome of a new way of being 'Jewish' on the old continent. The first precondition is that all Jews be 'voluntary', that is, that they have *freely* chosen to stay where they live because, after all, they have the possibility of moving to Israel. Such a choice to stay implies a positive sense of 'belonging' inside the society at large. The second precondition is that there should be many ways of being 'Jewish' without any State definition and without one single source of Jewish authority that rules over a tightly controlled community. Pluralism inside Jewish life must accompany pluralism in society at large. The third precondition is that Jewish life be an open crossroads where Jews of any given country interact freely with their counterparts elsewhere, whether in Europe, America, or Israel. Only with such individual and collective freedoms can one speak of a European Jewish setting. And it is in such a setting that a common sensibility will emerge through frequent 'pan-Jewish' interactions. European Jews will gradually discover that they have increasingly similar outlooks and priorities, both with respect to Europe's past and above all to its future, compared with their American and Israeli cousins.

European Jews are the only ones who conjugate their verbs in the future to perpetuate Jewry in Europe. Having made this existential choice to remain in Europe, they have two distinct types of responsibilities to confront: to promote historical, national, and religious reconciliation, and to fight for a tolerant democratic pluralism.

In the realm of reconciliation, the following tasks stand out:

1. Transcending the *Shoah* by transforming it from a uniquely Jewish abyss into a bridge, together with fellow Europeans.

2. Pursuing a qualitatively new inter-faith dialogue, not just with the Christians, but also with the Muslims of Europe.

3. Playing a central role in the quest for reconciliation inside Europe and with its neighbouring cultures, in the integration of immigrants and refugees in European culture and consciousness.

4. Reconciling what one asks of others with what one asks of oneself; in other words, going beyond the notion of the 'combat Jew', defined uniquely by the *Shoah*, towards a newly defined positive self-identification as European.

5. Encouraging the peace process between Israel and its neighbours by using the Jewish Space in Europe as a place in which one can carry out reconciliation and dialogue (for instance, conferences and encounters sponsored by Jewish community structures or leading newspapers). The dialogue might include mixed Jewish-Arab committees in the Diaspora.

The Jewish contribution to the fostering of a tolerant pluralist European democratic identity is best fulfilled by drawing the widest possible conclusions from the positive developments of the post-war Jewish experience in Europe. This implies:

6. Making the most of the Jewish Space as a space of dialogue and mutual enrichment.

7. Reflecting and extending to others the Jewish ability to live harmoniously with a highly complex identity, thanks to the notion of non-conflicting multiple loyalties.

8. Helping to define a democratic pluralism anchored in the double respect of universal values and specific identities, without falling into multiculturalist ghettos.

9. Combating anti-Semitism, of course, but also all other forms of intolerance and discrimination.

10. Delving behind the Israeli 'alibi' which has for too long obfuscated the reality of a European Jewish presence. This presence is vitally important as a bulwark against racist and fascist ideologies.

Reconciliation

Europe's Jews are the only ones who actually live on the continent which spawned the *Shoah*. Such an existential situation gives them a far greater understanding of Europe's cultural and human complexities, for they themselves are integral parts of Europe's living kaleidoscope, not just external carriers of a frozen memory of horror. Europe's older Jews not only continued to live with the people who witnessed or carried out the *Shoah*, but their descendants today share the same living cultural space with those who are the descendants of the perpetrators. For some Jews around the world such a cohabitation, especially in Germany, remains scandalous. One can instead argue that Jews should be in Europe because a *'judenrein'* Europe was precisely what Hitler had wanted to achieve. Beyond the philosophical debate of the validity of a Jewish presence in Europe lies the simple fact that Europe's Jews share some of the same heritage and a common destiny with their fellow Europeans and must articulate their own belonging on the continent. These cultural realities are less obvious for Jews in America or in Israel, for whom Europe still remains a foreign space overwhelmingly defined by its haunting *Shoah* past.

International Jewish organisations have played a central role recently in getting the *Shoah* into the headlines by addressing such crucial issues as reparations to the forgotten survivors of Eastern Europe, and more spectacularly by focusing on issues such as Nazi gold and the role of seemingly neutral countries such as Switzerland or Sweden in prolonging the ability of the Nazi war machine to operate. On both these counts, 'world' Jewish organisations have acted with the past in mind, seeking to settle accounts before closing the books, so to speak, as the *Shoah* slowly slips into the realm of non-witnessed history.

Jews in Europe, on the other hand, are faced with a different calendar. The day is fast approaching when there will be no more reparations to be paid out, when the last trials of crimes against humanity will have taken place, and when each state will have its Jewish museums, commemorative monuments, and revised textbooks, when all governments, churches and assorted institutions will have made formal apologies on behalf of their institutions' past crimes, callousness or indifference towards the Jews. And then what? The *Shoah* will finally become what it should have been all along: a non-Jewish, above all, 'internal' European issue, a chapter in each country's national history as well as a mirror of Western civilisation. With this change in Europeans' orientations, the *Shoah* will no longer function as an abyss separating Jews from non-Jews but will slowly become a bridge between them in the name of pluralist democratic values. In this realm, European Jews will play the central role for they can best draw the 'living' and future-oriented lessons of the tragedy. They can point out how it was not just rooted in absolute evil but in the all-too-human infinite series of bureaucratic, political, cultural, and personal stances, which are still present and which affect, obviously in a different manner, other ethnic groups today. Europeans are finally realising what the *Shoah* actually meant, and Europe's Jews should be central players in this new phase.

Jews in Europe are also destined to play a central role in a new interfaith dialogue based less on the old bland rhetoric of brotherly love. As Europe's churches integrate the *Shoah* into their own theology, Jews should play a crucial role in making sure that its humanist lessons enter both Christian and Muslim consciousnesses. They must also ensure that Judaism comes into its own as a coherent and vital spiritual force rather than as the background half of the much overused hyphenated 'Judeo-Christian' adjective. More practically, all religions in Europe must confront the burning issues of pluralist tolerance, bioethical and existential considerations in a continent which must reconcile its Enlightenment traditions with a pluralist religious spirituality. For the first time in millennia, Europeans are ready to relativise their Christian identity and to listen to the Jewish 'word'. Jews in Europe should be there to provide it, for such an inter-faith dialogue is neither an American nor an Israeli priority. American Jews live in a highly sociologised religious country where all churches, carrying no deeply rooted historical tensions, can coexist in an atmosphere ranging from friendly neighbourliness to benign neglect. Churches in America are as much about offering a sociological identity to their faithful as they are about religious transcendence, hence their ability to coexist in such harmony. In Israel, on the other hand, all religious issues are explosive both within the Jewish community and also with the surrounding Muslim world, which is not perceived as a significant 'other' inside the Israeli context. Europe is the only place where such a dialogue among historically and culturally 'heavy' religious identities can and must take place in a context of reconciliation.

The term 'reconciliation' lies at the very heart of post-war Europe's identity and of the European project as a whole. Having begun between France and Germany, the ancestral enemies who have since learned to think of the other as their best ally, reconciliation has now spread east to encompass German-Polish, German-Czech, and German-Russian relations. As the *Shoah* becomes increasingly a bridge rather than an abyss, Jews in Europe will be able to engage in their own form of collective reconciliation with 'Europe' as a cultural and historical concept. In the past, post-war Jews had made individual peace with their own respective countries, not with Europe as a whole. They may have been pro- or anti-European as citizens in their reactions to a supranational and most often technocratic project. They did not, however, bring together their positions on Europe with their Jewish identity. Today, instead, the European dimension, both in cultural and in political terms, is destined to become an increasingly important aspect of Jewish life on the continent. After all, there is now a fifty-year Jewish post-war history of harmony and peace in Western Europe which will carry ever stronger weight in a Jewish vision of Europe. The 'combat' Jew of the past, defined exclusively by the *Shoah*, will slowly give way to a 'reconciliation' Jew imbued with a positive Jewish religious and cultural identity, who will increasingly appear natural in the European kaleidoscope.

Jewish reconciliation with Europe can take place all the more easily because there has been a European rapprochement with Israel. Unlike in the 1970s, one cannot speak of Europe today as being anti-Zionist or latently anti-Semitic, as was the case previously in terms of foreign policy interests linked to Middle Eastern oil. The risk today is that Europeans will become potentially anti-Israeli because Israel itself is not measuring up to the democratic, human rights, and pluralist standards which Jews have come to expect of their European countries. To prevent such an ironic tragedy, Jews in Europe, qua Jews and qua Europeans, should work actively to pursue the peace process and encourage all forms of Israeli-Arab dialogue, benefiting from the fact that Jews and Muslims share the same minority and pluralist concerns inside European societies. European Jewish involvement on behalf of peace in the Middle East is a responsibility which stems directly from the Jewish stake in tolerant pluralist democracy within the Diaspora.

Nazism sought to destroy the Jews not only because it considered them an inferior race, but above all because it perceived them to be a traitor group working against the well-being of true Germans, precisely because they owed their ultimate loyalty to fellow Jews elsewhere and to an ill-defined 'cosmopolitan' and 'masonic' conspiracy. Because of the *Shoah* and in reaction to the tenets of Nazism, Western European countries allowed Jews to thrive in their midst by treating them naturally as equal citizens, but also by granting them implicitly the right to pursue multiple loyalties: that is, to live their individual and collective lives as fully-fledged citizens of their respective states, while also remaining loyal to fellow Jews elsewhere in the world, and maintaining a very strong and special tie with the state of Israel. This implicit pact was made possible only because of the *Shoah*, for it basically undermined the hallowed statist notion of a purely national belonging. Today, given Europe's increasingly variegated population and the complex co-existence of minorities and majorities throughout the continent, the time has come to spell out the content and the conditions inherent in such an implicit concept. Other groups (one can think of the Gypsies in particular, but also of other ethnic minorities, for instance Hungarians in Romania) could also profit from the Jewish precedent. If the concept of multiple loyalties were to take root as one possible form of a future European identity, then it would be a Jewish responsibility to underscore the rights, limits, and duties inherent in such a practice, lest it be denatured into a double loyalty, in other words, a double treason.

Tolerant Democratic Pluralism

Along the same lines, Jews in Europe have another role to play in the strengthening of pluralist democracy in Europe. As the inheritors of a religious tradition which since its inception has always sought to wed a specific identity with universalist principles, Jews must pursue this task even today. They are better equipped than most groups in the art of preserving their specificity while also militating for universal rights and values. Only in such a manner can one ensure that pluralism does not evolve into a ghetto multiculturalism which deprives individuals of the possibility of fashioning their cultural identity beyond the religious or racial characteristics linked to their ethnic origins. Similarly, nations within Europe should be able to define their own unique cultural and political cement, albeit in a spirit of pluralist tolerance. In this context, Jews can help guarantee such an open belonging while also providing a useful bulwark against the dangers of cultural relativism, with its 'pagan' overtones. For cultural relativism has never been a Jewish trait. Even in the Bible, non-Jews were supposed to adhere to the Noachide principles which contain the essential human duties. Today, to ensure a meaningful democratic setting, one must rethink the equivalent of the Noachide precepts which will allow a pluralist democratic setting to thrive beyond the inherently centrifugal tendencies of particularist interests. Jews can make an important contribution in this realm, for in this tragic century they experienced both the attractions and the dangers of acculturation. Since the *Shoah*, Diaspora Jews have managed to find a middle way in this dilemma, one which can be of use to others as well.

It goes without saying that Jews in Europe are in the front line in the struggle against anti-Semitism, but they should also be in the front line with respect to the equivalent struggle against racism, xenophobia and the hatred of all 'others'. Now that the *Shoah* is becoming a page of collective European memory, it is important for all to understand that the Eastern European Jews at the end of the war in Displaced Persons camps, not to mention the Jewish 'boat people' whom the British authorities prevented from reaching Palestine, were closer in terms of objective conditions to current day Gypsies, Tutsis, and Kurds than to their contemporary European counterparts. Such an awareness should condition Jewish positions with respect to Europe's treatment of refugees, asylum seekers, and immigrants. Jews, especially in the West, cannot behave as though they had always been traditionally rooted citizens of their respective countries, as though the *Shoah* had never taken place: this would be a dangerous form of false consciousness. By stating the degree to which they belong historically and culturally to Europe, Jews are in effect changing the parameters of what the very term 'belonging' implies. The concept will no longer be associated with mythical territorial and blood references (such as the Teutonic forest or the Thracian mountains) and will come to mean a far more voluntaristic allegiance to a language, a culture, and a multi-layered historical process, defined as much by differences and tensions as by the traditional references to harmony and unity.

For such a new European Jewish identity to develop in an open, pluralist setting, the Israeli 'alibi' must be abolished both for the Europeans and for the Jews themselves. In other words, both groups should squarely confront the implications of Jews living in Europe, rather than hiding behind the all-too-easy post-war equation made between Israel and the Jews, as though the latter were all Israelis and the few still found in Europe merely foreign aliens permanently resident in Europe's lands. Such an equation was remarkably convenient for reconverted German nationalists, conservative anti-Semites of all countries, and neo-Fascists who could find in the Zionist cause the fulfilment of their wish: a *'judenrein'* Europe and the consecration, through the Israeli example, of ethnically homogeneous nations. Lifting the Israel 'alibi' means precisely not confusing the Jewish cause on behalf of Eretz Israel with the opportunistic pro-Israeli sentiments of European extreme nationalists all too happy to close the door on any notion of a pluralist and open Europe with different cultural strains and identities.

There is also a second Jewish component to the lifting of the Israeli 'alibi': confronting the challenge of creating a meaningful Jewish life in Europe without pretending to be merely 'temporarily' on the European continent on the way to Israel. This mental attitude which was prevalent in the immediate post-war years has receded somewhat in the recent decade, but the stigma remains, and most Jews in Europe still feel uneasy about qualifying their life in the Diaspora as 'fully' Jewish. There can be no European Jewish identity without a redressing of the balance, all the more so now that most Jews in Europe and America are no longer in perfect concord with Israel's domestic and regional policies, precisely because of their commitment to pluralist democracy and a tolerant religious setting. Therefore, lifting the Israeli 'alibi' on both the European and the Jewish counts constitutes a vital clearing of the air, and a much needed lifting of one of the most important post-war taboos, namely, that implicitly, all Jews belong in Israel. Nowhere has this lifting of the taboo occurred more dramatically – albeit only partially – than in Germany.

Finally, the most important and creative cultural and religious Jewish responsibility in Europe is to fill the Jewish Spaces that are sprouting throughout the continent. These growing Jewish Spaces play a vital role in the strengthening of civil society throughout Europe beyond the purely Jewish sphere. They permit or even facilitate a pluralist dialogue opposed to monolithic nationalist discourses, while stimulating cultural debate and creativity. Such Jewish Spaces will carry a very real cultural and even political charge in Europe, one bearing no mathematical relation to the actual number of Jews populating them. Jews thus continue to hold a symbolic importance which well transcends their objective numbers. Jews and the Jewish Space inside Europe are thus destined to develop together, each reinforcing the other to the greater benefit of civil society as a whole. The Jewish existential wager in Europe will be won as much in the Jewish Space as in the strengthening of Jewish community life.

It is of course much too early to proclaim that there will be a European Jewish renaissance in the twenty-first century. American Jews and Israelis can furnish vital aid, but in the end, only Europe's Jews can make such a renaissance happen at the crossroads of a mutilated past and a pluralist future. They will have to prove that they have the necessary will and ability to forge a new religious and cultural creativity which they choose to cultivate within a democratically pluralist Europe. At the beginning of the twenty-first century, one can only stress that never have conditions been so favourable on the European continent to foster such a renaissance.

Whether it will take place will depend on all of us. One thing is certain. We, Jews and non-Jews, Europeans and non-Europeans alike, will be incommensurably richer if the entire European continent from Portugal to Russia were to harbour a living Jewish presence. Not only would such a presence embody the 'other' proof of Jewish resilience (besides Israel) against the absolute evil of this century. It would also open the road to a Jewish interaction and reconciliation with 'others' in a new pluralist, open and dynamic democratic Europe. Fostering a European Jewish identity implies cherishing both ideals.

Bibliography

Wasserstein, Bernard. 1996. *Vanishing Diaspora. The Jews in Europe since 1945.* Cambridge, MA, Harvard University Press.

Chapter 2

EUROPEAN MODELS OF COMMUNITY: CAN AMBIGUITY HELP?

Clive A. Lawton

In this chapter, I shall present a theory in progress. For every point made, there are counter-points as yet under-researched or considered. And so this essay stands as a start, and not as the last word, on the place and form of European Jewry in the twenty-first century.

Furthermore, I am conscious of writing as a British Jew, necessarily with a more optimistic attitude to life in Europe than those more closely and deeply scarred by the *Shoah* are likely to have. But I still insist on the possibility that, in the same way as Britain likes to believe that it straddles and therefore can mediate the gap between the two great blocs of the U.S.A. and the EU, so I think that European Jewry can usefully fill the space that lies psycho-politically between the two great blocs of Jewry, the U.S.A. and Israel.

In taking such a view, I am aware that it might appear smug or triumphalist. I may be seeming to urge the other communities of the world to 'do it like us', and to be claiming that European Jews have the solution to the difficult fact of being a Jew in the world. But I am not. I am well aware that European Jewry is fragile and dwarfed by its far more numerous and more vocal big brothers to the east and west. We certainly do not have all the answers, and perhaps not even many answers. But we do perhaps ask different questions, and in the process, add the capacity to look at things from a different angle. I hope by doing so to enrich the global vision of what the Jews might do and what Jews might be about.

I shall argue that the prevailing model of how to be a Jew in North America is essentially personal, individual – what I call 'privatised' – while in Israel the model is 'nationalised', that is, managed and defined by the State. While these two great blocs of world Jewry have diametrically opposed assumptions about how being Jewish 'works', I wish to point up a third model, often overlooked for a range of demographic, historical, and philosophical reasons: that of European Jewry, which strikes a middle path, centred on the contested but distinct framework of 'community'.

Because the concept of community is so variously defined, I am going to avoid a definition – it is anyway my contention that it is the very ambiguity of such concepts that characterises the European way of being Jewish – but suffice it for now to say that 'community' can be widely inclusive or narrowly restrictive; but one way or another, it lies as a form of identification, commitment, and association between the extended family and the political unit, be that municipality or state. In the former inclusive style, perhaps every person who identifies themselves as a Jew is counted and considered, while in the latter restrictive form, only those who have paid membership fees or attend services or fit a particular mode are taken into account. Given the huge diversity of all things European, I hope the following essay will posit sufficient frames and scenarios for the possibilities of the 'community' model to emerge.

It was perhaps sometime in the late eighteenth century, with the sounds of the French and American revolutions ringing in their ears, that Jews started to perceive a possibly different life for themselves in the modern world. Until then, whether under Christendom or Islam, Jews had been defined by the local doctrinal view and the relative benevolence of the ruler of the time and place. If the current Christian ruler was persuaded that the Jews were akin to the Antichrist then that determined the Jewish experience. If the local Muslim ruler was attracted to the Q'uranic teaching that Jews were first cousins to Muslims and so deserving of reasonable treatment and ready inclusion in social and political structures, then Jewish life flourished. This is not to say that the lot of the Jews had been continuously unpleasant under Christians or pleasant under Islam. At different times and in different places, life under either religious domination could be golden or catastrophic, but the Jewish communal structures and the Jewish place in the world were not determined by the Jews themselves, however much they resiliently maintained a strong and positive self-image as a people beloved by God, whatever others may have thought.

Contrary to the 'Oy vey' school of Jewish historical thought, many rulers of both Christian and Muslim lands have been enlightened (for their time) and generous to the Jews. A good few interpreted as generously as possible the theological leeway allowed for Jews either as *dhimmi* under Islam or, under Christianity, as wrong-headed but still the Chosen People of God. We can speculate as to the warmth of their motives, or the simple calculation of self-interest, but the outcomes were sometimes to accord Jews privileges which the ordinary downtrodden folk of the time might have only dreamed of.

By the nineteenth century, however, Muslim attitudes hardly mattered even in most Muslim countries. That century, it appeared, would belong to Europe and its Enlightenment. The growing movement for the rights of the individual that was sweeping across the Atlantic was producing powerful arguments for each person to be considered on his (or, shockingly, even her) own merits, regardless of nationality, birth or station. Now, individuals had status as individuals and were equal citizens under the law. Either they could be viewed as common descendants of the arbitrary ape, or they could claim the right to liberty, or they were indistinguishable in their common fraternity. That, at least, was how the theory had it.

Free-standing individuals the new Americans certainly were. Station and birth did not come into it, unless of course, you were a native of those lands, in which case the new science would explain how different humans were, like the different creatures of the natural world, some born to lord it over others. (This new science, which would eventually give rise to eugenics and a more virulent form of racism than ever before seen, was still in its infancy.) Whatever the mood sweeping through the soon-to-be post-Christian world, there were certainly strong signs that the Jews might have a better time of it under the new and slackening accommodations with Christian authority in Europe than under the preceding, more rigid Christian regimes.

However, the Enlightenment did not flow smoothly, nor entirely in the direction of the Jews. For many, Liberty and the rest were the godless overturnings of the Divine order, where every man knew his place (and the place of 'his' woman, too), and usually they knew that the Jewish place was near the end of the queue.

Not surprisingly, many Jews espoused the new thinking. They thus became associated with the revolutionaries or the individualists – proto-Communists or proto-Capitalists. But either way, this was not the stuff on which a stable Europe could be built in the minds of those who were starting to feel seasick due to the sea change that would soon engulf a queasy world. Any internationalists who were persuaded by the common destiny of mankind as exposed by the new science found themselves confronted by the new nationalists, striving for the particular destinies of their own little – or great – grouping of common heritage, language, or blood.

With God, it had been easy to argue that He was on 'our' side. Without God, as we were soon to find, it was even easier to argue that there was no common Fatherhood – and therefore no common Brotherhood. Although the taxonomy of Mankind was now based 'scientifically' rather than theologically, the concept of a hierarchy of humans survived, this time untempered by any concepts of charity to the unfortunate.

And so, before much of the talk of equality under the law could have its effect, by the end of the nineteenth century, spurious science and the forces of reaction were re-exerting their perception of the way the world should be. Whether through science or theology, Jews found themselves once again less than confident that the twentieth century in Europe would hold any real hope for them. And a proportion of them decided that something must be done. The new philosophies that had offered such hope were still there for the picking and Jews were still attracted to them. But which to choose?

In today's terms we can recognise the choice as 'privatisation' or 'nationalisation'. Some Jews decided that the future lay in 'privatising' their Jewish selves. I use the term to suggest the possibility of each Jew determining for him or herself what being Jewish entailed. Certainly a privatised Jewish identity was none of the State's business. It was a private affair, an accommodation between a Jew and God, or tradition, or culture, or whatever interlocutor appeared to demand a Jewish response. In all public matters, a Jew's Jewishness was expected to be irrelevant: in the public arena, the Jew was just a citizen like everyone else.

The early days of the French Revolution highlighted the issue. While eventually it was decided that 'to the Jews as individuals, everything; to the Jews as a race, nothing', the debates that led to this decision made clear the huge departure from traditional ways of being Jewish this required. Many speakers recognised that Jews were a group, collectively defining who they were for themselves, and some doubted that so distinctive a group of people could leave their Jewish selves outside the door to be equal loyal citizens to the State rather than to each other. Eventually, though, it was decided to let them try. Soon, French Jewry was to be characterised by spectacular levels of achievement and involvement in the life of France, though at the cost of an assimilation that might have done for French Jewry altogether if the influx of North African Jews in the 1950s and 1960s had not turned the tide.

While post-revolutionary, post-Napoleonic France theoretically offered the possibility of Jews rising through the ranks on equal criteria of merit along with their non-Jewish counterparts, the Dreyfus Affair was soon to knock a big hole in any confidence that observers might have had that such an option was secure. (The Dreyfus Affair was a late nineteenth-century scandal in France in which an entirely loyal French Jewish captain was falsely condemned as a traitor. The case exposed deep seams of anti-Semitism in France, until then thought to be the heart of European Enlightenment and freedom for the individual.) Even today, many French Jews are uneasy about the suggestion that it would be impossible to vote if election day fell on a Jewish festival. Indeed, when this happened a few years ago, appalled appeals were made to the then Chief Rabbi to grant some kind of dispensation to enable French Jews to vote and thus demonstrate that they were as French and as concerned for the body politic as the next Frenchman. The idea that the State might accommodate Jewish sensibilities by moving the date or making some other arrangements was a far less vocally proposed option.

Indeed, it was Theodor Herzl's experience reporting on the Dreyfus trial that propelled him away from his Austro-Hungarian assimilationist tendency. Such a tendency was also evident in most northern Protestant nations, which were increasingly tolerant of Jews but still in most cases had established churches, led by their monarchs. Jews would be accommodated, even allowed much, but it was not quite the full freedom under the law in full equality that might be hoped for. For example, throughout the nineteenth century, German Jews in particular converted to Christianity in clear conversions of convenience, to enable them more fully to play their part in the life of the nation.

Only the United States held out the possibility of an absolute separation of religion and State. Its dogmatic insistence on such a separation seemed to offer the only real hope of religion never entering into the matter. Jews flocked there in their hundreds of thousands – indeed, millions – and lived a privatised Jewish life which was soon to become nobody else's business.

And why, if it was nobody else's business, should any rabbi or tradition be allowed to tell you how to be Jewish? In the coming decades, Jewish life in America evidenced some of the most liberal and various Jewish behaviours ever observed in apparently organised Jewish communities. Jews trekked out into the Wild West, each on his own, being his own kind of Jew, making his own kind of accommodation with the modern world he found. More than in any other Jewish community in the world, Reform Judaism became the norm and Jewish practice became entirely according to the judgement of each individual. No-one could tell anyone what was 'properly' Jewish. Each person became his or her own Bet Din. In some circumstances, 'Jewish practice' became whatever it was that Jews did or defined for themselves as Jewish. No authority had the right to tell anyone what was the 'true' religion. After all, that was the way of dogmatism, benighted prejudice – and the Old World.

Meanwhile, other Jews in Europe found a different answer to the conviction that Jewish life in Europe was never going to improve. Instead of privatising their Jewish identities, they would 'nationalise' it. And so Zionism was born.

Of course, Jews had long dreamed of returning to the Land of Israel, and prayed for it. But such dreams and prayers did not have a political programme attached. The nearest to such a programme was the bold – some might even say absurd – demands of various pretenders to the role of Messiah who demanded the Land of Israel or Jerusalem for the Jews. But the point of the demands of such false messiahs was always to finish with politics as we know them, not to inaugurate a Jewish version of them in the community of nations. Indeed, until Zionism was properly underway, Jews did not really even have a name for the state they would like. Terms like Eretz Yisrael – the Land of Israel – the Holy Land, and Palestine (this last name has strong political overtones nowadays, but was even more charged in ancient times when the name was coined by the

Romans to accentuate the complete expulsion and dispossession of the Jews from their ancient homeland) were used interchangeably to describe the area loosely, but no-one particularly advocated any of these as the necessary name for any future Jewish polity.

Zionism was different. Become a Zionist and you no longer had to take individual responsibility for your Jewish life. The State would do it for you. At last, the law of the land would require *kashrut*, or the festivals, or the language or whatever it was that your sliver of Zionism perceived as an essential expression of Jewish life. Most Jews must know *olim* (immigrants to the State of Israel) who have commented that living in Israel has made being Jewish so much more effortless for them. It might be true to say that Zionism was for Judaism what the Welfare State was for the caring society.

Of course, this was not the universal dilemma for European Jews. The vast majority did what European Jews had done for centuries. They stayed put – more or less – and decided to sit out whatever the twentieth century held for them, as they had done for the last ten centuries or so.

Hindsight serves to considerably distort our vision of the way it really was. And no event more thoroughly skews and obscures our view of the past in European Jewry than the *Shoah*. Oddly, American and Israeli Jewry view the victims of the *Shoah* with more ambivalence than their genuine and vocal concern might suggest. There is a strand of thought amongst those supremely self-confident Jewish blocs that wonders why European Jewry did not do more to save itself. In some extreme forms this borders on contempt for European Jews going 'meekly like lambs to the slaughter'. American Jews like to believe they would have agitated for their rights and Israeli Jews know that they would have taken up arms. Even setting aside the fact that European Jews did both of these things in many instances, such simplistic views are aggravated by the fact that they are almost always only implied since they are so unacceptable, and therefore cannot so easily be challenged or examined.

Difficult though it may be to bear in mind with the vast shadow of the slaughter darkening every view, it is important to remember that no-one in the years leading up to the Second World War accurately predicted the *Shoah*. Even those who made apocalyptic warnings of the dire future for Europe's Jews did not envisage the inexorable machine of the Nazi genocide. Even Hitler, who clearly stated his aspiration of the total removal of Jews from Europe as early as 1924 in his manifesto book, *Mein Kampf*, may not have imagined how it might be done, and did not necessarily envisage the killing of so many millions. His first moves seem to suggest that a significant part of his plan was simply to expel Jews from his field of hegemony. As often in history, great dreams – even nightmares – could not be achieved in the absence of the right technology.

Since the War and the revelation of the horrors of the camps, the very mention of them makes us shudder. But we should remember that when the Nazis opened the first of the concentration camps, they held a press conference and opened it to the general public so that they could see this new step in penal reform, a much more aggressive, but no less heralded and lauded, version of the modern-day 'short sharp shock' in the U.K. or penal 'boot camps' in the U.S. There was nothing new about concentration camps anyway – they had been invented by the British in the Boer War forty years earlier – and similar kinds of camps existed around the world. The only thing that apparently distinguished the Nazi concentration camps was their show of efficiency and sterile perfection. At that time, the death camps may still not have been imagined even by the Nazis.

Those who escaped Central Europe with the rise of Nazism are really only using hindsight or believing their own hyperbole when they say that they left knowing that European Jewry was doomed to total death. What they really mean was that it was doomed to appalling oppression, not total destruction.

And if that is true, we should remember then that the *Shoah* was not a natural consequence for European Jewry. Certainly as anti-Semitism intensified, the Jews of different countries in Europe faced more and more severe oppression, restriction and suffering. But those European Jews who decided to sit it out were simply using proper historical knowledge. Sitting out oppression had proved to be a good strategy over the last thousand years. Despite our retrospective view of European Jewish history as being an endless catalogue of massacre, pogrom and expulsion, the reality on a day-to-day basis experienced by Jews – bearing in mind that nobody much, except a small and privileged elite, was having a good time in Europe for the last thousand years – was that life went on pretty ordinarily for a hundred years or so, and then it was disrupted perhaps for a decade until it settled back down.

In fact, of course, this proved to be true this time as well, but this disruptive decade exceeded all others. By the end of the *Shoah*, both Zionists and American Jewry knew that they were vindicated in their foresight. The *Shoah* 'proved' that it was impossible to live as a Jew in Europe.

But these alternatives to the European style of communal Jewish life were not the cause of the flourishing of American Jewry or the salvation of Israeli Jewry, nor was the way European Jews accommodated themselves to the State the cause of their near destruction. The easy assumption of 'cause and effect' has not been proven, and the self-satisfaction of Israeli and US Jewry in the post-war years has proved premature.

Nevertheless, for the fifty years or so following the war, the view of the Jewish world has been bipolar, with Israeli and American Jewry vying for the crown of most vibrant and most relevant resolution to 'the Jewish problem'. As indicated above, American Jewry became increasingly idiosyncratic, allowing the full freedom of individualism to impact upon different interpretations of Jewish life. On the other hand, in Israel, because of the state control of Judaism, ordinary folk became more and more alienated from it. Just as in the welfare state, when the government undertakes to do something for its citizens, they feel relieved of the responsibility of doing it for themselves. Israel, therefore, has proportionately the largest secular Jewish population of any country in the world. Perhaps 80 percent of Israeli Jewry thinks it needs to do nothing to preserve the future of the Jewish people except go about their daily lives. But worse than that, the sense of imposition resulting from state involvement and the legislative enforcement that some Jewish practices enjoy in Israel has given rise to widespread resentment and a feeling among many that Jewish things interfere with life rather than enrich it.

Of course, not all of European Jewry was equally savaged by the *Shoah*. Scandinavian Jews were already following the programme of German Jewry towards rapid assimilation into a tolerant and cultured Nordic world. Soviet bloc Jews were heading, more or less willingly, towards the atheistic ideology of Communism. British Jewry was gently punting its way along a sleepy stream surrounded by the dreaming spires of Cambridge, Westminster, or Edinburgh.

The responses of different national Jewries to the extent of each country's involvement in the *Shoah* also differ. Dutch Jewish questions, staring us in the face for all this time – if Holland was so tolerant and supportive of the Jews, how is it that a greater proportion of Dutch Jews died in the *Shoah* than in most other, less tolerant countries of Western Europe – have only recently emerged onto the international stage. (To be fair to the Dutch, it may be precisely because they were so tolerant, and therefore Jews felt too well integrated to protect themselves properly. The jury is still out on that one.) Swiss Jews have only recently engaged in public exposure of the fact that their accommodating State included them only by excluding others. French Jewry, post-war, struggles to confront the wilful amnesia in France, only now starting to break down, which served to maintain the fiction that Jews were indistinguishable citizens of the French Republic.

Oddly, though, and unwittingly, Israel put an end to any post-war tendency in Europe to try and fit in – to fulfil the French aspiration of equal citizenship through leaving Jewishness at home. The Six Day War of 1967, in which Israel was attacked by vastly superior forces from all sides, explicitly intending to wipe it off the map, acted as a wake-up call to Jews the world over and reminded them of their distinctiveness. More or less assimilated Jews in France and Britain found themselves, to their own wonderment, volunteering to help out in Israel. The Jews hidden behind the Iron Curtain in the Soviet bloc suddenly discovered an inspiring anchor for their own suppressed sense of Jewishness. On televisions around the world proud young Israelis, some of them sporting *kippot*, walked through the streets of Old Jerusalem, teaching Jews throughout Europe that it was possible to be proud and Jewish.

But the habits of a lifetime take a long time to break and any rising of the sap was imperceptible in the 1960s and 1970s. American and Israeli Jews were able to shout at each other across what they thought was the more or less dead carcass of what had once been the great centre of Jewish life and culture in Europe. It is still common for leaders from those two Jewish worlds to talk of Europe as a vast Jewish graveyard.

Any apparent communication between the East and West of the Jewish world was, of course, a dialogue of the deaf, each side convinced that it had found the best 'solution to the Jewish problem' – privatise or nationalise, neither prepared to give much time to the other's solution, and certainly not prepared to consider that there was any merit in the old European ways of doing things. The other possible great centre of Jewish life and culture of a classical sort – the North African and Arab Jewish communities – had been decimated following the founding of the State of Israel, the Suez debacle and the Six Day War. By the mid-1970s, it was possible to argue (especially if you were Israeli or American) that there were, frankly, no communities offering a way forward for Jews in the latter half of the twentieth century except those in the United States and Israel.

To complete the world picture, we should remember that there were also sizeable Jewish communities in South America, South Africa, Canada, and a growing community in Australasia. South African and Australasian Jewry were still fairly isolated from the rest of the world while Canadian Jewry, like its host country, was struggling with its sense of itself as an inheritor of the best of European life and culture while scrabbling on the scree to avoid being sucked down into the United States. In the 1970s, and to a considerable extent still, South American Jewry was attempting to model itself in Zionist terms, more successfully teaching its children to speak Hebrew than to light Shabbat candles, and striving to encourage high levels of *aliyah*. As we now know, such an intense focus on *aliyah* as the goal of Jewish education can be counter-productive. After all, in reality, making *aliyah* is probably an elitist goal for the minority in most places, and the exhortations to leave come to nothing for most people. So if most Jews are bound not to fulfil what they have been taught is the point of Jewish life, they are left with few alternatives to assimilation, especially if other ways of being Jewish have not been sufficiently explored.

By the 1970s, the growing assertiveness of the newly settled North African Sephardim within French Jewry in the West, coupled with the increasing vociferousness of nascent Jewish consciousness by the Soviet Jewish refuseniks in the East, necessarily drew attention to the possibility that all was not yet over for the Jewish communities of Europe.

At the beginning of the 1980s, there was a major increase in education about, and memorialising of, the *Shoah*. Some of it was a product of growing awareness that there will not be many eyewitnesses left alive for much longer. Some of it came from the media exploitation and exploration of the subject – from the two extremes of glossy Hollywood mini-series like *Holocaust* (1978) to the nine-hour documentary *Shoah* (1985).

In the strange dynamic of American perceptions of Europe provoking Europe into having perceptions of itself, there was also a corresponding rediscovery of the communities that were destroyed. America could tell the story of the *Shoah* less mournfully than Europe because after all, tragic though it was, it also seemed a vindication of (Jewish) American foresight. But such programmes as *Holocaust* allowed a European reassessment precisely because it was not too grim to look at. The very superficiality of which it was (rightly) accused is what made it such an effective Trojan Horse into European reluctance to consider the *Shoah* itself. The more positive but equally saccharine American version of pre-war European Jewish life manifest in the phenomenal success of *Fiddler on the Roof* (1971) several years earlier, and the increasing readiness of West German authorities to start to look their history in the eye – even the increasingly untenable position of countries within the Communist bloc, attempting to claim that they had had no part in the *Shoah* – provoked more and more attention to, and awareness of, European Jewish history.

It was the 1990s that finally jolted the smug duologue which had been the script for post-war Jewry. The existence of a dialogue between the Jews of the land of Israel and a major Diaspora centre was nothing new. Indeed, if anything, it was the norm for global Jewish life. From time to time, the centre of Diaspora Jewry had shifted from one place to another, but in general there was always a leading Diaspora community that would arrogate to itself the right to define what it was to be a Jew outside Israel. In earlier times it was Babylon, then Spain, Germany, the Ottoman Empire, then Poland and Eastern Europe, and now it was the United States.

The late 1980s and early 1990s saw two reports emerge in the U.S.A. and Israel respectively which caused both communities vertiginous fear that they may not, after all, be standing on foundations that might sustain them.

In Israel, the government sponsored the Shenhar Report ('People and World – Jewish Culture in a Changing World', Ministry of Education and Culture, 1994), which considered the state of Jewish awareness in young Israelis. Its findings shocked the Israeli Establishment to the core. It finally gave concrete evidence of something that many had been aware of before this time. It demonstrated that many Israelis did not feel any particular association with the history and collectivity of the Jewish people, that they were deeply ignorant of fundamental Jewish practices and facts, and that, in broad terms, large parts of the Israeli education system were aggravating rather than mitigating this erosion.

Meanwhile, in the United States, the largest demographic survey to date (U.S. National Jewish Population Survey, The Council of Jewish Federations, 1990) uncovered the fact that American Jews were assimilating at an alarming rate. Intermarriage figures of over 50 percent and evidence that non-Orthodox communities in particular were haemorrhaging from generation to generation forced a major rethink among the leadership and organisers of the American Jewish community.

Thus was born the Jewish Continuity movement, accentuating more assertively the need for Jewish education, association with the local community, the re-evaluation and encouragement of traditional practices, the cultivation of ethnic particularities and, in particular, a reassertion that the 'successful' Jew not only had a strong Jewish identity of his or her own, but also was committed to successful strategies for transmitting being Jewish to the next generation. At last, mainstream American Jewry started to accept that how you were Jewish was not just your own private business.

It does not require much perception to recognise that these two discoveries met each other in the middle. More than that, rather than conducting a strident shouting match, each confident that they had found the way to the future survival of the Jewish people, both communities briefly fell silent and looked at their feet. And what did they find there? Slight though indubitably green shoots of Jewish life across Europe.

The collapse of the Iron Curtain allowed for a flood of Judaic enthusiasm to sweep across the Continent. Even in Western Europe, the newly discovered connections with Eastern European Jewry breathed new life into sometimes fairly moribund communities. For example, the long existing European Council of Jewish Communities (ECJC) suddenly sprang into much more dynamic life. Without doubt, such a revival could not have been possible without the commitment and dedication of both American and Israeli Jewry. In particular, the American Joint Distribution Committee (the JDC or the 'Joint') and the Jewish Agency for Israel (JAFI) worked to nurture such a renaissance. Through them, both personnel and resources were made available to European Jews slowly and tentatively emerging into the light of a new world.

Fortuitously, these developments coincided with the start of the Oslo Peace Process and the possibility that the Jewish world faced no other urgent cause. The Israeli personnel who were despatched to build on this renaissance discovered, as they had already discovered in Western European communities, that it was fairly difficult to propagate any sense of Jewish awareness without engaging in traditional, not to say religious, forms. The Joint, temperamentally or instinctively more dedicated to the individualistic patterns of American Jewry, was tempted to support the development of self-determining communities along the lines of the secular, non-denominational Jewish community centres of North America. But even they found that they had to work with the grain of the instincts of European Jews.

And the sleeping giant started to stir.

The European contribution to the set is to offer a kind of middle way between the privatised Jewish identity of America and the nationalised Jewish identity of Israel. This 'third way' (Tony Blair, the British Prime

Minister, called his socialist-capitalist model the 'Third Way') is the ambiguous and politically elusive model of the community. Europe and European Jews, older and both more compromising and compromised than their younger national siblings are, once again resurrected the as yet poorly articulated multi-layered identity of the European Jew.

Across Europe, prior to the catastrophe of the *Shoah*, Jews had been moving at various speeds into emancipation. Often the issue of 'rights' was not as important as the winning of concessions or exceptions from acceptedly Christian nations. Frequently, the community had some kind of status in law – the capacity to levy taxes or contributions – to provide parallel arrangements for Jews to opt out of the otherwise universal Church arrangements. In Britain, for example, where trading on Sundays was forbidden, the Board of Deputies of British Jews was charged with the responsibility of licensing those who could trade on Sundays because they closed their businesses instead on Shabbat.

In general, this mixture of legal definition and concession tends to be less pluralistic in Europe than in America, though more accommodating of diversity than Israel. After all, European Jewry is as much defined by 'the other' as it is defined by itself. Since there seems to be more of a consensus as to what is, for example, Polish (and less room for diversity within that definition than in the U.S.), Poles tend to see Jews as 'not quite as Polish' in terms of national culture. Jews are aware of this, and are conscious that, by celebrating Passover and not celebrating Christmas, they are seen in this way. The definition of what is Jewish therefore is not only not entirely in the hands of each individual Jew, but is contested between the Jews and those around them. In this respect, as a minimum, Jews need to act collectively to ensure that they are not defined in ways they cannot accept.

At the same time, though, Jewries are not usually established and maintained by the State. In general, the non-Jewish states of Europe do not try to adjudicate as to what is acceptably Jewish, and usually whatever Jews say is Jewish is judged as being eligible for any of the exceptions and accommodations that the State is prepared to concede. However, the states recognise some Jewish organisations but not others. In doing so, they are not deciding matters of Halachah, but making (political) decisions about which organisations to recognise as representing Jews. They make these decisions based on considerations generally unrelated to religious or other differences within Jewry. Furthermore, unlike in Israel, where the only form of Judaism that is State-supported is Orthodox Judaism, and where Orthodoxy is sufficiently numerous and powerful to not care (enough) about the loss or indifference or exclusion of others, in many small communities round Europe, sheer pragmatism would require that all Jews, however affiliated, work together at least in matters of representation to government or securing concessions for Jews as a whole, although in practice, that is not always the case.

Of course, there is the possibility of a secular cultural Jewish identity. Such an identity existed in Western Europe, but it is not clear how much this was a product of resistance to the total inclusion of Jews into general non-Jewish society or the residual sense of affiliation – 'running on empty', as it were, from previous generations. Certainly, a secular Jewish culture was rife and thriving in Eastern Europe before the *Shoah*. This – to oversimplify it – 'Yiddish' identity had a key prerequisite of any identifiable culture, that is, a definitive language or voice that set it apart from others. Jewish culture in the United States still has something of this, though as Jewish writers, artists, and film-makers become more and more acculturated there is less and less of their output that can be said to be distinctive. It seems reasonable to conclude, therefore, that such a cultural aspiration is hardly a mainstream option nowadays where there are not sufficient numbers to enable the culture to exist through the inert power of numbers. If Jewish identity is to exist at all powerfully in the small communities in the different countries of Europe, it will exist by virtue of their conscious effort to express themselves as Jews in contradistinction to the society within which they live.

These differences of culture – which give rise to the three models of how Jews 'construct' themselves in wider society – and the assumptions implicit in how one expects a Jewish world to be are played out with intriguing results in different countries around the world. Reference has already been made to the strange hybrid of Canadian Jewry which is both British/French in some of its forms and yet distinctively North American in many others. It is far more traditionalist than U.S. Jewry, and yet far more accommodating of non-Orthodox strands than most European communities.

Another country in which one can detect the odd interplay of these different models is Hong Kong. The resident Hong Kong Jewish community is Sephardi in origin and British in development. Its unarticulated assumptions (in classic Sephardi/British form) are that the community should be Orthodox, whatever the private practice of individual Jews is. However, a significant proportion of the Jews of Hong Kong are now expatriates or transitory American business people who expect a much more pluralistic model in their community. The predominantly American Reform community of Hong Kong cannot understand why the resident community feels it should be a little more suppliant and modest in its demands to be treated on equal footing as a sizeable part of the resident community. Why, for example, can they not use the community centre for their religious services, given that the only actual synagogue in Hong Kong is Orthodox? At the same time, the resident community finds it difficult to understand how to respond to the expectations of the Reform community to be treated as equals, when they appear not to be adhering to tradition in the way that the 'official' community has always been led to believe is the proper form. (The situation is further complicated by the fact that several of the 'guardians' of the status quo are themselves not deeply committed to Orthodox practice.)

This results in a rerun in miniature of the global dialogue of the deaf, crammed into this small, overcrowded island, giving rise to moments of tension which have, from time to time, threatened to crack the community in two. After all, if members of the Reform community are subscribers to the Community funds, should they not be allowed to use the community buildings as they wish? A threat to secede from the 'official' community would have weakened the whole community to no-one's benefit, but to have pressed their 'rights' to do as they wish would have driven the Orthodox out of the community structures. It is a great credit to all players on the different sides that they have managed to find the statesmanship and sensitivity to keep the community ship afloat despite their occasionally bewildered incomprehension of the other side.

So what are the realities arising from trying to live with this more ambiguous model of Jewish interaction with the wider world?

The first step, I think, is to recognise the huge oversimplification utilised above. The 'community' model has many different forms. To be fair to European life and, at its best, the European refusal to choose between the private and the national, requires the difficult but honourable insistence of a both/and position, rather than an either/or one, intentionally accommodating difference while not implying that the differences do not matter. But the vast majority of Jews and their communities in Europe actually just flip back and forth between being utterly Jewish sometimes and entirely non-Jewish at others. At the heart of most European Jews' daily Jewish life lies equivocation, ambiguity and compromise – not, let me stress, necessarily negative attributes. They bring to life the valuable recognition that an individual's decisions and behaviour may not always be right for everyone else. But the pressure placed upon Jews in Europe by the evidence – and general self-confidence – of the other models now available demands of communities in different countries that they finally clarify where they stand. This is not necessarily to anyone's benefit, but the trend appears irresistible.

For example, in German speaking countries, the *Einheitsgemeinde* or 'unified community' is the norm. In theory – often in collaboration with the State – the community is a single entity, collecting its resources and distributing them centrally. This is not dissimilar to the American 'Community Chest' form of fundraising through a Federation; but the *Einheitsgemeinde* tends to work mainly through synagogue communities, though it also has responsibility for welfare provision and education. Before the war, the predominance of Reform communities in German-speaking countries made those the ones who defined the norms of the community; some of the Orthodox felt they had to secede and were left to manage as best they could. Nowadays the situation is reversed, with Orthodox voices defining the 'official community', thus tending to exclude the Progressive communities from *Einheitsgemeinde* resources in most places so that they have to maintain themselves with little State recognition or support. It seems that this is not likely to be sustainable for much longer.

Italy, on the other hand, has a long tradition of its own brand of 'Italian Jewry', standing proudly as neither Ashkenazi nor Sephardi, and determinedly including all Jews more along the lines of Sephardi communities than the much more doctrinally insistent Ashkenazi world. But post-war, until recently, Italian Jewry has failed to produce its own rabbinate, thereby putting at risk its traditions and traditional inclusive tolerance. It has started to fall to the more divisive pressures of alien Ashkenazi forms – Lubavitch and others – as rabbis needed to be imported, or Italian young men were trained in the yeshivot of non-Italian forms. Recent signs suggest that Italian traditions are reasserting themselves with a few indigenous young rabbis coming back on to the local scene, which gives some hope for the future of this uniquely integrated community.

Central and Eastern European Jewry, however, faces other challenges. All the various denominations and groups have flooded into this field, thirstily soaked up by a parched Jewry which does not know how to differentiate or discriminate between the blandishments of each. There are rival Orthodox groups – for example, rival Chief Rabbis in Russia – but also developing Reform communities, sponsored by communities in particular in the United States, who sometimes cannot find recognition from the fairly conservative State religious structures of newly freed Eastern Europe.

The Scandinavian communities have a long tradition of liberalism, giving rise to a distinctive traditionalism which was at ease with a fairly tolerant and inclusive wider society, and was near enough to Orthodoxy to pass muster in a more fragmented world. But Scandinavia can no more stay independent of the currents flowing through world-wide Jewry than the Central and Eastern European Jews mentioned above. They can no more define their own standards of Jewish life with indifference to the opinion of other authorities in other communities in the world than the economy of one country can nowadays afford to ignore that of another. This globalisation of Jewish life is putting them under pressure to draw the lines more firmly in matters of conversion, for example, than was the case hitherto. These comfortably inclusive communities are sometimes thus finding themselves being forced to split or exclude in ways which may not be helpful to them, by the uncomprehending pressure emanating from the more bullish Jewish worlds of Israel and America – who, given their numbers, seem to believe they can afford the luxury of excluding large swathes of Jews from the officially recognised communities.

All of this has practical consequences. Jews in Europe, given their undefined status – neither legally structured entities in European law, nor merely citizens in a world that does not engage in religious issues – find themselves potentially recipients of government funding or legal exemptions or whatever. But then who is to say that someone has a right to such legal features? In Britain, for example, the government funds Jewish schools – to a considerable extent anyway – but then can the Jewish community exclude people whom the government might consider Jews but this or that section of the community does not? What happens when a self-defining Jew claims his/her right to a place in a government-funded school and the Jewish community claims that they are not Jewish?

What happens when the State is ready to hand back a piece of property for the rebuilding of a synagogue or the establishment of a community centre in a town where the most numerous Jewish group is not the 'official' Jewish community? Who gets it? Who defends the 'Jew for Jesus' when he claims the right not to work on Shabbat under European human rights legislation?

The ambiguities of community and communal existence require that these kinds of questions remain unresolved in any categorical way. If they must be addressed, it should be in a piecemeal manner and on a temporary basis, allowing the ambiguities to remain for another day. Each case must be judged on its merits and each country's community must find its own accommodation with the country at large. For example, French Jewry faces a very different set of national assumptions to Spanish Jewry. Russian Jews face a different political and social heritage to German Jewry. British Jews work within a different legislative framework to Ukrainian Jews. The relationship of the State to religion in the Czech Republic is different to that in the U.K. or Russia. Spanish Jews were overwhelmed by the visit of King Juan Carlos to their synagogue in Madrid, whereas Danish Jewry expects its Queen to turn up from time to time. For similar reasons of local political culture and norms, French Jews agonise when the national General Elections are scheduled for a Jewish festival day – should they vote or not? – while it is obvious to Jews in Britain that accommodation must be made by the State. And it is also why American Jewish organisations and Israel bluster uncomprehendingly about the way the French government and French Jewry reach their own resolutions on responses to what they (Americans and Israelis) would see as incontrovertible and unacceptable levels of anti-Semitism.

Every community's relationship with being Jewish and with the world at large is always work in progress, unresolvable in a once and for all way, given the flux of the world in which the Jews are living and the fact that in Europe, Jewish forms are more responsive to the context in which they exist than they are in their bigger and more self-defining fellow community constructs of the U.S.A. and Israel. The very flexibility of the European model is what has enabled its continuing survival, mirroring and resisting the patterns of other religious communities in the country in question. Jews in Europe juggle skilfully and sophisticatedly with ethnic identity, quasi-national associations with the State of Israel, patriotism with the country of residence, occupying with good reason the ancient European persona of jaded elder in the world, having seen it all before, finding it impossible to sign up to any ideology completely, but espousing participation as an ideology.

If, though, the community model is so indefinable and various, can it serve any useful purpose as a form, except to distinguish European ways of dealing with the interaction with the world at large from those of the U.S. and Israel? Huge amounts have been written recently about the 'Communitarian' school of thought, offering a middle road between the private loyalties of family and the national loyalties of patriotism. Some argue – fairly convincingly, in my view – that it is community that teaches people to care for more than their own. It offers a human-sized scale on which to practice not being entirely selfish and self-centred, and, of course, Jews are not the only ones to use it. Most religious groups in Europe utilise the community model and, as more new religious communities immigrate, it becomes an increasingly common model of loose organisation for many.

Following the disintegration of the Communist bloc on the one hand and the growing status of 'spirituality' as a domain for human concern and well-being, most (or all?) European countries are rediscovering religious identity as a key feature of human self-definition. At various paces, different countries in Europe are having to recognise that, though we are no longer a 'religious society', each person's religion and religious aspirations must be accommodated in law. (Some countries are only at the stage of trying to hold back this fact with probably unintended negative consequences on the Jews. Until relatively recently, Jews, as the only identifiable religious minority in most European countries, could be accommodated without much difficulty if the desire was there. Now that Muslims, Hindus and others have arrived on the scene in significant numbers, some countries have tried to withdraw those concessions, arguing that to give them to everyone will wreck common national norms. This expansion of the place of religion in civic life may frighten off the legislators, finally forcing them towards a more American model of separation.) But the growing awareness of European legislators that religion is also a function of ethnicity – or is it the other way round? – means to say that there is a progressively more subtle understanding of the spheres within which religion is relevant.

The tentative, ambiguous relationship between recognised but not controlled religious communities and the State allows much leeway for each group to organise itself as it sees fit, while providing it with a recognised space in the civic realm. Such a capacity to occupy a place in the public eye also imposes a need to be a little more coherent and 'official' than might otherwise be the case.

Besides this need to be able to operate in the public sphere in a manner that secures the respect and understanding of the non-Jewish world within which the community exists, such communities also need to develop their own methods of sustaining themselves, both in terms of financial and personnel resources and of development to adjust to the changing world they occupy. After all, they exist in an open world in which their survival is not protected or promoted by the State.

So what are the skills required by a European community to continue to survive and, hopefully, to thrive?

As has already been mentioned in the case of Italian Jewry, a community needs to produce its own personnel. The local culture of each national Jewish community is subtle and distinctive. While we like to enjoy the global nature of the Jewish world, we should not lose sight of the special flavours of Swedish Jewry compared to that of Greece. 'One rabbi fits all' is not a useful policy and each community should have regard to growing its own leadership, both in the lay and the professional field.

To do that, we need a more discerning lay leadership that can recognise when it is being offered something unsuitable for its own clientele. Unfortunately, most of our community leadership currently is not particularly skilled in understanding the needs and challenges of community development or the subtleties of Jewish life and distinctions. Give a chap a hat and a beard and he'll look good enough as a rabbi for most of our leadership – at least until he's given a job in the community, and then the trouble starts. And everyone then blames the rabbi. But he is probably only doing what he always said he would do: it is almost certainly the community leadership that did not sufficiently think about or understand the needs of the community to seek the kind of person that would suit them in particular.

I dwell on rabbis more than on other personnel because this is the field of employment in which people are more likely to suspend their own judgements most destructively for their communities. When appointing a community director or head of the local Jewish school or old people's home, community leadership tends to feel able to ask all the right questions. But with rabbis, they frequently feel that this is not a field they understand and so they are often bamboozled into making the wrong appointment or under the wrong terms.

In Israel, many rabbis are appointed by the State and are State functionaries. The same is true of many other community workers. In the United States, rabbis are frequently the chief executives of their community organisation, given the power and held responsible in the same way that chief executives of companies are. But in Europe, the appointing board frequently fails to be specific enough about what it wants from its rabbi. Rabbis are often given little power but held to account: while the rabbi is nominally in charge, s/he is often given far less leeway than is necessary to do a really good job. Just one example is that frequently rabbis in Europe are not given budgets or expense accounts to carry out their work. The individualistic nature of each synagogue community in the

United States allows each to do its own thing, more or less unconfined by anyone else's definition of what should be done, and the rabbi is the definer of the community's standards. But in Europe many communities are federated, and they try to keep together in some way. The rabbi is then neither entirely free, nor given clear guidelines as to the boundaries constraining options. While the collegiate possibilities for rabbis working in groups or in loose federations is very intriguing, just as often, these federations act as a constraint on individual initiative, forcing each rabbi to go at the pace of the slowest.

So personnel and the manner in which it is employed is key, as are the range of institutions on offer. Many of our communities in Europe have institutions which either were constructed for a different world or are the wrong size to fit the community we have now. Many communities are occupying unsuitable buildings or using them unsuitably for their current needs because that is how they have always been. In Jewish tradition, the only building the Jews were sentimental about was the Temple, and that no longer stands. All other buildings should either be functional or not of interest to us. However, the heritage movement, which has been an important stage towards the European Jewish world rediscovering itself, is now in severe danger of saddling the Jewish communities of the twenty-first century with responsibilities and preoccupations with buildings and property management issues. However important these may seem, they will inevitably distract the community leadership from the challenges of staying flexible and responsive to current situations and future needs.

While not wanting to decry the preservation of significant sites of historical interest, this is as much the business of the State authorities as it is of the Jewish community in particular. If the site is of genuine historical interest, local Jews should strive to persuade the State to take responsibility for it and include it in its tourist trails and so on. If the State will not take it on, it may well be that we are either failing to ensure that the country as a whole recognises the history of the Jewish community as an intrinsic part of the history of the country, or we are being unnecessarily sentimental about something that has little intrinsic worth. Either way, the challenge is to get our past into perspective for our own sake and then learn to move on. We certainly already have enough memorials and cemeteries to commemorate the past; we do not really need more for their own sake.

One might think that the creative management of property would be something that most communities could find skilled volunteers to manage. With restitution issues looming large on the current agenda of many European communities, creative use of the buildings and property becoming available is an urgent priority. The huge multiplex synagogues and community centres of the United States are rarely a useful model for the much smaller communities of Europe, while the functional synagogue without any community facilities of most of Israel is far too restrictive for

European community purposes. One might imagine that the beginning of the twenty-first century in Europe would see the flowering of a hugely creative surge in Jewish community building design, but by and large it is not happening yet.

While we must have regard to the personnel and physical resources of our communities, we also need to consider ways of raising funds. The funding of local communities is also something that works differently in different places, but in each case it tends to reflect the 'mixed economy' of Europe rather than either the dogmatically individualistic model of America or the nationalised provision of Israel. Forms of communal fund-raising tend to reflect local assumptions on general taxation. American Jews are encouraged both nationally and communally to think of a balance between low tax and a high individual responsibility to give, while Israeli Jews have a high tax culture with correspondingly less sense of a need to shoulder social burdens on their own.

Jewish communities in Europe utilise the donations, large and small, of individuals and philanthropists, but also expect a level of State funding for key institutions – schools and welfare provision, for example – where these provisions cater for those who otherwise would become a call upon the State anyway. At the same time, most communities levy some kind of community taxation, membership fee or whatever to cover the basic needs of all identifying Jews, imposing the expectation of every Jew that they have to give their modern equivalent of the half-shekel.

In the main, European Jewish institutions and communities are not as fortunate as their U.S. counterparts in the large-scale benefactors that bless and enrich American Jewry. The individual's responsibility is wonderfully manifest in the huge largesse of key individuals and foundations. The Federation, usually an alliance of all the key communal organisations, is the machinery through which local state or city communities raise their funds year on year. Federation campaigns are exactly that – exhorting people to feel that they should give voluntarily. The case needs to be sold each year. In contrast, European Jews tend to collect people's dues on an annual basis as a matter of course through various systems, while at the same time conducting top-up campaigns to raise money for specific needs.

Israelis Jews, on the other hand, know nothing of paying fees to synagogues or community centres, unless their particular synagogue or centre is not formally recognised by the State. Even in those cases, frequently they will then be supported by communities abroad in acts of solidarity with this or that provision. It is only fairly recently that Israelis are learning the habit of giving to 'communal' charities. (They have a pretty good record of giving to medical charities and the like. The conventional canard that Israelis do not know about charity is not true: they just have not been encouraged to recognise Jewish life as a recipient for it.)

So while European Jews can learn something from the experience of funding from abroad, not least creative forms of making donors feel good about giving, mostly the mixed economy model serves well. In some countries, where the government actually collects the 'religious levy' on behalf of the churches, it does so for the Jews as well, but this leads to some of the problems explored earlier as to who has a right to be a recipient of the money raised this way. (It is probably only the diffidence of European governments post-*Shoah* that prevents them from feeling able, indeed duty-bound, to decide 'who is a Jew', at least in reference to the ability to be a recipient of monies raised for Jews. When/if that comes about, that would surely be a strange mirroring of the Israeli problem.)

Overall, therefore, European Jewry stands at a key moment in its history. It has proved itself to be more resilient than we might have given it credit for thirty years ago. It is starting to wake from its sleep and flex its muscles. It is still woefully short of its own systems of training and development for its own leadership, though programmes like Le'atid, the European Leadership Training Institute, do fill that gap to some extent and certainly show a way forward. This programme provides for the fairly sophisticated training of both voluntary and paid personnel – rabbis, community board members, senior community personnel – through short courses, focusing on the interplay between concepts of community development, pertinent Jewish ideas and management theory and practice. Not only are the courses good in themselves (I should state an interest – I am on the faculty) but they also serve to develop a cadre of leadership across Europe, further bolstering the sense of European Jewry as opposed to isolated national Jewries. (Le'atid is largely funded by the Joint, but co-sponsored by the European Council of Jewish Communities – ECJC – and shows what is possible if only communities were prepared to spend money on securing their future, not just their past.) Most (all?) European communities have not resolved the new challenges of the much more plural forms of Jewish self-definition that have emerged over the last century. At the same time, the flexibility of the community model thrives on such challenges.

Postmodernism teaches us that things might be both/and rather than either/or – an ancient Jewish insight that lies at the heart of the Talmud and has just started to come back into its own, after the pressures of doctrinal simplicities and the certainties of the nineteenth century. When things can be both waves and particles at the same time, and the most powerful features of the universe are the things that we cannot see and, to the layman at least, do not exist, it is a brave person who would argue that we need systems for community survival which are more defined rather than less.

So in the face of the growing clamour for resolution and simplicity, I plead for complexity and ambiguity, equivocation and pragmatism. The wonderful experiment that is the enlarging European Union faces similar challenges just now. Some wish to see things made more uniform for the sake of clarity and equality. How does one include the minority – or in the European Union case, the small countries – with equal respect to that necessarily seized by the more powerful? But others are concerned that the particular aspects of differences that make the patchwork of Europe the fascinating continent it is should be preserved and allowed – even encouraged. That capacity to live with dilemmas rather than always trying to resolve them seems the best way to solve the human – and in particular the Jewish – condition in Europe today. Such an approach to dilemmas has always been a strength of European Jews, and long may it continue. The nineteenth-century distraction of demanding inflexible ideologies by which all things could be resolved proved in the twentieth century to be not only a dead end but a frighteningly destructive trend. Europe – and European Jewry – has retreated from that, but the relinquishing of such tendencies is not yet complete either among Jews or Europe as a whole.

The subtlety, the maturity – the humility – required to manifest the virtue of accommodating others without judging them, while accepting the same virtue in others, is an ancient Jewish quality cultivated over centuries in the crucible of European Jewish life. The world has never needed it more. I hope that European Jews will continue to accelerate their re-emergence onto the European and world stage to take up their historic and rightful place again as one of the most vibrant forces for good on every issue that Europe and the world face.

Chapter 3

CONCEPTS OF DIASPORA AND GALUT

Michael Galchinsky

Jews tend to think they know what it means to live in Diaspora. After all, Jewish tradition invented the concept, Jewish people lived the concept, and Jewish scholars and writers elaborated the concept during 2,500 years of dispersion throughout the world. Who should know what Diaspora means if not the Jews? Yet this assumption that Jews already know the meaning of Diaspora may cause them to ignore important recent developments in the concept, and they may miss out on information they need.

The dissolution of the European colonial empires, the development of information technology, easy and cheap mass transit, and the disappearance of the Berlin Wall – these developments have contributed to increased migration across national borders in Europe. More visible than ever before are enclaves of Turks, Kurds, Sinti, Afro-Caribbeans, Filipinos, Iranians, Poles … and the list goes on. In the last two decades, many of these migrants have come to understand themselves as members of diasporas. They have both adopted and adapted the concept of diaspora from Jewish tradition, so that in their use the term does not necessarily have the same meaning as it does in a traditional Jewish context.

This redefinition of diaspora has so far had little effect on Jews. American Jews, at any rate, have tended to ignore these newcomer diasporas, regarding their own community as unique and exceptional in world history and therefore as incomparable. For that matter, American Jews have regarded their diaspora as unique and exceptional in Jewish history as well. But by regarding their condition as incomparable, American Jews have neglected to participate in cross-cultural conversations to which they might make valuable contributions. They have reinforced their reputation among other diasporic communities as inward-looking and isolationist. They have alienated themselves from Jewish history as well as from potentially crucial resources, information, and support. And, not least, they have hampered their efforts to forge a constructive relationship with the state of Israel.

I wish to suggest that European Jews might succeed where American Jews have largely failed, by leading the way towards a dialogue of diasporas. And I want to try to demonstrate that such a dialogue may help Jews develop an identity better suited to the late twentieth century than that so far developed by American Jewish intellectuals. In any case, American Jewish attitudes towards diaspora are almost certainly not adequate for European Jews, particularly in the wake of the dissolution of the Soviet Empire and in the face of the consolidation of the European Union, and there are already several indications that European Jews have begun to articulate what distinguishes their diaspora from the American model. The revitalisation of the European Jewish Studies Association in 1996, after it lay defunct, suggests that a new European Jewish identity is in the air. As Diana Pinto argues in Chapter 1, we seek today to understand European Jews as both contributors to and beneficiaries of a new concept of diaspora that is even now under construction.

I will attempt to describe here the contours of this new concept. I will first describe the way intellectuals from former European colonies understand diaspora, then compare their understanding with the traditional Jewish narrative the very different American Jewish understanding. Finally, I will suggest a synthesis of these narratives that may prove of use to the reformation of European Jewish identity at the beginning of the new millennium. By engaging in systematic comparisons of their condition with the analogous conditions of other late-twentieth-century diasporas, I will suggest, European Jews may be able both to learn from and to contribute to dialogues of inordinate importance in a time of global population shifts and the thrilling but frightening restructuring of nations.

Postcolonial Theories of Diaspora

Until recently, the proposition that Jews might engage in dialogue with other migrants might have seemed absurd to all but the most naïve Jews. After all, theorists of other diasporas have generally been migrants from former European colonies. These postcolonial intellectuals have generally understood 'Jews' as members of the white power structure, 'Zionism' as an expression of Western imperialism, and 'Israel' (especially after the 1967 War) as an American imperial proxy and colonialist entity. Rejecting each of these assertions as limited or distorted, Jews have considered themselves outsiders to postcolonial models, just as postcolonial theorists have considered Jews outsiders to their theories.

But recent postcolonial theorists have begun to re-evaluate and diverge from this initial analysis, offering Jews a potentially constructive new direction. First, they have begun to recognise that the entities to be resisted are not only comprised of 'people of colour' dominated by 'whites' (Appadurai 1993);[1] they realise that the global phenomena they seek to interpret cannot be explained according to any theories of racial 'essences'. Second, while earlier theorists saw Jews at best as pawns or victims of nationalism, and at worst as among nationalism's most heinous exploiters, recent theorists have begun to understand Jews' history and theories of 'diaspora' as crucial to their attempts to critique nationalism. The new adaptations of the concept of 'diaspora' emphasise the hybrid and fluid communities created by both forced and voluntary migrations. Post-colonial theorists suggest that in the era of decolonisation, these 'diasporic' communities can be subversive of nations. They argue that the multiply-ing number of diasporas whose members pour information, funds, and affection back and forth across national boundary lines works to unsettle nations' ongoing attempts at 'imagining communities' that are self-contained and non-porous (Anderson 1991). While criticising these theories where necessary, I hope to show that they may serve a crucial function for European Jews in enabling them to articulate a new and necessary kind of self-understanding.

The news that the term 'diaspora' has become an important analytical tool for those engaged in describing various postcolonial situations has become quite commonplace since 1989. In the spring of 1991, Khachig Tölölyan, a professor at the Zoryan Institute for Armenian Studies in Cambridge, Massachusetts, edited the first edition of a new journal titled *Diaspora: a Journal of Transnational Studies*. A short list of groups to whom various writers in the journal have since applied the term 'diaspora' includes Irish, Native Americans, Cubans, Eritreans, Kurds, Palestinians, Sikhs, Tibetans, Lithuanians, Turks, Nigerians, Indians, Pakistanis, Egyptians, Sri Lankans, Filipinos, Iranians, Franco-Maghrebians, Mexicans, and under certain conditions, women (cf. Koshy 1994; also, Boyarin and Boyarin 1993). The beautifully designed coffee-table book *The Penguin Atlas of Diasporas* by French Marxist historians Gérard Chaliand and Jean-Pierre Rageau appeared in French in 1991 and in English in 1995 and attests a similarly diverse list (Chaliand and Rageau 1995). Other journals have since begun paying attention to 'diaspora' and 'diasporic groups' (Lie 1995). Historians, sociologists, political theorists, literary critics, and philosophers have all used the concept (Anderson 1994; Anzaldúa 1987; Appadurai 1993; Gilroy 1993; Said 1993; also cf. Sollors 1989).

Although postcolonial theorists have employed the concept of 'diaspora' increasingly, they have disagreed with one another about what the term actually means and how it is to be employed. 'There is no ambiguity about the term <u>diaspora</u>', Chaliand and Rageau claim, 'when it is used in relation to the Jewish people' (Chaliand and Rageau 1995: xiii; Cohen 1997) – a problematic statement, as we shall see below. But they admit that once the term is 'applied' to other groups, 'it becomes im-mediately apparent how difficult it is in many cases to find a definition that makes a clear distinction between a migration and a diaspora, or between a minority and a diaspora' (ibid.). *Global Diasporas*, an introductory volume by Robin Cohen, suggests that there are at least five different types of 'diasporas', which Cohen calls, 'victim, labour, trade, imperial, and cultural diasporas' (Cohen 1997: x). Cohen tries to relate these types to one another by suggesting they share several features or elements. These features include the experience of dispersion, a collective memory of the homeland, desires to support or restore the homeland and to return to it, and a resolve to remain partly separate from their host societies (op. cit. p. 23).

Despite its somewhat incoherent definition, postcolonial theorists have found the concept of 'diaspora' useful in developing a new understanding of migration. The traditional understanding imagined migration as immigration – that is, as a singular move from one well-defined national territory to another. According to sociologist John Lie, immigration 'entails a radical, and in many cases a singular, break from the old country to the new nation'. Migrants are 'uprooted' and 'shorn of premigration networks, cultures, and belongings' (Lie 1995: 304). The 'melting pot' assimilates them by permanently removing what is unique to them. While they may retain a sentimental attachment to the old world, eventually they construct new networks in the new world and cease to consider return a serious possibility.

But postcolonial theorists have been attempting to describe a trajectory different from singular international immigration – a trajectory of multidirectional transnational migrations. A transnational community maintains its networks in the old world and continues to exchange information, political support, contractual obligations, funding, and perhaps above all affection with members of its ethnic or religious group in the old world. Lie remarks that '[m]ultiple, circular, and return migrations, rather than a singular great journey from one sedentary space to another, occur across transnational spaces' (op. cit.). The availability of cheap international telephone rates and the technologies of the fax, overnight express, email, and other outgrowths of the information age have made it increasingly possible for migrants to maintain living and not merely nostalgic connections with those they have left behind (Anderson 1994). The 'homeland' is not understood to be a unified field, not 'a comfortable, stable, inherited, and familiar space, but instead … an imaginative, politically charged space' (Mankeker 1994). According to many of the writers in *Diaspora*, this new narrative entails an altered attitude towards both the old world and the new. The new diasporans' mobility, and the fact that they occupy experiential 'border zones', engender in them multiple allegiances and resistance to the seemingly impermeable boundaries of the nation (op. cit.).

The belief that diasporas are subversive is nowhere more apparent than in the writing of the editor of *Diaspora* himself. Recognising from the outset that 'the term [diaspora] once described Jewish, Greek, and Armenian dispersion', Tölölyan argues that the term now 'shares meanings with a larger semantic domain that includes words like immigrant, expatriate, refugee, guest-worker, exile community, overseas community, ethnic community. This is the vocabulary of transnationalisms ...'. In the understanding made possible with this enlarged vocabulary, 'diasporas are the exemplary communities of the transnational moment', because 'they embody the question of borders, which is at the heart of any adequate definition of ... the nation-state. [A nation] always imagines and represents itself as a land, a territory, a place that functions as the site of homogeneity, equilibrium, integration'. But this imagined unity is disrupted by the existence of diasporas. According to Tölölyan, in fact, the increased visibility of diasporas is the ground condition for an entirely new vision: 'the vision of a homogeneous nation is now being replaced by a vision of the world as a "space" continually reshaped' by heterogeneous groups in constant negotiation. As a social formation that forces nations to recognise the limitations of their harmonious and unitary self-perception, 'diaspora' is potentially subversive (Tölölyan 1991; see also Tölölyan 1994).

'Diaspora' inserting heterogeneity into the nation-state might not be possible except that it forces an awareness of 'hybridity' and 'impurity' into the public discourse. Many postcolonial theorists seem to share a vision of 'diaspora' as a state of hybridity and impurity as against an empire or nation-state that is ideologically concerned with promoting homogeneity and purity (Said 1993: xxv, 14). For example, literary works written by diasporans include both elements of the cultures of their host societies and their homelands and therefore, as one critic remarks, are able to 'interfere with apparently stable and impermeable categories founded on ... nationality ... '. Such literary works are 'far from being fixed and pure' (op. cit. pp. 111–12).

In this view, because diasporans do not share the homogenising impulse of the nation, they (or at least some of them) are able to attain a powerful critical perspective. According to one postcolonial theorist, diasporic intellectuals can 'distill and articulate the predicaments that disfigure modernity – mass deportation, imprisonment, population transfer, collective dispossession, and forced immigrations' (op. cit. pp. 332–3). For many postcolonial theorists, the 'hybrid counter-energies' (op. cit. p. 335) that can resist nationalism may only be articulated by a diasporic consciousness.

A good example of a postcolonial theorist who makes claims for the subversiveness of diaspora and the critical potential of diasporans is Paul Gilroy, an Anglo-African historian at the University of London. In *The Black Atlantic: Modernity and Double Consciousness*, Gilroy demonstrates the hybridity and creative impurity of the thought and art that results from the encounter of African-American, Afro-Caribbean, and Anglo-African cultures, both with each other's artistic and intellectual heritage and with the non-black European and American artistic and intellectual traditions. He does so in order to argue that a fluid Black 'diaspora' culture traverses back and forth across the Atlantic Ocean. For Gilroy, 'diaspora' is valuable as a concept 'lodged between the local and the global' that offers 'an alternative to the nationalist focus which dominates cultural criticism' (Gilroy 1993: 6). He believes that nationalist ideology is totalising, and that since the concept of diaspora by definition cannot be forced into a single national mould, it can function as a crucial part of a subversive cultural criticism and politics.

Gilroy is aware (as some postcolonial theorists are not) of the 'dangers of idealism … associated with this concept' (op. cit. p. 81). He is aware that the condition of diaspora is often misery. But Gilroy asserts that even the suffering of diasporans 'has a special redemptive power, not for themselves alone but for humanity as a whole' (op. cit. p. 208). By making visible the terror at the heart of modern rationality and modern social formations such as slavery, diasporans' suffering can force nations to acknowledge and repent for their brutality. Like Said, Gilroy believes that '[w]hat was initially felt to be a curse – the curse of homelessness or the curse of enforced exile – gets repossessed. It becomes affirmed and is reconstructed as the basis of a privileged standpoint from which certain useful and critical perceptions about the modern world become more likely' (op. cit. p. 111). These privileged perceptions do not, however, seem available to every diasporan but only to exiled intellectuals. Gilroy sees 'diaspora' as a privileged and clear-sighted 'position' from which engaged intellectuals might mount effective resistance against nationalist power.

Here, there is room for criticism of the developing postcolonial model. For diaspora is not always subversive of nationalism: on the contrary, the condition of diaspora may inspire nationalist sentiment (Anderson 1994). True, Jonathan Pollard, the American Jew who spied for Israel, certainly represents the potentially subversive character of diaspora, since Pollard gave the Israelis information classified to protect U.S. national security. But diaspora does not always have this kind of subversive effect. The political theorist Benedict Anderson suggests that 'the rise of nationalist movements and their variable culminations in successful nation-states' can be accounted for as 'a project for coming home from exile, for the resolution of hybridity, for a positive printed from a negative in the dark-room of political struggle' (op. cit. p. 319). Nationalism is not necessarily expunged during periods of exile; indeed, it can be inspired by the experience. Exile can be described as the progenitor of the violence of nationalism as well as the motive for subverting the nation. Anderson's corrective is necessary so that the idealisation of 'diaspora' does not obscure the ambiguity of its relations with state power.

Even Anderson's corrective might itself need correction before it can be useful to European Jews, however. For like the other theorists, even

Anderson continues to favour the idea of 'diaspora' over the idea of the nation almost reflexively, as if diaspora communities were clearly more ethical than other types of 'imagined communities' – in particular, than the nation. If this interpretation of the relative ethics of 'diaspora' and 'nation' were applied uncritically to Jewish history, then 'diaspora' would appear to be Jewish history's grandest contribution to world history. By contrast, the formation and continuing existence of Israel as a national state would seem to be, at best, a highly unethical moment in Jewish history, which obviously needs to be subverted. This decontextualised understanding of the emergence of Israel as a nation-state is not a view that many Jews will accept (for an exception, see Boyarin and Boyarin 1993).

Despite its somewhat incoherent efforts to find a generalisable definition for 'diaspora', its insufficient appreciation for diasporans' suffering, and its rather inflexible ethical vision, the postcolonial discourse of 'diaspora' may have much to offer Jews. For one thing, since the new theories demonstrate that various ethnic minorities have features in common, these theories may prepare the ground for alliance-building between Jews and other such groups.

For example, Paul Gilroy acknowledges Black intellectuals' debt to Jewish history, and he extends an invitation to Jews and Blacks to engage in specific comparative analyses of their respective diasporas. He hopes that the links that would be revealed by such analyses 'might contribute to a better political relationship between Jews and blacks at some future distant point' (Gilroy 1993: 206). In fact, he initiates such a comparative analysis himself by tracing the influence of modern political Zionism in the nineteenth century on such Black liberation projects as the establishment of Liberia (op. cit. pp. 205–12). He also suggests that Jews might benefit from a renewed alliance since, unlike Jewish culture, Black Atlantic culture has developed strategies for relating to a diaspora that is a permanent condition and something other than a curse (op. cit. p. 208; see also Safran 1991).

Without engaging in comparative analysis of the kind for which Gilroy and other postcolonial theorists appeal, there is no way to gauge whether any of the strategies developed by other groups might be useful for European Jews.[2]

Jews' Traditional Narratives of Diaspora

But perhaps there is no need to look outside of Jewish history and intellectual tradition for theories of diaspora. Perhaps postcolonial theory has only repeated what Jews already know from their own experience. Once again, who knows Diaspora if not the Jews? By investigating the traditional Jewish narratives of diaspora – biblical, prophetic, and rabbinic – I will show that postcolonialism is actually proposing quite a different way of understanding diaspora than that found in traditional Jewish narratives. Perhaps the traditional narrative and the postcolonial discourse can each make visible what is missing in the other's approach.

In justifying their invocation of the concept of 'diaspora', a number of postcolonial commentators have noted that the term was first used in the Septuagint, the Egyptian Jews' translation of the Hebrew Bible into Greek c. 250 BCE. The literal meaning of the term 'diaspora', 'to be scattered' (like seeds), shows that the translators accurately reproduced the original Hebrew term from Deuteronomy 28:64, *'v'hefitz'cha'* ('you will be scattered'). But the Greek word 'diaspora' is not only an equivalent of the Hebrew word: it is an indicator of the very condition that the term describes. The translation of the Hebrew Bible into Greek would not have been necessary had Jews not already been scattered throughout the Greek (and subsequently Roman) empires. That is, the term is a mark of the Jews' experience of being colonised. Was the Greek Jews' Diaspora the vital and subversive existence predicted by postcolonial theory? Before we can fully appreciate the answer, we must be aware that there was already another narrative in whose light the Hellenised Jews themselves must have understood their existence. This narrative was first articulated in the very text from which the term 'diaspora' was derived.

'Diaspora' is first introduced in Deuteronomy when Moses, nearing his own death, recounts the history of the people of Israel to a new generation. All but two of those who had been liberated from Egypt with him are dead. In an attempt to inspire this new free-born generation of Israelites, Moses describes the manifold blessings that will accrue to the people if they uphold the Covenant – pledged at Sinai by their parents – after they have crossed the Jordan and taken the land of Canaan by military force. These blessings will benefit the people if they 'obey the Lord your God to observe faithfully all His commandments' (Deut. 28:1). On the other hand, if they are forgetful, neglectful, or rebellious, and do not 'obey the Lord your God to observe faithfully all His commandments and laws' (Deut. 28:15), they will be cursed – the most extreme of the curses being 'diaspora'. Thus, 'diaspora' makes its first appearance as the divine punishment for breach of contract.

Such a breach proves to have devastating consequences. For the text predicts that 'The Lord will scatter you (*v'hefitz'cha*) among all the peoples from one end of the earth to the other, and there you shall serve other gods, wood and stone, whom neither you nor your ancestors have experienced' (Deut. 28:64). In diaspora, Jews shall be made to commit the Bible's ultimate transgression, idolatry, and Deuteronomy goes on to predict that scattered Jews will experience profound political and spiritual degradation (Deut. 28:65–8).

Moses's curse is the first of many elaborations in biblical, prophetic, and rabbinic literature of the narrative of Israel's transgression against God and subsequent exile from blessing. While the term 'diaspora' seems to have a potentially positive connotation – the notion that, like seeds, those once scattered can take root and continue to thrive amid foreign flora – this meaning is increasingly foreclosed in prophetic literature by the replacement of the term *'t'futsoth'* (scatterings, 'diaspora') with the more strongly negative term *'galut'* (exile). As the above discussion suggests, Deuteronomy conceives the condition of diaspora to have both political and metaphysical dimensions. On a political level, it reminds Jews that property and security are gifts from God that can be taken away. On a metaphysical level, diaspora represents expulsion from nurturance, alienation from nature, and estrangement from God, others, even oneself, from all potential sources of blessing. Deuteronomy depicts the time of diaspora as Jews' bleakest hour: they are trapped in a condition of political and spiritual homelessness, in the aftermath of a glorious past, in a present full of danger and discontent, with only dread for a future (Eisen 1986; also see Eisen 1987). Thus, the attitude envisioned by the first use of the term 'diaspora' is alienation from home and hopelessness in the present host land.

While the vision of alienation in this text is profound, there is a promise hidden in Deuteronomy's narrative that is exploited by subsequent prophetic and rabbinic tradition: Jews might be able to seek redemption from diaspora if they atone for their many transgressions against God (Eisen 1986: 33). If they pass their time of trial through acts of atonement, Jews can expect a 'return' to and fulfilment of Deuteronomy's blessings. In contrast to Gilroy's understanding of the automatic redemption brought about by diasporic suffering, the traditional Jewish narrative understands diasporic suffering as only *potentially* redemptive: it may be redemptive only if Jews respond to it with the proper action, known as *'teshuvah'* – often translated as 'repentance' or 'return'. Appropriate *teshuvah* has been interpreted variously in Jewish history as prayer, social justice work, mysticism, national liberation struggle, or most frequently, the multitude of daily acts defined in the *halakhah*, the Jewish code of daily ritual observance. The mere fact of suffering, without an appropriate active response, does not guarantee redemption. This appears to be a difference between traditional Jewish thought and that emanating from the Black diaspora, the latter of which has been influenced by Christian interpretations of suffering and redemption.

According to the prophets, if Jews do respond appropriately, the 'scattered seeds' will be 'ingathered', the Jews restored to their homeland in Zion, and peace and prosperity will reign once more. The metaphysical and political alienations will cease. As Anderson suspected, the pain of 'diaspora' does generate an intense longing to return to the 'homeland' (although not necessarily a homeland defined in 'nationalist' terms). For the prophets, however, the homeland is understood not merely as a geographic source, nor merely as a source and origin of cultural integrity, but as a *sacred* source that represents the promise and proof of God's continuous care over the obedient covenantal community.

The cyclical narrative of Jewish history in which 'diaspora' is embedded might be schematised, then, as follows: Prosperity – Transgression – Diaspora – Repentance – Redemption. From this vantage point, the term seems to have little in common with the way postcolonialists use it. The premodern rabbis would have been able to make little sense of the postcolonial theorists' idealistic vision of 'diaspora' as a 'border zone' or hybrid consciousness filled with vital impurities.[3] In the Mishnah and Gemara, they repeatedly sought to separate the 'pure' from the 'polluted', through systems of halakhic regulations such as *kashrut* or *mikvah*. They did so in order to create a means by which it would be possible to ensure Jewish cultural survival in the midst of pressures to convert and assimilate. Indeed, the halakhic system gained such centrality that, unlike the prophets, medieval diasporic Jews expressed political aspirations to return to the homeland only infrequently: for centuries, the desire to return to the homeland meant primarily a metaphysical desire for wholeness. In this way, the Land remained a 'center of aspiration', but was on the 'periphery [of] actual existence' (Eisen 1986: 51).

Nor does the traditional narrative conceive of the condition of diaspora as inherently subversive of the systems of power in the midst of which the scattered must survive. If anything, the rabbis' interpretation of diaspora as a punishment made them rule warily when questions of obedience to the imperial Greco-Roman, Christian, or Ottoman rulers arose, to avoid bringing further harm to their vulnerable communities. While they succeeded in recreating Jewish time outside the Land, they were not always able to fend off threats to their security – the Jews were perhaps 'subverted' more often than their hosts. This evidence of the limitations of 'diaspora's' subversive potential may not be welcome to postcolonial theorists, but for medieval Jews (or later, for Soviet or Ethiopian Jews), for whom 'migrant consciousness' was not merely an intellectual exercise, the curse of exile remained potent.

Ultimately, however, neither postcolonial theory nor the traditional Jewish narrative proves fully accurate, at least when applied to the Hellenised Jews. While the existence of the Greek term 'diaspora' indicates that the Deuteronomic curse did to some degree come true – Jews had to read even their sacred text in the language of the dominant power – the fact that a translation of the Hebrew Bible came into being at all suggests that living in 'diaspora' was not quite as alienating as the Deuteronomic curse predicted. Life within the Greek and Roman empires was precarious for Jews: tributes were exacted from them, and they were prohibited at various times from sacrificing at the Temple (while it still stood) or from praying in their synagogues after the Romans destroyed the Temple in CE 70. Some, like the Maccabees and the zealots at Masada and in the Bar Kokhba uprising, lost their lives in resistance. Many were forced into slavery, others displaced from their homes. But that at least some Jews were able to read their sacred text (if only in translation) meant that at least some of them were not being made to 'serve other gods, wood and stone'. A community that could produce such a translation was probably not as powerless as Deuteronomy's narrative had foretold.[4] But neither was it as powerfully subversive as postcolonial theory would imply.

Thus, the traditional Jewish narrative is useful in pointing out the excessive idealism of the postcolonial model.

American Jews' Exceptional Diaspora

In turn, postcolonial discourse may be useful in calling attention to some of the flaws in American Jews' attitude towards their diaspora. Analysing American Jews' diaspora provides an excellent example of what European Jews should probably try to avoid.

Twentieth-century American Jewish intellectuals have generally resisted many of the elements of the traditional Jewish narrative. In particular, they have rejected the equation of the United States with *galut*, and the state of Israel with Zion. For the most part not Orthodox, they have been unwilling to see their diaspora as a divine punishment for their transgressions. Moreover, while American Jewish intellectuals have conceded that Israel is the Jewish cultural centre in the second half of the twentieth century, most have resisted the notion that Israel is the spiritual centre. Most have not seen Israel as the 'homeland' in the metaphysical sense, rejecting the notion that the Land is a sacred source of wholeness.

The conclusion Arnold Eisen reaches upon completing his survey of twentieth-century American Jewish thought is that 'America is not home, yet neither is Israel. [Israel] *is* the Center and is certainly not exile, but neither can the [U.S.] be compared to any previous diaspora. 'America is different'. Nor should its rich Jewish resources be underestimated. The two communities [are] interdependent' (Eisen 1986: 156–80). I hope to show that this ideological consensus is, however, only partially accurate and has some quite negative consequences. As a result of their attitude that they are different, exceptional, American Jews are isolated from other cultural groups in the United States, and alienated from any except a sentimentalised Jewish history.

America's 'difference' is usually justified by pointing to the relative absence of systematic persecution, and, concomitantly, to the many freedoms American Jews enjoy. Since the colonial period, American Jewish intellectuals have maintained that this New Jerusalem (as the Puritans called it) was a place of promise – a Promised Land – unlike any other. The Jews' embrace of the basic goodness of the Bill of Rights has perhaps most recently been exemplified in Lynne Sharon Schwartz's short story 'The Opiate of the People', in which David the Russian Jewish immigrant memorises the Constitution in order to be more American than Americans themselves (Schwartz 1990). (Imagine a German Jew memorising the Basic Law.) An attitude towards their condition that includes trust in the United States, trust that the United States is not *galut* but a hothouse nurturing self-expression and experimentation, pervades American Jewish theology and literature. There is no need to look abroad for Zion when Zion is right here – or more accurately, when Zion is right *now*, a time rather than a place, an experience rather than a territory, to be reached through the practice of a particular kind of attention, or *kavanah*.

In contrast to this vision of America as *heimisch* – familiar, secure, and creative – the State of Israel has seemed to many American Jews what Freud would have called *unheimlich*, uncanny (Freud 1963). While the traditional narrative of Diaspora functioned to unite scattered Jews from diverse locations in a common dream of return, the realisation of that dream by the ingathering of Israel's hundred diasporas has had the ironic effect of producing an awareness of Jews' heterogeneity. For many American Jews, for whom Jews appear fairly homogeneous – Ashkenazi, white – the hundred diasporas call attention to Israel's diversity and unfamiliarity. For many American Jews, then, this heterogeneity is another indication (alongside Israel's continuing national insecurity and economic deprivation) that Israel is not Zion, that Israeli nationhood is not the fulfilment of a sacred promise but the partial, haphazard, sometimes elating and sometimes distorting realisation of generations of Jewish dreams and nightmares.

Even the familiar Western aspects of the modern state, like its parliamentary structure and principle of majority rule, can produce an awareness of Israel's distance from the traditional vision of Zion, for if the state is comprised in part of political and cultural institutions transplanted to the Land from *galut*, then the centre begins to seem less distinct from the periphery after all. These 'impurities' associated with Israel's realisation must conflict with the prophetic promise of a return to wholeness and the rabbinic vision of spiritual purity. When Philip Roth's Portnoy makes his brief and catastrophic journey to the Land, the state appears exotic, dangerous, even emasculating (Roth 1969). American Jews may still 'sing the songs of Zion in a strange land', but they do so with the consciousness that the land in which they sing is not so strange, and the land of which they sing not so familiar.

If American Jewish writers have longed to return to any Zion, it is not to Jerusalem but to Bialystok. For many, the Old World is the American Jewish homeland. To be sure, it is an imaginary homeland, not remembered in its particularities, a homeland sentimentalised as a quaint and timeless place of Jewish wholeness, a seamless Yiddishkeit. The important differences between German and Russian Jewish immigrants – and between Jews from Galicia and Warsaw, for that matter – have been replaced by a pan-Ashkenazi 'American' Jewish identity. American Jews are alienated from the reality of this homeland more even than from the

Israeli nation. Thanks to the *Shoah*, they believe they are separated from it by a distance of anguish that cannot even be imagined, much less traversed. The desire to return to the Old World has gained a certain tragic pathos in the work of many American-Jewish writers who try to bridge the gap between the New World and an Old World to which, because of the *Shoah*, American Jews cannot return (Glatstein 1987; Ozick 1983; cf. Singer 1972; Spiegelman 1986; Spiegelman 1991). Short story writer Steve Stern has taken this desire to make contact with the Old World in a more nostalgic direction in his collection, *Lazar Malkin Enters Heaven*. He creates a *shtetl* in Memphis, Tennessee, in which no pogroms ever occur, and all the Jews are Americans. He brings the sentimentalised version of the Old World to America (Stern 1986).

Alienated from both 'homelands', American Jews have felt they have no choice but to create an existence unlike any their ancestors ever knew. Because of their ideology of exceptionalism, they have not, for the most part, looked to other eras of stability and promise in Diasporic Jewish history for aid in understanding their situation. In consequence they suffer an emotional and intellectual distance not only from Israel and the Old World, but also from the rest of Jewish history. For this reason, American Jews' commitment to the promise of America simultaneously affirms the solidity and the fragility of their freedom. The triumphal tone that since 1948 has seemed a hallmark of certain kinds of American Jewish thinking about the 'periphery's' relation to the 'centre' hides a deep anxiety of rootlessness. In less defensive moments, what American Jews celebrate as their freedom from the dictates of tradition, they also lament as the loss of their continuity with the past.

What makes American Jews since 1948 truly exceptional is not in any case the absence of anti-Semitism, nor the economic or cultural opportunity provided by *die Goldene Medineh*. There have been many such eras. Rather, American Jews' exceptionalism rests on two startlingly new facts of Jewish history: that they are among the first Jews in two thousand years to have had the option to make real the notion of 'return' – and that for the most part they have chosen not to be 'gathered in'. Along with European Jews, American Jews are faced with two questions that their ancestors never had to confront: what sort of attitude is appropriate towards a 'Zion' that has been realised as a nation-state? And what does it mean to desire to continue living outside of that 'Zion'?

Clearly, for American as for European Jews, the old narrative that interprets Diaspora as a curse and Israel as sacred and whole will not suffice. Yet how can Jews justify abandoning elements of the traditional vision if they have no parallel examples with which to compare themselves? Alienated by the *Shoah* from the Old World and its certainties, and alienated in many ways from the new homeland, American Jews, at least, have so far seemed unable to find another standard according to which they might build a more appropriate identity.

Towards a Dialogue of Diasporas in Europe

The conference *Galut 2000* seems to suggest, however, that European Jews may be more adventurous and more willing to search for alliances among diasporas than American Jews. Perhaps European Jews are more willing than their American cousins to participate in a dialogue of diasporas. If, rather than gauging their experience relative to the traditional Jewish narrative of Diaspora, European Jews begin to see their experience within the framework of transnational migrations, they might discover that they are not exceptional. They might find analogies for their experiences in other diasporic communities. For it appears that in the late twentieth century, diaspora is a condition for which Jews have not been uniquely chosen. Turks in Berlin, Blacks in London, Maghrebins in France, may be having analogous, if not precisely similar, experiences. While German-Jewish history has incomparable elements which make it unique, today's German-Jewish community may find that it shares features with other diasporic communities. It may also find that members of these communities have been able to articulate a different vision of 'diaspora' from that expressed in the traditional Jewish narrative. Given European Jews' attempt to remain in existence side by side with an existing Jewish state, elements of this alternative vision may be of more use to them at present than the traditional narrative.

For postcolonial theorists have described a diasporic consciousness not based on a hierarchical distinction between centre and periphery, nor on a coding of the homeland as whole and sacred as against the cursed and fragmented Diaspora. The diaspora's relationship to the homeland is not imagined as a sinful community's repentant desire for a prior sacred place, but as a living and ongoing exchange of information, financial and political support, contractual obligations, and above all, affection. These communities do not regard violation of the relationship as a sin against the sacred, but as a transgression against kinship, friendship, and contract. The ideal form of the relationship towards which they work is interdependence, mutual support, and respect. The homeland (like the diaspora itself) is recognised as 'impure', a site of hybridity and struggle, and is not held up to the unforgiving standard of moral exemplarity. But the diasporans do have the right and the responsibility, as engaged yet distant participant-observers, to criticise the homeland if it participates in oppression, and to pressure it to cease.

European Jews stand to gain much by adapting this vision to their particular needs. By carrying out comparative analyses, European Jews may discover practical strategies for supporting Israel, as well as models for emotional attitudes towards it appropriate to the statehood era, which is exceptional in Jewish history. They may also gain practical benefits through engaging in multicultural alliances with other diasporas, such as enlarging their base of support on issues ranging from the legal definition of citizenship to altering asylum laws. In all these areas, Jews can learn from engaging in comparison and exchange.

Not only will European Jews be able to learn from the ongoing dialogues, they will also be able to enrich these dialogues with information and ideas emerging from their own histories and experiences. European Jews' experience as the historical 'test case' for civil and human rights throughout the EU may enable them to offer insights and even at times to speak out on behalf of newer diasporas who cannot yet speak for themselves. European Jews' organisational knowledge and capacity may enable them to aid younger diasporas attempting to build organisations and gain political influence. And Jews' experience in building an ongoing relationship with Israel may be of use to diasporas in their relationships with their own homelands.

By taking up the challenge to engage in comparative analysis, Jews will make significant gains in information exchange and cross-cultural understanding. If European Jews are to thrive in what some have called 'the time of nations' – which is necessarily also the time of diasporas – they will need to draw from and to confront their own histories and traditions, as well as the histories and traditions of their partners in dialogue.

Notes

This chapter has been adapted with permission of the University of California Press from Michael Galchinsky, 'Scattered Seeds: A Dialogue of Diasporas', in Biale, Galchinsky and Heschel, eds., Insider/Outsider: American Jews and Multiculturalism (Berkeley: University of California Press, 1996), 185–211.

1. Multiculturalists who have begun to theorise whiteness include Takaki 1993, who includes chapters on Irish and Jews, McLaren 1994, and Frankenburg 1993.
2. For an interesting case of cross-cultural dialogue between Jews and Tibetan culture, see Kamenetz 1994.
3. The term 'mestiza' has been put most prominently to use in Anzaldúa 1987.
4. I do not go as far as Ruprecht (1994), who traces the impact of Jews on Hellenism and reverses the standard view that 'Hellenism' triumphed over 'Hebraism'. See also Biale 1987.

Bibliography

Anderson, Benedict. 1991. *Imagined Communities: Reflections on the Origin and Spread of Nationalism*. London, Verso.

Anderson, Benedict. 1994. 'Exodus'. *Critical Inquiry* 20 (winter): 314–27.

Anzaldúa, Gloria. 1987. *Borderlands/La Frontera*. San Francisco, Aunt Lute Books.

Appadurai, Arjun. 1993. 'The Heart of Whiteness'. *Callaloo, Special Issue on Post-Colonial Discourse* 16 (autumn): 796–807.

Biale, David. 1987. *Power and Powerlessness in Jewish History*. New York, Schocken Books.

Boyarin, Daniel and Jonathan Boyarin. 1993. 'Diaspora: Generation and the Ground of Jewish Identity'. *Critical Inquiry* 19 (summer): 693–725.

Chaliand, Gérard and Jean-Pierre Rageau. 1995. *The Penguin Atlas of Diasporas*, trans. A. M. Berrett. New York, Viking Penguin.

Cohen, Robin. 1997. *Global Diasporas: An Introduction*. Seattle, University of Washington Press.

Eisen, Arnold M. 1986. *Galut: Modern Jewish Reflection on Homelessness and Homecoming*. Bloomington, Indiana University Press.

Eisen, Arnold M. 1987. 'Exile'. In *Contemporary Jewish Religious Thought*, ed. A. A. Cohen and P. Mendes-Flohr. New York, The Free Press.

Frankenburg, Ruth. 1993. *The Social Construction of Whiteness: White Women, Race Matters*. Minneapolis, University of Minnesota Press.

Freud, Sigmund. 1963. *Das Unheimliche: Aufsätze zur Literatur*, ed. K. Wagenbach. Frankfurt am Main, Fischer.

Gilroy, Paul. 1993. *The Black Atlantic: Modernity and Double Consciousness*. Cambridge, MA, Harvard University Press.

Glatstein, Jacob. 1987. *Selected Poems of Yankev Glatshteyn*, trans. and ed. Richard J. Fein. Philadelphia, Jewish Publication Society.

Kamenetz, Rodger. 1994. *The Jew in the Lotus: A Poet's Rediscovery of Jewish Identity in Buddhist India*. San Francisco, HarperSanFrancisco.

Koshy, Susan. 1994. 'The Geography of Female Subjectivity: Ethnicity, Gender, and Diaspora'. *Diaspora: A Journal of Transnational Studies* 3 (spring): 69–84.

Lie, John. 1995. 'From International Migration to Transnational Diaspora'. *Contemporary Sociology: A Journal of Reviews* 24 (July): 303–6.

Mankeker, Purnima. 1994. 'Reflections on Diasporic Identities: A Prolegomenon to an Analysis of Political Bifocality'. *Diaspora: A Journal of Transnational Studies* 3 (winter): 349–71.

McLaren, Peter. 1994. 'White Terror and Oppositional Agency: Towards a Critical Multiculturalism'. In *Multiculturalism: A Critical Reader*, ed. D. T. Goldberg. London, Basil Blackwell.

Ozick, Cynthia. 1983. *The Shawl*. New York, Vintage Books.

Roth, Philip. 1969. *Portnoy's Complaint*. New York, Random House.

Ruprecht, Jr., Louis A. 1994. 'On Being Jewish and Greek in the Modern Moment'. *Diaspora: A Journal of Transnational Studies* 3 (autumn): 199–220.

Safran, William. 1991. 'Diasporas in Modern Societies: Myths of Homeland and Return'. *Diaspora: A Journal of Transnational Studies* 1 (spring): 83–99.

Said, Edward. 1993. *Culture and Imperialism*. New York, Vintage Books.

Schwartz, Lynne Sharon. 1990. 'The Opiate of the People'. In *America and I*, ed. J. Antler. Boston, Beacon Press.

Singer, Isaac Bashevis. 1972. *Enemies: A Love Story*. New York, Farrar, Straus and Giroux.

Sollors, Werner. 1989. 'Introduction: The Invention of Ethnicity'. In *The Invention of Ethnicity*, ed. W. Sollors. Oxford, Oxford University Press.

Spiegelman, Art. 1986. *Maus I*. New York, Pantheon Books.

Spiegelman, Art. 1991. *Maus II*. New York, Pantheon Books.

Stern, Steve. 1986. *Lazar Malkin Enters Heaven*. New York, Penguin Books.

Takaki, Ronald. 1993. *A Different Mirror: A History of Multicultural America*. Boston, Little, Brown, and Co.

Tölölyan, Khachig. 1991. 'The Nation-State and Its Others: In Lieu of a Preface'. *Diaspora: A Journal of Transnational Studies* 1 (spring): 3–7.

Tölölyan, Khachig. 1994. 'Note from the Editor'. *Diaspora: A Journal of Transnational Studies* 3 (winter).

Chapter 4

'HOMO ZAPPIENS':
A EUROPEAN-JEWISH WAY OF LIFE
IN THE ERA OF GLOBALISATION

Lars Dencik

Introduction

A process of globalisation is permeating the world and shaping new life conditions in Western societies. This, of course, affects the Jews in Europe, too. But how? How – if at all – do they live as Jews in globalised modernity? Are there any particular ways that Jews *as Jews* are influenced by these ongoing transformations? How does European Jewry cope with the challenges of globalisation today? How are the identities of Jews in these societies transformed?

Judaism and the Modernisation of Modernity

Modernisation is part and parcel of modernity. Hence contemporaneous modernity is constantly replaced by the changes that further modernisation brings about. *Post*modernisation is the term we use to denote the social processes that make this happen: the continuous modernisation of modernity. In our time – at the threshold of the third millennium CE – one of the main features of postmodernisation, if not *the* most penetrating characteristic, is globalisation. In contemporary social science, '"globalisation" refers to the processes, operating on a global scale, which cut across national boundaries, integrating and connecting communities and organisations in new time-space combinations, making the world in reality and in experience more interconnected' (McGrew 1992: 99). In that sense humankind now lives in what might be called a new era – *the era of globalisation*. New communication technologies shape new time–space relationships. Globalisation today takes place in all fields of human life: wherever one is, the economic order, the political system, the technological infrastructure, and the cultural field are constantly and often profoundly affected by what goes on elsewhere. Globalisation is 'extra-territorial': the dimensions of space and locality are rapidly losing much of their previous social significance, whereas the dimensions of time and mobility are becoming increasingly important for the *condition humaine*. Wherever an event occurs, it may have almost instant repercussions anywhere. Virtually everything becomes 'here and now'; but any 'here' is linked to many 'theres'. And faster than ever the present becomes the past. The 'now' becomes shorter and shorter: contemporaneity has never before been so fleeting. Thereby society as we know it is being replaced rapidly and continuously by new social conditions. Therefore, social collectives as well as individuals today continuously have to find new ways to cope with their existential conditions, in order simply to remain in their positions in society, for example as a culturally identifiable group (cf. Dencik 2001).

One of the few things of which one can now be certain is that nothing is really certain. Nothing is per se or automatically valid just because it was in the past.

Leading sociologists tend to agree that contemporary Western societies can be characterised both as 'post-traditional' societies and as societies penetrated by a process of continuous 'reflexive modernisation' (cf. Bauman 1991; Beck et al. 1994; Castells 1998; Giddens 1991; Giddens 1994). In order to cope adequately with their situation, individuals can no longer just carry on the cultural traditions transmitted to them. Traditions are no longer automatically socially relevant when it comes to how one should lead one's life. Instead, individuals in all spheres of life constantly need to reflect upon and make their own decisions about which traditions to maintain and how to carry them out. This, however, does not imply that all traditions have become obsolete. Whereas culturally transmitted traditions previously served as clear, stable and unquestionable guidelines to what people should do and when to do so, today, each and every individual has to rely more and more on his or her own reflections and decisions as to what to do and when to do it. Postmodernisation (cf. Crook et al. 1992; Arvidsson et al. 1994) places people in a situation of chronic 'cultural release/freewheeling' (*'kulturelle Freisetzung'*), as the German professor of education Thomas Ziehe (1982; 1989) has labelled it.

Judaism, based as it is on ancient myths and codes of behaviour, is one of the oldest and most profoundly tradition-based cultures in existence.[1] But the social situations of Jews living in the Western world have been undergoing fundamental and rapid transformation over the last century, not only because of major events in Jewish history itself, such as pogroms, the *Shoah* and the establishment of the state of Israel, but also because of the immediate impact of the (post)modernisation process – with all the rationalisation, secularisation and individuation of social life it has brought.

Rationalisation implies that effectiveness, utility and profitability become superior considerations in all spheres of life.

Secularisation has opened up the opportunity for critical questioning of established values and religious traditions.

Individuation has meant that individuals have become singled out socially, 'disembedded' from their social background, as the leading British sociologist Anthony Giddens puts it (Giddens 1990), and are nowadays – ideally – treated only as representatives of themselves, and not of any ascribed collective, be it kinships, ethnic or religious affiliations or anything else of that kind. The idea of equal rights for all, regardless of race, sex and social background, has become widely accepted across the Western world.

How are the members of one of the world's oldest cultures and the adherents of one of the most traditional religions coping with the challenges of these ongoing transformations?

In investigating the possible transformations of Jewish identities, it should be understood that any ethnic, national or religious identity, *I*, always refers to and is based on several elements: mythical beliefs, historic traumas and events, traditions and cultural habits, values, attitudes and outlooks, rites and rituals, and so on. Not all elements are equally significant in defining someone as having the identity *I*. Nor does a particular element always have the same *Stellenwert* ('status') in the hierarchy of elements. In different epochs and in certain conditions a particular element may surface as more significant than others. What at a certain period in time, or in a particular social context, actually constituted the most decisive element in defining a person as having the identity *I* – for instance, the belief in one unified God and the participation in certain religious rituals – may in a different era become less significant, whereas some other elements, such as a shared historic fate and the sense of belonging to a particular people, may instead become the salient elements in defining what constitutes the same identity *I*.

Thus, we ask: how do members of the Jewish communities in Sweden, one of the Western European countries where this process of continuous postmodernisation is most pronounced, cope with the ongoing modernisation of modernity? How do Jews in one of Europe's most advanced countries maintain a Jewish identity (if they do), while their customs, lifestyles, outlooks, and values change (if they do)?

Below, I will briefly report some of the findings of a study aimed at elucidating, among others, these questions.[2]

Globalisation: Challenging Jewish Existence?

The processes of globalisation and the breakthrough of new technologies – such as biotechnology and digital information technology – are reinforcing each other and profoundly reshaping the conditions of social life and of human existence in the highly modernised part of the world. Furthermore, the pace of change is accelerating. Continuous processes of social transformation constantly challenge the individual's life situation. The time span during which almost everything – traditions, technologies, production methods, communication systems, family patterns, gender roles, scientific 'truths', normative values, customs, lifestyles and so on – is valid in society becomes shorter and shorter. More obviously than ever before, change is becoming the natural order of life.

Leading sociologists of our time agree almost unanimously that human conditions are changing dramatically because of the current processes of globalisation. For example, Manuel Castells claims that 'Globalization of for instance capital, multilateralization of power institutions, and decentralization of authority to regional and local governments induce a new geometry of power, perhaps inducing a new form of state, the network state' (Castells 1998: 346).

It should, however, be kept in mind that globalisation is not an entirely new phenomenon: 'Something akin to "globalization" has a long presence within the history of capitalism', states David Harvey (2000: 54). Nevertheless, allowing this should not mislead us into underestimating the new qualitative aspects of the radically increased level of globalisation in the present historic era – the *era of globalisation*. The profoundly European sociologist Zygmunt Bauman – a leading social analyst of our time – considers the currently ongoing globalisation processes as having profound repercussions on all levels of society and social life, and hence also for the shaping of trust, identities and solidarities between groups and individuals.

In his book *Globalization* (1998) Zygmunt Bauman elaborates why and how large segments of the population will become socially expelled and superfluous in the wake of the current processes of globalisation. As a consequence they will become confined in their localities, out of touch with the dynamics that make the world move, and their localities in turn will erode both economically and culturally. The world moves, but they do not. Globalisation turns them into 'vagabonds' of postmodernity.

At the other end of the spectrum are those who make the world move by themselves moving around freely as a kind of perpetual 'tourists' of postmodernity, increasingly disconnected from any binding attachments to local environments and national borders.

> 'Globalization' means that we are all dependent on each other. Distances matter little now. Whatever happens in one place may have global consequences. With the resources, technical tools and know-how we have acquired, our actions

span enormous distances in space and time. However locally confined our intentions might have been, we would be ill-advised to leave out of account global factors, since they could decide the success or failure of our actions. What we do (or abstain from doing) may influence the conditions of life (or death) in places we will never visit and of generations we will never know.

This is the condition under which, knowingly or not, we make our shared history today. Though much, perhaps everything or almost everything, in that unraveling history depends on human choices, the condition under which choices are made is not itself a matter of choice ... Globalization in its current form means the dis-empowerment of nation states and (so far) the absence of any effective substitute. ... Retreat from the globalization of human dependency, from the global reach of human technology and economic activities is, in all probability, no longer in the cards: Answers like 'circle the wagons' or 'back to the tribal (national, communal) tents' won't do. (Bauman 2001)

If Bauman's perspective, suggesting that identities and social communities will become fragmented as a result of globalisation, may perhaps be described as a pessimistic scenario, other theoreticians of globalisation, such as Stuart Hall in the volume *Modernity and its Futures* (1992), rather sees new possibilities for community and identity formations in the wake of the globalisation processes. But both perspectives agree that basic conditions for belonging, solidarity, and collective as well as individual identities, are changing drastically. Many, like the geographer Ajun Appadurai (1996), find that, as a consequence of globalisation, people will tend to come together socially across national borders and the frameworks of the nation states – they will form groups based on common experiences, struggles and culture rather than on spatial confinements and territorial areas. People's *bio*graphy rather than their *geo*graphical closeness will constitute the social glue that makes them join and form collectives.

Does globalisation as such then represent a threat to Jewish self-understanding? Does it force the Jews of Europe to adopt a way of life new and alien to them? Is globalisation really challenging 'Jewish identity'?

This, of course, depends on how one defines 'Jewish identity'. First of all one has to acknowledge that there are, and have almost always been, more than one kind of Jewish identity – one should rather speak in plural of 'Jewish identi*ties*': some define their 'Jewishness' in terms of their faith, others by their lifestyle, some in terms of a biological and/or cultural heritage, others in terms of emotional attachments, and some in terms of observance of certain rules and customs. Clearly, if Jewish identity is defined as observing certain religious rules and practising certain cultural customs, then it is quite obvious that most Jews in Europe today lead a different life in this respect than most Jews did only one or two centuries ago. The consequence of modernisation and globalisation is that Jews, like people all over the Western world, are certainly less observant in general than their ancestors were. Most European Jews have 'stepped out of the ghetto' and adopted many of the habits and ideals that characterise the larger Gentile society. If Jews previously could be easily recognised and identified by having been confined to a particular living area, by their dress code, language, food habits, and so on, the division between 'Gentile' and 'Jewish' is no longer clearly visible. If this division is at all valid in the world of today, then it is much less related to exterior social characteristics of the groups than to interior, psychological factors of the individual members of each of the categories.

Today the Jews in Europe are at least as 'modernised' as anybody else. Several writers and scholars (for example, Kundera 1984; Bedoire 1998) even propose that the Jews in Europe were both individual forerunners and as it were social midwives with respect to cultural modernism and the modernisation of European societies. As long as traditional Jewish identity is defined in terms of observance of certain religious rules and outwardly visible customs, there is no doubt that the processes of modernisation and globalisation have had almost revolutionary repercussions on 'the Jewish way of life'.

But, 'a Jewish way of life' in Europe is not necessarily defined by the observance of certain religious rules. The practice of some cultural traditions and a particular philosophical approach to life, including certain attitudes to the societies in which they live – such as a consciousness of living in Diaspora – may also be significant elements in what constitutes a 'Jewish way of life'. This being so, it is not at all clear that globalisation means a challenge to traditional Jewish self-understanding. Jews in Europe have always understood themselves as living in a Diaspora (for an interesting discussion of the implications of this, see Marienstras 1975), are at the same time citizens in European nation-states – and in that sense 'insiders' and often fully-fledged participants in the social affairs of that country – and to some degree also 'strangers' in that nation-state – and in this sense 'outside observers' of the civil life in the country. Simultaneously being both different and the same, at the same time belonging to a particular group and being regular citizens, has become the existential condition in which Jews in contemporary Europe find themselves.

Evidently this dual situation has constituted one of the bases for tremendous tragedies for European Jewry and for Europe as a whole. But it has also constituted a tension that has resulted in extraordinary cultural and intellectual creativity among members of the group – contributions of such significance for Europe and European culture that without them Europe would not be what it is.[3] Attempts to transcend this duality have also encouraged strongly felt aspirations towards 'normalisation' – either in the form of assimilation, or in the form of Zionism.

Because of the built-in duality with respect to belongingness, Jews in Europe traditionally have been forced to cope with ambiguous perspectives and tensions caused by ambivalence. In many respects this has coloured the 'Jewish way of life' in Europe. Postmodernisation and globalisation bring about increased mobility – today many peoples and groups other than Jews, such as Palestinians, Hungarians, Turks, Kurds, and Bosnians share the traditional Jewish experience of living in a Diaspora. In that respect a 'Jewish way of life', or even 'being Jewish', has in a sense become prototypical for many other groups and nationalities now residing in Europe. At the same time, the very same processes have contributed to make Jews less 'special' and 'alien' in contemporary Europe. From this perspective, therefore, globalisation could better be understood as a social transformation process accentuating, and in structural congruence with, a traditional social pattern of large segments of European Jews, rather than being a threat to Jewish self-understanding.

Indeed, globalisation is a powerful phenomenon, changing the conditions of life for many in our time. Individuals, groups and even nations find themselves forced into new ways of life. Many fear becoming 'uprooted'. Among many, uneasiness grows at the increasing numbers of 'strangers' in their neighbourhoods and at the influx of foreign ideas and customs into their lands. The diminishing social significance of locality and territory challenges their traditional feeling of identity, based as it often is, in a sense of belonging to a geographically defined homeland (in German: *Heimat*) – as if their collective identity or *Volksgeist*[4] (popular soul), to use an illustrious German expression, somehow emanates from the very soil (in German: *Boden*) itself.

The Neotribalist Backlash

During the last decade such established and territorialised identities have been challenged dramatically. Globalisation, increased migration into Europe and mobility within it have contributed to diminishing the congruence between soil and soul – between *Blut* [blood] *und Boden,* to use a renowned and infamous German phrase – on the European continent. This in turn has had repercussions in the form of manifestations of xenophobia and populist politics in several European countries. The terrorist attacks on New York and Washington on 11 September 2001 accentuated these trends and caused latent anti-Muslim sentiments to be voiced openly in public debate. Two of the tendencies that have become manifest in the aftermath are, on the one side, a strengthened emphasis on national unity and national culture, and on the other, increased militancy of those groups that feel targeted by xenophobia. The way in which immigration from non-European and mainly Muslim countries into Europe has been handled over the last two decades has contributed to this. In the wake of the failure – or perhaps rather unwillingness – to let immigrants become integrated into their host countries a strengthened tendency towards a 'new nationalism' in several of the European states has emerged. Populist political parties such as Front National in France,

Jörg Haider's nationalist so-called Freedom Party in Austria, Lega Nord in Italy, Vlamske Front in Belgium, Pim Fortuyn's Party in the Netherlands, and Dansk Folkeparti (the Danish People's Party) in Denmark have more or less successfully exploited this. With some variations between the countries, the policy these parties have launched could be described as a kind of 'diet version' of *Blut und Boden*. The tendencies expressed by these parties have not been confined only to these and similar outspoken populist parties and movements: also, well-established and respected democratic political parties and groupings in some of the countries mentioned have now jumped onto that band-wagon.

Denmark, one of Europe's most advanced liberal welfare states and most enlightened countries, may serve as a case in point. Not just a small, ethnically homogeneous and seemingly peaceful country on the Nordic edge of the European continent, Denmark is also the European country which in 2002 was judged by the European Monitoring Centre on Racism and Xenophobia (EUMC) to have the most xenophobic public debate and government policies.[5] One significant reason for this is the influence of the populist Dansk Folkeparti. This political party combines a strongly islamophobic anti-immigration and anti-asylum-seeker position with political protection of central aspects of the social welfare state. According to them, social rights granted the Danes (such as certain welfare measures, free medical care and allowances for retired persons) should not be shared (or, as they imply, 'destroyed') by ' strangers'. The political platform of the party may be described as 'welfare state chauvinism'. In the last public elections the party gained approximately the same following as many other right-wing populist parties in other countries of Europe, about one-eighth of the vote, but in contrast to what has happened in many other countries, the populists in Denmark have gained a dominant influence both on the public debate and on government policies as far as immigrants, asylum seekers and foreign citizens – in their rhetoric lumped together as 'strangers' – are concerned. Contributing to this has been the strategy chosen by the two major established political parties in Denmark, the Social Democrats and the Liberal Party ('Venstre'), in combating the challenge posed by the up-and-coming Danish People's Party. In what, at best, could be understood as an attempt to pre-empt the challenge, they co-opted the anti-immigrant and anti-multiculturalist arguments put forward by the Danish People's Party – thereby in effect legitimising the very discourse launched by the populist agitators. This development was greatly helped by a populist tabloid press and by a certain brand of Danish publicists and intellectuals, many of whom were previously active on the extreme left, and who are influenced by the popular nineteenth-century Danish Christian priest, writer and philosopher Frederik Grundtvig. A celebrated notion in his philosophy is the notion of 'the people' (in German: *Volk*). In his understanding, 'the people' is synonymous with 'the Danes' – entrusted with a particular *'folkesjæl'* (soul or spirit of the people) and constituting a certain *'folkestam'* (human tribe).

In the public debate in Denmark of today, such notions are still often used. The political exploitation of these ideas apparently hit deep cultural resonance in the Danish population. When referring to the celebrated notion of 'the people', what is denoted is the Danish *ethnos*, rather than a *demos* corresponding to the 'the inhabitants of Denmark'. As a consequence of this, much of the political discourse in Denmark of today centres around blatantly ethnocentric and outspokenly anti-multiculturalist propositions.

Accordingly, a tendency towards neonationalism may penetrate deep into the sentiments of many 'native' European populations. But not only among them: several of the newly arrived groups on the European scene seem to be developing an equally ethnically defined social identity, too, probably in part as a consequence of the processes just described. Paradoxically enough, in the shadow of ongoing European integration in the economic and political arenas, a kind of neotribalism seems to be emerging in the European social and cultural spheres.

Thus, a tendency towards a strengthened neonationalism among some of the indigenous European populations on the one hand, and an equally strong tendency towards increased 'Muslim militancy' in several European societies on the other, may in fact be related. Sooner or later, each of these tendencies by itself tends to manifest itself in xenophobic standpoints and actions. More interestingly, however, the decreasing tolerance and acceptance of differences in cultural lifestyle that accompanies the new nationalism negatively affect the possibilities for the growing extra-European and mainly Muslim groups in these countries to become integrated into their host societies. Some groups within these populations then tend to become culturally marginalised and radicalised to the extent that they identify strongly with anti-Western, and therefore also anti-European, standpoints,[6] which they manifest in violent action – that again foster xenophobic neotribalism in large sectors of the 'native' populations of the European countries. A political spiral is set in motion: neonationalistic tendencies encourage increased marginalisation of the growing numbers of immigrants (regarded as 'strangers') in European countries, leading to increased ethnic radicalism, which in turn breeds even more xenophobic sentiments in several indigenous European populations. As has become the case in Denmark, for example, this may amount to a kind of neotribalism manifesting itself in hostile attitudes towards immigration and 'strangers', against giving asylum seekers refuge, and against in actual practice granting equal human rights to all, regardless of origin, religion and ethnicity.

The neotribalist backlash to the ongoing globalisation processes, both in the form of neonationalism among the European 'natives', and in the form of ethnic militancy among immigrants to the European countries, is essentially anticosmopolitan. A negative attitude towards initiatives to further European integration very often accompanies the neotribalist rhetoric. From a Jewish perspective, however, another aspect of the neotribalists' anticosmopolitan standpoint becomes more palpable. The 'new nationalism', accompanied as it is by decreased tolerance and acceptance of difference in both Denmark and Sweden, has recently led to proposals to prohibit male circumcision and to hinder the establishment of schools for specific ethnic or religious groups. The 'Muslim militants', on the other hand, have engaged in at times violent anti-Israeli and anti-Jewish standpoints and actions. Catalysed by the ongoing Israeli-Palestinian hostilities, both tendencies, the neonationalism among certain of the European 'natives', and the ethnic militancy among primarily the Muslim immigrants to the European countries, seem to find outlets increasingly in overt, and at times also violent, anti-Semitism, each in its own way. In this indirect way, of course, globalisation may mean a threat to Jewish life and interests in Europe.

Living Traditions and Identity Transformations

Societal changes invariably lead to cultural traditions becoming trans-formed. Some elements of what used to be may be left behind, other elements might be given new interpretations; supposedly 'old' habits may be resumed and new elements may be added for the purpose of cultural survival. Traditions are continuously invented and reinterpreted, as the great British historian Eric Hobsbawm (Hobsbawm and Ranger 1983) has noted; not just now, not just in Europe, and not just Jewish traditions. As the American scholars Goldscheider and Zuckerman (1984) observed, the Jews in the U.S. have undergone profound transformations already in order to save their cultural distinctness. Adapting traditional habits and lifestyle to new conditions by assigning new meanings and interpretations to some traditional customs is what makes cultures survive. This means neither giving them up – hitting the culturally suicidal road of assimilation – nor rigidly sticking to traditional forms or manifestations that have become obsolete or in reality non-practicable under the new social conditions – the death march of fundamentalism. Living traditions are just that – living, that is, changeable and in constant transformation.

Coping adequately with the challenges of globalisation demands of any social group that wants to survive as such a considerable openness for cultural transformation. Several social entities, such as many nation-states and political interest groups, are emotionally and intellectually ill-prepared for that. The Jews, however, based on their long experience as a Diaspora people, might have a relative advantage in these matters. European Jews have a long experience of combining the necessity to adapt with the necessity to preserve. Living in contemporaneity and making traditional cultural patterns and customs relevant to one's current social situation is certainly nothing new in Jewish history: in this respect the European Jews have always been modernistic. But how do things evolve in this respect today, in the era of globalisation? How do Jews in Europe today cope with the impact of contemporary globalisation and the social and political events of particular relevance to Jews? Are the tendencies towards assimilation (often disguised as 'normalisation') gaining force? Are there perhaps, on the contrary, signs of increased fundamentalism among Jews in Europe? Or are the European Jews of today continuing to modernise their culture and way of life? If so, in what ways are these transformations occurring and manifesting themselves?

Typical but Special? – Swedish Jewry

In the years 1999–2000 a questionnaire[7] comprising a dozen questions relating to local conditions in the respective communities and a general section of seventy-two questions – many of them with several subquestions – focusing on Jewish life and attitudes towards Jewish issues was sent to the members of the Jewish communities of Sweden.[8] Some basic data on Swedish Jewry will serve to put the results in context.

According to recent estimates, approximately thirty thousand Jews live in Scandinavia and Finland. Just over half of them live in Sweden, and out of these at most two-thirds may be counted as a 'core' group of Jews, meaning that, even if not religious, they observe Jewish practises to some extent. Seen in relation to the population as a whole, the Jews in Sweden today amount to 1.7 out of one thousand Swedes.[9] Never before in history have as many Jews been living in Sweden as at present.[10] About one-third of the approximately eighteen thousand Jews living in Sweden are members of one of the three Jewish communities in the country. Each of them is what in the European Jewish tradition has been called an *Einheitsgemeinde*, that is, open to membership for any Jew, regardless of his or her religious or political orientation.[11] Today they actually constitute a Jewish civil society within the larger Swedish society. This includes a wide variety of community activities such as religious services, kosher food supply, burial societies, social work, services for the elderly, nursing homes, kindergartens, youth groups, summer camps, educational programmes, a school, sporting activities, and activities directed at society as a whole, such as the publication of periodicals and cultural events.

During the last three decades of the twentieth century the social makeup of Sweden changed from an extraordinarily homogeneous ethnic composition – that served as the social basis for quite effective collectivistic welfare policy measures – towards heterogeneity comprising a majority of ethnic Swedes and a considerable number of newly arrived immigrants and refugees from many different countries and several different ethnic groups. Sweden has now officially proclaimed itself to be a multicultural and multi-ethnic society. In connection with ratifying the European Council's Framework Convention for the Protection of National Minorities in 1999, the Swedish Parliament also passed a law officially acknowledging five national minorities, among them the Swedish Jews.[12]

Many of the Jews in Sweden are immigrants from other countries. Only one-third of the Jews living in Sweden today were born there and have parents who both were, too. Those who were either themselves not born in Sweden and/or whose parents (both of them) were not born in Sweden constitute as many as 44 percent of the present members of the Jewish communities in Sweden. The rest are children of a Swedish-born and an immigrant parent. More than 10 percent of the members of the Jewish communities in Sweden are 'Jews by choice', that is, they have converted to Judaism – out of these, approximately 80 percent have some kind of Jewish family background.

Jewish life in Sweden today – at least in Stockholm, where more than two-thirds of the Swedish Jews currently live – can be characterised by vitality, self-assertiveness, openness towards society, and visibility.[13]

On the whole, 'Jewish culture' (or rather, what is perceived as such) has a high standing among the Jews in Sweden today.[14] The Swedish government has also given some support for 'Jewish issues'. In 1997, the 'Living History Project', a research and educational campaign focusing on the *Shoah* and its legacy, was launched. In January 2000, the Swedish government convened an International Holocaust Conference attended by top-level politicians and scholars from all over the world. This was followed up a year later by declaring 27 January, the day of the liberation of Auschwitz, an official 'Holocaust Memorial Day against intolerance and racism'. At the same time the Swedish government gave a grant for the establishment of a European Institute for Jewish Studies in Sweden called *Paideia* (see www.paideia-eu.org). The fact that the Jews in Sweden were granted the status of national minority in the year 2000 does not mean that the State keeps, or intends to keep, any genealogical records of 'who is a Jew'. The implication of the law granting the Jews national minority status is not to single out certain individuals. The rights associated with it are purely collective, meaning, for example, that the schools in Sweden, when teaching about Sweden, are obliged to include the Jewish minority as part of Sweden's cultural composition, that there should be at least one department at a Swedish university devoted to Jewish Studies, that a certain part of the public support for culture should go specifically to support Jewish culture, and so forth.

How Do You Jew?[15]

As the conditions of social life change, so does the formation of individuals' identities. In the light of ongoing globalisation and post-modernisation processes, how do the Jews transform their way of being Jewish? Do the very ways they identify as Jews change? If so, how? Do they give up traditions? Do they attach new meanings to them? Are new components added to the Jewish way of life?

We know that modern life-patterns, including the rise in interethnic and interreligious ('mixed') marriages make it a conundrum to define in a relevant way 'Who is a Jew?' But the impact of the postmodernisation processes on Jewish life in Europe today also makes it increasingly relevant to ask, 'How do you Jew?' And perhaps also, 'Why do you Jew?'

Major events in Jewish history such as the *Haskalah*,[16] the *Shoah*, and the establishment of the State of Israel contributed in different ways to changing the basis for Jewish life in Europe. More recently, events such as the collapse of Communism in Eastern Europe, the rise of the European Union, the Palestinian *intifadas*, and the political developments in and around Israel have affected the existential conditions of European Jewry. In practice it is difficult, not to say impossible, to distinguish the impact of these events from the general influence of the processes of modernisation and globalisation on contemporary Jewish life. All of these factors contribute to why 'Jews do Jew the way they do' in Europe today.

How, then, do European Jews as individuals in the globalised post-modern world of today handle their Jewishness? How 'Jewish' are they?

The results of the study mentioned above indicate that nine out of ten members of the Jewish communities in Sweden state that they identify strongly as Jews. Asked how they conceive of the Jews as a group it turned out that only a few, less than 5 percent, regard the Jewish group 'mainly as a religious group', whereas two-thirds of the respondents see the Jews in Sweden mainly 'as part of the Jewish people.' Most members of the Jewish communities in Sweden do not object to being considered an official Swedish 'national minority'. Whereas approximately eight out of ten state that 'a feeling of being Jewish in essence (as a personality, way of thinking, and so on)', 'loyalty to Jewish heritage', and 'a sense of belonging to the Jewish people' is very important to their personal feeling of 'Jewishness', less than one out of four attribute high importance to religious activities, and close to one out of five declare that religious activities are of no importance to their 'being Jewish'. As far as contemporary affiliated Swedish Jews are representative of modern European Jewry, we may conclude that Jews (but perhaps not non-Jews) primarily conceive of Judaism in ethno-cultural terms. In the context of the multicultural setting of contemporary Europe, 'being Jewish' today first and foremost means manifesting what may be called 'symbolic ethnicity'.

Secular tendencies in Western societies have had a strong influence on the lifestyle and attitudes of members of the Jewish communities in Sweden. Thus, a majority of the respondents agree that women should be given a role equal to men in Jewish life, including in synagogue life. Most members of the Jewish communities today in Sweden have an open and tolerant attitude towards 'mixed' marriages. A majority of them agree that the Jewish Diaspora and Israel are moving towards different kinds of Jewry. Only a small minority agree with the proposition that only by being Orthodox can Jewry survive. Further, a majority of respondents *dis*agree with the proposition that 'in the long run Jewry has a chance only in Israel'. On the contrary, a vast majority of the members of the Jewish community state that the future of Jewish life lies in supporting Jewish cultural and social activities in the country where they reside – in this case, in Sweden.

It seems that Swedish Jewry, after years of dwelling in the shadows of the traditional mentality of the Jewish ghetto – and for the last fifty years also in the mental shadows of the *Shoah*[17] – has begun move towards a greater self-awareness, and perhaps also out of the grip of Jewish nostalgia.[18] The results of our investigation clearly indicate that a majority of the members of the Jewish communities in Sweden now would give priority to outwardly directed activities such as campaigns against anti-Semitism, participation in public debate, and the manifestation of Jewish cultural activities in the form of Jewish theatre, film festivals, book fairs, and so on.

In his book *Vanishing Diaspora. The Jews in Europe since 1945* Bernard Wasserstein (1996) predicts: 'On current projections the Jews will become virtually extinct as a significant element in European society over the course of the twenty-first century'. In his analysis, the possibility may seem bleak that the today considerably fewer than two million Jews living in Europe (as compared to ten million in 1939, just before the *Shoah*), 'who have jettisoned religious observance in the spirit of a secular Europe, and who have lost their cultural distinctiveness to such an extent that many acknowledge their heritage solely through the "entry and exit rituals of male circumcision and Jewish burial"'[19] may survive Jewishly. Our findings about contemporary Swedish Jewry, however, may give a glimpse of another possible perspective. The Jews of Sweden today constitute an officially acknowledged national minority. As such they are distinguishable as an ethno-cultural group in society, and at the same time quite integrated into it. Their Jewishness manifests itself in strong Jewish self-awareness and a clear-cut ethno-cultural identification as Jews combined with a high level of activity within the field of Jewish culture.

As individuals, they typically practise a free choice and combination of Jewish customs, and they often attribute new meanings to those traditional Jewish practices that they observe. The dominant pattern is to choose freely among the religiously prescribed practices – which to observe and which to refrain from observing – and to decide individually how to combine them with other non-Jewish traditions and customs in society. Their way of 'being Jewish' is to combine the traditions they choose to observe in a personally relevant way: for instance keeping a kosher or partly kosher household at home (38 percent), but consuming shrimps in restaurants (67 percent), or within the family sometimes lighting *Shabbat* candles (73 percent) but also giving Christmas gifts (35 percent), or having a *mezuzah* at the entry door to one's house (80 percent), but having a Christmas tree inside it (15 percent), and so forth. In this selective choosing and combination among the customs one often attaches new subjective meanings to these practices, meanings socially relevant to the individual in contemporary society.

So traditions become transformed. But cultural transformation, even cultural 'creolisation' (Hannerz 1996), in a way is the opposite of assimilation; it is to make traditional cultural patterns and customs relevant to one's contemporary social situation. Doing so is certainly nothing new in Jewish history – on the contrary, in a sense it is by this process that Judaism has managed always to be modern.

This propensity to adapt to new conditions in the contemporary era of globalisation and secularisation has become increasingly penetrated by a general tendency towards rationalist calculations, that is, to organise one's life and choose among alternatives according to what one considers pragmatic, appropriate and workable in a particular situation.

This presumes considerable flexibility in the ways one clings to what one regards as basic values in Judaism. Seen in this perspective, what we have found are particular expressions of that phase of modernisation that we have called 'postmodernisation'. In line with this we may label the kind of Jewish life that we see emerging in Sweden, and, as other studies show (see Gitelman et al. 2003), also in other parts of Europe – a 'postmodern "Swedish smörgåsbord" Judaism'. It is important to understand that this is not only a way of being 'postmodern', but also a way of being Jewish.

Cultural Polyvalence

Globalisation means, among other things, increasing mobility and the growing factual and virtual presence of 'foreign' cultures in one's vicinity. The globalisation process is two-sided in a paradoxical way: at the same time as it makes many places around the world – cities, buildings, airports and hotels – come to resemble each other more and more, and in that sense homogenises the world, globalisation also breaks up the cultural homogeneity in most local places, making habits, lifestyles, food, ways of thinking and so forth from many different places of the world present in almost any local community of the Western world at least. In that sense, globalisation brings plurality and the availability of alternatives into the immediate environment of most human beings in Western societies. While formerly the Jews and a Jewish way of life – together with the gypsies – were more or less the only 'strangers' in European societies, and hence frequently harassed as such, today inhabitants even in remote villages in Europe will on a daily basis, for instance when shopping, be reminded that there are many ways of living, eating, and being other than their own. Accompanying this is the diminishing political, economic and cultural significance of national borders. At the same time, Jews in all European countries today have become fully-fledged citizens of the country in which they reside.

From a Jewish perspective, this means, among other things, that most Jews have become relatively less distinct wherever they are. So, how does the self-conception of Jews as 'being Jews because they belong to the Jewish people' harmonise with the fact that they are also members of another people, in this case, the Swedish people? We asked the members of the Jewish communities in Sweden: 'Do you feel more Jewish or more Swedish?' Half of the respondents state that they feel more Jewish than Swedish, whereas only a few, seven percent, state the opposite. Slightly more than one-third say that they feel equally Swedish and Jewish.

We have seen that Jews in Sweden today identify very strongly as Jews – close to nine out of ten indicate that they feel quite Jewish, and more than 50 percent say that it is very important to them. Does this mean that the Swedish Jews do *not* identify as Swedes? No. Rather, it indicates that the question put – whether one is Jewish *or* Swedish – is becoming obsolete in today's increasingly multicultural, globalised world. Almost all of our respondents are Swedish citizens, their children go to regular Swedish schools, and as young men they do their military service like all others. Their level of participation in public affairs and in general elections is at least as high as among other Swedes. Like many persons and peoples today, Jews are not 'either – or', nor 'fifty – fifty'. On the contrary: Jews in Sweden, as in many other European countries of today, appear to be able to be both fully 'Jewish' and fully 'Swedish' (or whatever their citizenship or other national belonging may be). In fact, many Jews in post-*Shoah* Europe seem to have developed a capacity to be 100 percent of both.

As if things were not complicated enough by that, most Jews also have a close relationship to a third national entity – the state of Israel. Our data show that the Jews in Sweden maintain intense contact with Israel: 95 percent have visited Israel, and 83 percent have close relatives or friends there; 58 percent indicate that they 'feel strong solidarity', and an additional 37 percent that they 'feel some solidarity' with the State of Israel.

Still, there are more members of the Jewish communities who agree than disagree with the proposition that two distinct Jewries are emerging – a Diaspora Jewry and an Israeli Jewry. Further, almost twice as many of the respondents disagreed as did agree with the proposition that 'in the long run Jewry has a chance only in Israel'.

Jews in the era of globalisation clearly have complex patterns of national and social affiliation. Does this mean that European Jews are in a more or less permanent state of ambivalence with respect to their attachment to different nations?

As Eric Hobsbawm (1990) stressed in his study of the history of nations and nationalism, a person's identifications may be related to a multiplicity of objects, institutions, groups, values and symbols on the social and cultural level. Social psychologist Peter Weinreich (1991) has pointed out that the strength and importance of the individual identifications may vary in individual cases, situations, and over time. In her study the Polish historian Antonina Kloskowska discusses the effects of living on cultural borders – in her case between the German and the Polish. She points out that her case is 'comparable to the millions of other members of national minorities or periphery groups, or people living on ethnic and national borders in contemporary Europe ... and ... that this [living on ethnic and national borders] is ... gaining importance in the modern, or postmodern societies as the twentieth century approaches its end' (Kloskowska 1994: 91). She observes two distinct variations of coping with such borderline situations:

> A model example of these two variations was the situation of Eastern and Western Jews in Europe before the Holocaust. The Eastern European Jews, separated in their mass from the majority Slav populations, preserved internal collective identity, and thus created their own rich culture, although it was an object of distrust and animosity. The Western European Jews lost much of their identity without achieving full acceptance from the majority groups and were living in a state of ambivalence. (op. cit. p. 92)

In his book *Modernity and Ambivalence* (1991), Zygmunt Bauman gives an insightful analysis of the critical predicament of the Jews in Germany and Austria in the nineteenth and twentieth centuries. His proposition is that in postmodernity, living with ambivalence is unavoidable. Kloskowska objects, stating that ambivalence refers to unresolved love-hate attitudes. As an alternative she proposes the term 'bivalence':

> to denote such non-conflicting interlinking of elements selected from two cultures, possessed, approximately, in the same degree and accepted as close to one's value system ... Cultural bivalence is not necessarily tantamount to double national identification, but it may even contribute to such a solution. ... cultural bivalence which accepts a double national identification as legitimate, and even enriching, because it allows one to enjoy the possession of twofold cultural heritage and to feel obligated to participate in two national traditions. (op. cit. p. 93)

Kloskowska realises that beyond the limits of any imagined national synthesis, composed of items selected from various cultural systems, there lies a realm of other neighbouring (geographically or virtually) national or regional cultures: 'In terms of individual experience this means not just bivalence but polyvalence of cultural participation ... fostered in the modern and postmodern world' (op. cit. p. 94).

Referring to the Jews in contemporary Europe, we may now speak of at least a 'trivalence' of national attachments: to the Jewish people, to the country in which one is a citizen, and to the state of Israel. Perhaps it is justified even to describe contemporary European Jewish identity as 'quadrovalent': hardly any other segment of the European population seems to be so prepared to take on board also the idea of being 'Europeans' and to support European integration as are the Jews in Europe. The tendency (described above) towards a 'new nationalism' in many European countries is usually not supported by the Jews, for obvious reasons. On the contrary, as seen when Czechoslovakia was divided into two independent nation states, the Czech and the Slovak Republics, the Jews living there tended to remain 'the last Czechoslovaks'. Similarly, when upsurging nationalism caused Yugoslavia to dissolve into the new nation states of Bosnia and Herzegovina, Croatia, Macedonia, Serbia and Montenegro, and Slovenia, the Jews there were among those who to the end retained the idea of a unified Yugoslavia.

Globalisation makes it ever clearer that today a person's identities should be understood in terms of actual social and cultural relationships rather than in terms of 'roots' in some local and more or less mythological *Heimat*. The relationship between being and feeling mentally, socially and geographically 'at home' is becoming increasingly complex (Huber 1999), which makes it increasingly important for people to develop an ability to feel at home in homelessness: or put otherwise, to be at home in several and differing settings. This capacity to harbour cultural polyvalence is precisely what the Jews of Europe have learned through the history and the social predicaments they have experienced. A Jewish cosmopolite like the poet and Nobel Laureate Nelly Sachs, a refugee from Nazi Germany in Sweden, once expressed it this way: '*An Stelle von Heimat halte ich die Verwandlung der Welt*' ('In place of homeland I place the transformation of the world').

The Magen David (Star of David) of the Diaspora[20]

A diasporic identity is always complex, but not necessarily a negative or burdensome condition, neither for society nor for the individual. Post-modernisation implies that what formerly was seen as a disadvantage, a so-called 'double identity', may now become instead an asset in the new conditions of society and living, both for society at large and for the individual.

In accordance with the idea of poly- and bivalence mentioned above, we can speak of people (Jews) having a multiple or dual identity. Such an identity provides the individual with the possibility of oscillating between several perspectives, and thus see the world 'stereoscopically'. The increasing number and differing kinds of diasporic situations into which people are drawn under globalisation provide the individuals with a wider basis for developing enhanced abilities to critically understand their own existence and society – increasingly important now that people find themselves facing demands of mobility and the need to move between and 'perform' in several different social arenas.

For some it may seem problematic to keep their identity and to guard their integrity while shifting between manifesting various of their latent social identities. However, every person contains a multitude of latent identities, and when moving between the social contexts in which the person finds him/herself, they may become manifested. In the perspective of postmodernisation, being able to oscillate between them becomes imperative.

Like other ethnic or national identities, Jewishness is a *transformative phenomenon*. What constitutes 'Jewish identity' is furthermore partly optional. To some it may be religious observance, while for others it may be a particular historic consciousness, for instance of having been a potential victim of pogroms and the *Shoah*. For others still it may be identification with a particular political cause, such as Zionist ideals. Many may oscillate between these elements, one being more significant at one moment and another element at another moment in the person's life history. The relative salience of the elements that may potentially be referred to in identifying oneself or anyone as 'Jewish' changes.

Diaspora Jewish experience may actually be quite prototypical for what many more individuals and peoples will experience in the course of globalisation. The results of our study indicate that contemporary Diaspora Jewish identity can be framed within what somewhat heretically may be called a modern 'Jewish trinity'. The cornerstones of this trinity are:

a) *Judaism as a religion*. Some Jews are observant with respect to the rules and rituals prescribed by the religious system of Judaism, others are not – yet they are still Jewish. Even to those Jews who are not religious, the Jewish religion as a social and historical phenomenon is something they cannot avoid relating to in one way or the other.[21]

b) *Jewishness as a prism through which one experiences the world*. All Jews belong to the Jewish people. Which means that regardless of whether they live in, say, Copenhagen, Berlin, Budapest, Buenos Aires, New York, or Tel Aviv, Jews are part of the same collective historic experience. From a sociological point of view it does not really matter whether these are mythical images (for instance, about the Exodus from Egypt) or real events (such as the expulsion from Spain in 1492 or the *Shoah*).

Collective experiences of specific ethnic and historic bonds express themselves not only in cultural manifestations (food, folklore, music, and so on) but also on the individual level in certain more or less subtle idiosyncratic sensitivities, reaction patterns and perspectives through which one experiences the world.

c) *The State of Israel as an existing reality.* Some Jews are Zionists – their Jewish identity corresponds largely to their commitment for the establishment and survival of the state of Israel. Other Jews are less involved in this, or even opposed to the Zionist ideal. Many are a-Zionist, that is, neither Zionist nor anti-Zionist. But regardless of how one is Jewish, it is virtually impossible to be a Jew today without relating somehow to the fact that Israel exists as a Jewish state.

The *'Jewish trinity'* may be depicted graphically as a triangle like this:

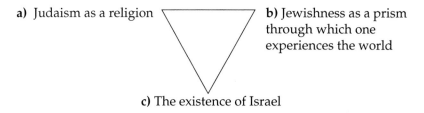

a) Judaism as a religion   **b)** Jewishness as a prism through which one experiences the world

c) The existence of Israel

Figure 4.1 'Jewish trinity'.

We may conceive of this triangle as the existential life-space of Jewish identity. Individual Jews of course differ in their orientations and their perceptions of themselves as Jews: some are closer to one of the corners than others, who may be closer to another corner or perhaps far from all of them. But regardless of where a person stands as a Jew, the 'Jewish trinity' constitutes the frame within which any modern Jewish identity exists.

As has been stated, however, any Jew in the Diaspora is not only Jewish: Jews in Europe today are also citizens of European countries, often of the country where they live. As a Jew one may be Danish, French, Hungarian, or, say, Swedish. Being Swedish, for example, means that one is also located between some fundamental cornerstones of Swedish existence: as a Swede one lives in a particular culture, is part of a certain national history, and is a citizen of a particular state. Like Jewish identity, Swedish identity can be framed as a triangle. The cornerstones of this *Swedish trinity* are:

d) *Citizenship in the State of Sweden.* As a citizen of a state, one has certain rights and duties, such as the duty to defend one's country or the right to participate in general elections. Some citizens have strong affiliations to their 'fatherland', others have more relaxed feelings, but regardless of whether one feels pride or shame, one is inevitably part of the country to which one belongs.

e) *'Secularised Lutheranism' as a cosmology.* Although Sweden is a country in which most of the citizens by tradition belong to the recently abolished Lutheran *State* church[22] (now the 'Swedish Church'), Christianity *as a religion* does not characterise the life of any large segment of the population. Nevertheless, most Swedes' everyday world view and daily life ethics are profoundly coloured by certain Christian or rather Lutheran values: the Protestant ethic (cf. Weber 1904) of hard work and diligence, combined with a particularly rational way of handling human affairs. In the formation of the modern Swedish welfare state, this is amalgamated into a 'higher' cosmological unity that for want of a better label could be described as *secularised Lutheranism.* In this cosmology, virtually everything is measured according to its utility, nothing is really 'holy', and religiosity is a question of private inner beliefs. The very categories by which one organises and evaluates social affairs in Sweden are tinted by the tacit values and viewpoints of secular Lutheran cosmology.

f) *Swedishness as a prism through which one experiences the world.* By growing up in Sweden, by having Swedish as one's mother tongue and by having spent one's formative years in a Swedish school, one acquires a Swedish way of perceiving the world. This may manifest itself in the way one perceives society and interprets social justice, but also in a rather special devotion to nature as such. There is a way of appreciating wild forests, red cottages, empty landscapes, and beaming sunshine that is more or less 'typically Swedish'. The fact that the songs of Swedish folklore and the special products of Swedish cuisine evoke positive associations and feelings among some Swedes is only because they are 'Swedish'.

Like the *'Jewish trinity'* discussed above, a *Swedish trinity* may be depicted graphically as a triangle like this:

d) Sweden as a homeland

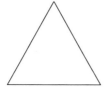

f) Swedishness as a prism through which one experiences the world

e) Secularised Lutheranism as a cosmology

Figure 4.2 Swedish trinity.

Thus, the identity of a modern European Jew is always to be found within the existential triangle defined by the 'Jewish trinity'. However, living in the Diaspora, the Jew is at the same time inevitably also circumscribed by another triangle, in this case the Swedish trinity. The two triangles are not mutually exclusive. As already demonstrated, one may well be both Jewish and Swedish at the same time. And since both of the triangles form a fairly complete cultural frame of reference for the individual concerned, they are not complementary – it is not the case that the one contains what the other lacks. Nor is it the case that you are half this and half that. On the contrary, a person may have both identities, and each of them to 100 percent, and simultaneously. The triangles thus overlap, but in a rather peculiar way: we may collapse the two trinities to describe the comprehensive socio-cultural framework of a Jewish individual in the contemporary Diaspora. The two triangles then form a well-known pattern:

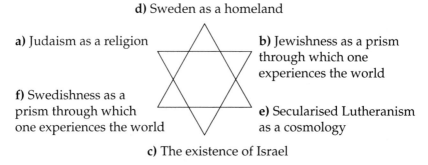

d) Sweden as a homeland

a) Judaism as a religion

b) Jewishness as a prism through which one experiences the world

f) Swedishness as a prism through which one experiences the world

e) Secularised Lutheranism as a cosmology

c) The existence of Israel

Figure 4.3 The Star of David of the Diaspora.

We call this the *Star of David of the Diaspora*. As a simple model of a complex identity, it is certainly valid not only for Jews. (Actually, considering the complex social attachments of Jews in Europe today, it may be an oversimplified model.) Nor is the reasoning behind the model restricted and relevant only to Sweden. *Mutatis mutandis*, the argument holds also for, for example, Muslims in Denmark, Turks in Germany, Iranians in France, and Palestinians, Bosnians, and many others who have been forced to leave their local environments because of war, political reasons or other hardships. An increasing number of peoples and individuals today are in some way or other diasporic.

The ongoing globalisation of information and of economic and cultural influences implies that the time of locally and nationally unified culture has passed. In its place we have what may be called 'globalised minority cultures'. Even if some neotribalist restrictions recently have become introduced, for instance in Denmark, everyone may on the whole retain their respective cultural practices, maintain food habits, have access to their own culture – wherever they live. Today the people who constitute a particular cultural minority may well be scattered all over the world. Being a member of this group, then, is significantly facilitated thanks to modern information and communication technology. Everywhere we may meet people from various 'digital diasporas', as we may call them. At the same time, those who wish may enclose themselves in the 'global ghettos' of the internet.

What once tied people together in a locally or nationally unified culture, such as those in Scandinavia, was the geographical closeness to others in the same village, town or country. This is no longer so to the same extent. Today people may also stay in touch at a distance and feel close to others who do not live in their locality but with whom they share their views, lifestyle, and fate. Even if you still cannot serve chicken soup to your loved ones, you can exchange concerns via the internet, and gather family by relatively cheap jet flights for a seder. People tend to become less 'citizens' (in French, *'citoyens'*) of the place (in French, *'cité'*) where they live, and more *'netizens'* (in French, *'netoyens'*) of the social networks within which they live and between which they move.

Jews in this respect have certainly been *netoyens* for some time now. Perhaps more than any other group in Europe until now, Jews have been moving around geographically, socially and intellectually. Jews in Europe have always understood themselves as living in a Diaspora – digital or real. As long as Jews have been on the European scene they have been 'globalised'. Globalisation, looked at from this perspective, seems rather to underpin such a 'Jewish way of life'. Oscillating between several affiliations and attachments while having a 'portable fatherland' in one's culture,[23] as the exiled German Jewish poet Heinrich Heine once put it, has for many been a Jewish way of life. In the era of globalisation, man (with Jews as prototypes) is not only *Homo sapiens*, but is also becoming a *Homo zappiens*.

Notes

1. A frequently asked question is why the Jews have been able to keep the Sabbath, i.e., sanctifying a weekly day for rest and contemplation, throughout the millennia. A typical Jewish answer to that is: 'It is not we who have kept the Sabbath, it is the Sabbath that has kept us (as Jews)!'
2. A full report of the study, entitled '"Jewishness" in Postmodernity: The Case of Sweden' is available online at www. paideia-eu.org; a somewhat shorter version can be found in Gitelman 2003.
3. In his book *Wien ohne Juden. Ein Roman von übermorgen* [*Vienna without Jews. A Novel from the Day after Tomorrow*] that was published in Vienna in 1922, the writer and journalist Hugo Bettauer gave an almost prophetic perspective of this. The book served as the basis for a widely distributed film, and also inspired a similar book to be written a few

years later about the city of *Berlin ohne Juden* [*Berlin without Jews*]. *Post hoc*, the Czech writer Milan Kundera published a penetrating essay entitled 'The Tragedy of Central Europe', dealing, among other things, with the 'intellectual void' in Europe caused by the extermination of the Jews of Central Europe. See Kundera, 1984.

4.   The idea that each separate people has a particular *Volksgeist* was elaborated philosophically by the German philosopher G.F. Herder (1744–1803). This idea was subsequently also adopted by the influential Danish philosopher N.S.F. Grundtvig (1824–83).

5.   A poll published on 5 June 2003 by *Jyllandsposten*, the largest morning daily in Denmark, showed that more than 80 percent of Danes admit that in Denmark 'racism' now prevails against those that have arrived in the country as refugees and immigrants.

6.   Cf. e.g., the radical Muslim group *Hizb-ut-Tahrir*, active in the U.K., Germany and Denmark, where, among other things, they have set up a website and distribute pamphlets referring to the Jews, urging: 'And kill them wherever you find them, and expel them from wherever they expelled you.'

7.   An English version of the questionnaire called 'Questions about Jewish Life' can be ordered from lade@ruc.dk.

8.   My colleague and co-worker sociologist Karl Marosi in Denmark and I applied the same questionnaire in studies of the members of the Jewish Communities in Finland and Norway. There are only a few marginal differences between the Jews in these three Nordic countries with respect to how they respond to the questions. Parallel studies have recently also been carried out in other countries such as the U.K., Hungary, the Netherlands, and South Africa.

9.   Estimate by the demographer Prof. Sergio Della Pergola at the Department of Contemporary Jewry of the Hebrew University Jerusalem.

10. This is largely due to the particular position of Sweden as a neutral country during the Second World War. Up to the beginning of the war Sweden received approximately three thousand Jewish refugees from Germany and Central Europe; during the war the Danish and some Norwegian Jews were given asylum in Sweden; and after the war Sweden received another six thousand who had survived the Nazi concentration camps. As a consequence of political and anti-Semitic events in countries like Hungary, Czechoslovakia, Poland, and the Soviet Union, Sweden received another approximately five thousand Jewish refugees from the then Communist bloc during the second half of the twentieth century.

11. The Stockholm Jewish community is by far the largest in Sweden. It runs three synagogues, the Great Synagogue is *Masorti* ('Conservative') and the two smaller ones have Orthodox services. There are also regular egalitarian services held in the Community Centre. The Gothenburg Jewish community defines itself as liberal, but for the time being both of the two synagogues there are Orthodox. The Malmoe Jewish community defines itself as an Orthodox community.

12. The other groups are the Same people, the Roma people, the Finnish Swedes and the Tornedalians – a group living in the valley of the river Torne along the border of Sweden and Finland at the base of the Baltic Sea. They speak the language of *meänkieli*, a variation of Finnish. In connection with the simultaneous ratification of the European Charter for Regional and Minority Languages, Yiddish was also acknowledged as a minority language in Sweden (Statens Offentliga Utredningar 1997a and 1997b).

13. A French Jewish magazine in the year 2000 presented contemporary Jewish life in Sweden under the heading '*Vivre son judaïsme en toute liberté*' (*EuroJmagazine* 8, 2000). These tendencies are in sharp contrast to what was found in a study of Swedish Jewry thirty years ago (Gordon and Grosin 1973).

14. The periodical *Judisk Krönika* (*Jewish Chronicle*) is regarded as one of the leading cultural magazines in Sweden; there are also a high-quality institutional Jewish Theatre (*Judiska Teatern*), an active Jewish Museum featuring exhibitions of Jewish art, a Jewish Library,

a yearly Jewish Film festival, annual appearances at the Swedish national book fair, several klezmer music bands, etc.

15. This section of the present chapter borrows large parts of its content from my article 'Jewishness in Postmodernity', published in Gitelman 2003.

16. *Haskalah* is the Jewish Enlightenment movement; its central figure was the German-Jewish philosopher Moses Mendelssohn (1729–86).

17. One may remember here that, according to a Jewish saying, it took forty years for Moses to take the Jews out of Egypt because he needed a generation 'to take Egypt [i.e., the mentality of slavery] out of the Jews'.

18. In a public discussion at the Jewish Community in Stockholm on what type of Jewish culture to launch in Sweden today, a desire to be able to develop something other than 'old shtetlach nostalgia and modern Israeli kitsch' was expressed.

19. Quoted from the book flap, hardcover edition.

20. Substantial parts of this section have previously been published in my articles 'Hemma i hemlösheten' ('To be at Home in Homelessness') (Dencik 1993) and 'Transformations of Identities in Rapidly Changing Societies' (Dencik 2001).

21. George Klein, an eminent Swedish scientist and a brilliant writer of Hungarian background, is a prominent Jew and an outspoken atheist. That he is, in his own words, in a typical Jewish way: in several of his books and essays he deals with Jewish religion and Biblical themes.

22. In neighbouring Denmark the People's Church (*Folkekirken*) still is a state-run institution.

23. 'What are roots good for if you can't bring them with you?' as the American Jewish author Gertrude Stein once mused.

Bibliography

Appadurai, Arjun. 1996. 'Sovereignty without Territoriality. Notes for a Post national Geography'. In *The Geography of Identity*, ed. Patricia Yeager. Ann Arbor, University of Michigan Press: 40–58.

Arvidsson, Håkan, Lennart Berntson and Lars Dencik. 1994. *Modernisering och välfärd – om stat, individ och civilt samhälle i Sverige* [Modernisation and Welfare – on State, *Individuals and Civil Society in Sweden*]. Stockholm, City University Press.

Bauman, Zygmunt. 1991. *Modernity and Ambivalence*. Ithaca, Cornell University Press.

Bauman, Zygmunt. 1998. *Globalization – Its Human Consequences*. Oxford, Blackwell.

Bauman, Zygmunt. 2001. 'The Ethical Challenge of Globalization'. In *New Perspectives Quarterly* (Center for the Study of Democratic Institutions) 18(4).

Beck, Ulrich, Anthony Giddens and Scott Lash. 1994. *Reflexive Modernization. Politics, Tradition and Aesthetics in the Modern Social Order*. Cambridge, Polity Press.

Bedoire, Fredric. 1998. *Ett judiskt Europa. Kring uppkomsten av en modern arkitektur 1830–1930. [A Jewish Europe. On the Rise of a Modern Architecture 1830–1930]* Stockholm, Carlssons.

Bettauer, Hugo. 1922. *Die Stadt ohne Juden. Ein Roman von Übermorgen [The City without Jews. A Novel from the Day after Tomorrow]*, Vienna, Gloriette.

Castells, Manuel. 1998. *The Information Age: Economy, Society, and Culture* II: *The Power of Identity*. London, Blackwell.

Crook, Stephen, Jan Pakulski and Malcolm Waters. 1992. *Postmodernization. Change in Advanced Society*. London, Sage Publications.

Dencik, Lars. 1993. 'Hemma i hemlösheten' ['To be at home in Homelessness']. In Jakubowski, Jackie. *Judisk Identitet [Jewish Identity]*. Stockholm, Natur och Kultur.

Dencik, Lars. 2001. 'Transformation of Identitities in Rapidly Changing Societies'. In *The Transformation of Modernity, Aspects of the Past, Present and Future of an Era*, eds M. Carleheden and M. Hviid Jacobsen. Aldershot, Ashgate: 183–221.

Dencik, Lars. 2003. '"Jewishness" in Postmodernity: The Case of Sweden'. In *New Jewish Identities: Contemporary Europe and Beyond*, eds Zvi Gitelman et al., Budapest, Central European University Press: 75–104.

European Monitoring Centre on Racism and Xenophobia. 2002. Anti-discrimination Legislation in EU Member States. A Comparison of National Anti-discrimination Legislation on the Grounds of Racial or Ethnic Origin, Religion or Belief with the Council Directives. Denmark. http://eumc.eu.int/eumc/material/pub/Art13/ART13_Denmark-en.pdf

Giddens, Anthony. 1990. *The Consequences of Modernity*. Cambridge, Polity Press.

Giddens, Anthony. 1991. *Modernity and Self-identity*. Cambridge, Polity Press.

Giddens, Anthony. 1994. 'Living in a Post-traditional Society'. In *Reflexive Modernization. Politics, Tradition and Aesthetics in the Modern Social Order*, eds. Ulrich Beck et al. Cambridge, Cambridge University Press.

Gitelman, Zvi, Barry Kosmin and András Kovács, eds. 2003. *New Jewish Identities. Contemporary Europe and Beyond*. Budapest, Central European University Press.

Goldscheider, Calvin and Alan S. Zuckerman. 1984. *The Transformation of the Jews*. Chicago, The University of Chicago Press.

Gordon, Hans and Lennart Grosin. 1973. *Den dubbla identiteten. Judars anpassning i historisk och psykologisk belysning [The Dual Identity. The Adaptation of Jews in Historic and Psychological Light]*. Stockholm, Department of Education, Stockholm University.

Hall, Stuart. 1992. 'The Question of Cultural Identity'. In *Modernity and Its Futures*, eds Stuart Hall, David Held and Anthony McGrew. Cambridge, Polity Press: 274–316.

Hannerz, Ulf. 1996. *Transnational Connections: Culture, People, Places*. London, Routledge.

Harvey, David. 2000. *Spaces of Hope*. Edinburgh, Edinburgh University Press.

Hobsbawm, Eric J. 1990. *Nations and Nationalism since 1780*. Cambridge, Cambridge University Press.

Hobsbawm, Eric J. and Terence Ranger, eds. 1983. *The Invention of Tradition*. Cambridge, Cambridge University Press.

Huber, Andreas 1999. *Heimat in der Postmoderne [At Home in the Postmodern]*. Zürich, Seismo Verlag.

Jakubowski, Jackie, ed. 1993. *Judisk identitet [Jewish Identity]*. Stockholm, Natur och Kultur.

Kloskowska, Antonina 1994. 'National Conversion. A Case Study of Polish-German Neighbourhood'. In *The Neighbourhood of Cultures*, eds Richard Grathoff and Antonina Kloskowska. Warsaw, Polish Academy of Sciences, Institute of Political Studies.

Kundera, Milan. 1984. 'The Tragedy of Central Europe'. In *The New York Review of Books* 31(7) (26 April 1984): 33–8.

Marienstras, Richard. 1975. 'The Jews of the Diaspora or the Vocation of a Minority'. In *European Judaism* 9(2).

McGrew, Anthony. 1992. 'A Global Society'. In *Modernity and its Futures*, eds Stuart Hall, David Held, and Anthony McGrew. Cambridge, Polity Press: 61–116.

Statens offentliga utredningar. 1997a. *Steg mot en minoritetspolitik. Europarådets konvention om historiska minoritetsspråk* [*Steps towards a Minority Policy. The European Council's Frame Convention on Historic Minority Languages*]. Stockholm, SOU 1997: 192.

Statens offentliga utredningar. 1997b *Steg mot en minoritetspolitik. Europarådets konvention för skydd av nationella minoriteter* [*Steps towards a Minority Policy. The European Council's Frame Convention for the protection of national minorities*], Stockholm, SOU 1997: 193.

Wasserstein, Bernard. 1996. *Vanishing Diaspora. The Jews in Europe since 1945*. London, Hamish Hamilton.

Weber, Max. 1904. 'Die protestantische Ethik und der Geist des Kapitalismus'. In Max Webers Gesammelte Aufsätze zur Religionssoziologie I. Tübingen (1934).

Weinreich, P. 1991. 'National and Ethnic Identities. Theoretical Concepts in Practice'. In *Innovation*, 1.

Ziehe, Thomas and Herbert Stubenrauch. 1982. *Plädoyer für ungewöhnliches Lernen* [*Plea for Unusual Learning*]. Hamburg, Rowohlt.

Ziehe, Thomas. 1989. *Kulturanalyser: ungdom, utbildning, modernitet.* [*Cultural analysis: youth, education, modernity*], Stockholm, Symposion.

Chapter 5

ISRAEL AND DIASPORA: FROM SOLUTION TO PROBLEM

Göran Rosenberg

The question 'What is a Jew?' or 'Who is a Jew?' is not only becoming increasingly difficult to consider and contemplate, but also increasingly embarrassing, sometimes sounding more like a joke or a provocation than a seriously meant inquiry. This is not because it is an unreasonable question, but, on the contrary, because the answers have become so diverse, so random, so self-contradictory and so vested with hidden meanings and agendas that it now can only be asked either by someone who is not interested in the answer or by someone who knows it – often – all too well.

The fact that I have been invited to give my view on Jewish identity and culture, albeit recognising that we are dealing here with many identities and many cultures, testifies to the amorphous nature of this subject. Almost anyone can say almost anything on this subject.

So let me say something about myself. Or rather, ask: in what way am *I* a Jew? I surely do not practice any part of the Jewish religion and tradition except to go to my mother's place for Seder and Rosh Hashanah, and that has mostly become an occasion for a family reunion. I am not even a member of any synagogue (of the *församling*) in Stockholm. I do not participate in any Jewish social activities, except when I am invited to talks and discussions. I am even by some Jews considered anti-Jewish because of my positions on Zionism and on the relation between Israel and Palestine. In addition, I am married to a Swedish, non-Jewish woman, and our three daughters have been brought up well aware of their dual background. If and when and how they wish to identify themselves as Jewish is completely up to them. Of course, in this case the Orthodox matrilineal tradition weighs heavily against them, although this tradition does not weigh too heavily in Stockholm, not any more. Patrilinear Jewish heritage has for all practical purposes been accepted by the leading liberal faction of the *församling*. But of course not by everybody. And, of course, not by the ruling orthodoxy of Israel.

So already within one family, my family, we can see how the question of who and what is a Jew quickly disintegrates and slips away.

Still, I would not hesitate to call myself a Jew. Or rather, if anyone asks, I will answer 'yes'. Well, the obvious criteria of course apply. There are Jews on both my mother's and father's side as long as living memory has it. My mother came from a famous (or perhaps infamous) *shtetl* in Eastern Poland, Chelm (known for its fools), where she grew up in a large orthodox family of rabbis, craftsmen, merchants, and strong women. My father's family belonged to the aspiring Jewish middle class in Lodz and was more assimilated and secularised than my mother's. Both families perished in the *Shoah*, with the miraculous exception of four youngsters, two from each family.

That two of them, who were on the same transport from Lodz to Auschwitz, managed to find each other after the war, and eventually make some kind of home in a country called Sweden, and there give birth to a son – me – is in my eyes more than enough to make me a Jew by default. Or to be more precise, to make me a Jew by history and heritage. A very specific history and a very specific heritage. I am a Jew of the *Shoah*. I am a Jew of Hitler and of genocidal anti-Semitism. I am also a Jew of the survival – of the collective postwar Jewish experience of state-building and nationhood. I am a Jew defined by a recent past and an imminent future. I am thus a Jew determined by external events and by external definition – not by inner conviction and choice.

It is probably fair to say that Jewish communal life in Europe during the first post-war decades was held together mainly by the trauma of the *Shoah* and the promise of Israel. Both factors defined in their own way the future limits and options of Jewish life. Neither demanded much of Jewish inner spiritual and cultural renewal. To remain a Jew in Europe was to have escaped Hitler and not yet have fulfilled the Zionist mission. To be a Jew was to engage in an act of solidarity with the annihilated – thus denying Hitler a posthumous victory – and to participate in the birth of a Jewish nation.

Some things in life you do not choose. They are chosen for you. My Jewishness is such a thing. It makes it both simple – and complicated. Simple, because it is by default. Complicated, because it has nowhere to go – and nothing to sustain it beyond one generation or two. A Jewish identity, defined by the experience of the *Shoah* and by the obligations to Israel, must weaken when the experience fades – and the obligations lose their moral force. And I believe this is happening right now: the two pillars of Jewish post-war existence, the *Shoah* and Israel, are rapidly losing their ability to define a distinct Jewish existence. As a consequence, we are now witnessing a rapid disintegration of common Jewish positions and interests and beliefs and lifestyles and definitions.

In many ways we are brought back to that juncture in Jewish history when the questions 'Who is a Jew?' and 'What is a Jew?' were raised for the first time, when the option of choosing between different ways of being a Jew originally occurred, in the wake of the European Enlightenment, with its revolutionary ideas of national citizenship, religious freedom, and individual human rights. Before that, no one would have had any problem with the question 'Who is a Jew?' Jews lived in separate communities, within separate social and religious jurisdiction, within a system of traditions and beliefs that was more or less the same all over Europe. The question 'Who is a Jew?' thus had a very specific and concrete answer.

With the rapid dissolution of the Western European ghetto – the Jewish kehillah – in the late eighteenth and early nineteenth centuries a whole panorama of new Jewish lifestyles opened up. Jewishness became a matter of choice. For the first time in millennia, Jews had to *ask* themselves what it meant to be a Jew. Did it mean a continued life in the relative seclusion and protection of the Jewish kehillah, or did it allow for an exit into the tempting modern secular world of education, politics, business – and tolerance? Were there many ways of being a Jew? Could one be a good Jew at home and a respected citizen on the street? Could one stop being Jewish by an act of will and/or conversion?

Some tried to reform Judaism, to make it into a 'modern' religion; others resisted, and there were soon as many opinions on how to modernise as there were on how to resist. Many Jews tried to leave Judaism altogether, whether they formally converted or just simply joined in the secular movements and passions of the time. Within a few decades the Jewish community of Western Europe had undergone a radical transformation which completely changed its conditions of existence – and survival.

It did not take long before the answers were as many as the questions, and it did not take much longer to realise that none of the answers 'solved' the dilemma of modern Jewish existence. On the contrary, the dilemma rapidly turned into depression, despair, and delirious utopianism. We all know the problems that ensued; on the one hand, an ongoing inner disintegration of Jewish life; on the other, a growing external pressure of modern anti-Semitism. We also know how the Jews of Europe eventually tried to respond and react. Two options seemed at the time more promising to bewildered modern Jews than others; one was Communism – the other, Nationalism.

In that sense we are better off today. We do not need to explore again these two answers to the questions of Jewish existence. They have both been thoroughly tested – and proven wrong. You might of course also conclude that we are worse off than the Jews two hundred years ago – since we now have less hope of ever finding an answer.

In what way then have the previous answers been proven wrong? Well, about Communism we do not need to argue any more. About Nationalism we do. The incorporation of a nationalist element into Jewish existence, which was the goal of Zionism, was and still is a most persistent part of modern Jewish existence. After the *Shoah*, the nationalist element of Judaism became the new defining paradigm of Jewish life. Zionism went almost overnight from a sharply contested ideology and movement to an almost indisputable symbol of post-war Jewry. The little blue-and-white donations box for the Jewish National Fund was prominently displayed in nearly every Jewish home in Europe and the U.S. Even Jews who had no intention whatsoever of emigrating personally – and that went for most Jews in America, Britain and incidental havens like Sweden – firmly engaged in support for those who so wished and for the Zionist idea as such.

The underlying assumption here was that Jewish post-war life would quickly gravitate towards the new state. Some argued provocatively, like Arthur Koestler (1954: 51 ff.), that the option of freely emigrating to Israel was in fact a historically unique, one-time option to remain a Jew or not. The choice of remaining Jewish or not was the choice of Israel. The national dimension of Judaism was the only one remaining. It was still difficult to imagine a rift between the interests of the Jewish state and Jewish interests beyond the state.

Nevertheless, the potential of a rift was obvious. A state is a state, with its own agendas, interests, and responsibilities. Its main loyalty must be to the well-being of its voters and taxpayers, not to people and communities outside its legal web of rights and obligations. The interest of Zionism and of Israel was indeed to transform the Jews of the world into a homogeneous collective of national citizens and put an end to the ambiguities of the Diaspora. The Zionist definition of Judaism tacitly assumed that all Jews either should become citizens of the Jewish state or begin to regard themselves as national exiles in relation to it. Their relation with Israel would then resemble the relation of exiled Greeks or Poles or Turks to their countries of origin: not a complex and diffuse religious-cultural Diaspora any more, but a clear-cut ethnic community, albeit with common religious traditions to go with it.

In any case, this was the very solution that held the long-awaited promise of Jewish 'normalisation'. Only to a Jewish national, to an actual or soon-to-be citizen of the Jewish state, could the perks of the Herzlian utopia be offered in full. The option of a 'secular' Jewish existence, of remaining a Jew while shedding Judaism, was the option of becoming an Israeli Jew, or an Israeli Jew in temporary or permanent exile. For Jews who wished to identify otherwise, who actually, God forbid, would conclude that life in the Diaspora was preferable to life in the Jewish state, or for whom the values of their particular Judaism could not be accommodated within a national–ethnic framework, for whom the ethics of Judaism were more important than its 'ethnics', this solution had more ominous implications.

Most importantly, it created an inevitable rivalry between sharply diverging interpretations of Jewish existence, at first hard to see and admit but after fifty years of Israel increasingly open and obvious. The once self-evident role of the Jewish state in the life of post-war Jewry is far from self-evident any more. The conflict of interest between an increasingly self-contained and single-minded Jewish nationalism on the one hand and an increasingly independent-minded Jewish Diaspora in the U.S.A. and Europe on the other cannot be subdued any longer. It now loudly manifests itself in both the religious and the political sphere, both inside Israel and outside. The national institutions of the Jewish state, for instance, now claim the right to interpret who is a Jew or who is not, disavowing the legitimacy of large Jewish Diaspora communities. The national institutions in Israel, in their daily decisions and actions, tacitly claim to speak for the Jews of the world and not only for the Jews of Israel, which is a position increasingly hard to maintain in the face of the deep internal and external controversies surrounding the most crucial of these decisions and actions, some of them concerning the nature of the Jewish state as such.

Emphasising the nationalist part of Judaism is thus proving to be a false or insufficient solution to the Jewish dilemma. Or rather, it has transferred the dilemma from one arena to another, extended considerably the range of Jewish self-interpretation, and thereby has caused further conflict and further Jewish disintegration.

Many of the questions once associated with the so-called Jewish problem have vanished – together with the so-called solutions. The seemingly unavoidable accusation – or sometimes self-reprehension – of having dual loyalties, for instance, was intimately connected with the rise of the nation-state, with modern citizenship, and the ensuing demand that Jews become loyal Swedes or Frenchmen or Englishmen. It could only occur in an ethnic–national context, not in a confessional–religious one.

Whatever specific Jewish loyalties there were, to Jews in other nations, to other historical myths, to other places, to another God, to other values, they soon became the focus of resentment, hatred, and self-doubt. This was a historic trap with no escape. Jews, no matter how much they tried to prove their undivided loyalty, could still be singled out as the weed in the national garden, a foreign and harmful element in the pure stock of Swedes or Germans, the carriers of national ambiguity and cosmopolitan ideas.

Later, the issue of dual loyalties became explicitly connected to Jewish solidarity with Israel. Arthur Koestler, and many Zionists as well, subscribed to this view of things and called for a final choice of loyalties. The loyalty of Jews was to be to the Jewish State of Israel. Or they should not remain Jews at all. In time, this would solve the problem of dual loyalties. I still remember that, as a bunch of Jewish kids in a Jewish summer camp outside Stockholm, we asked ourselves whom we would support if Sweden and Israel were to play the final game in the World Cup. I do not remember our answers, but I vividly remember myself some years later being the only person in the whole stadium of Tel Aviv cheering like a madman when Sweden scored against Israel.

Still, I believe that the question – or accusation or problem – of dual loyalties belongs to the past. Europe has become a society of migrations and migrants, many of its citizens have open and uninhibited ties with other countries, other religions, and other cultures. The Foreigner has moved next door. The Foreigner is you. The borders of the European nation-state have opened up. The Jew is not the only show in town any more.

There *is* a genuine problem – or rather a situation – of dual or multiple loyalties, but that is today a problem (or rather a condition) of many people and individuals, not only Jews. It has the advantage of putting this version of the Jewish problem on a par with a more general problem of the modern post-nation-state society. The problem is how to combine pluralism and diversity with decency and social order, various loyalties if you so wish, with one binding loyalty. In addition, the Jews of the world have *not* accepted a national definition of their Jewishness. They have certainly not heeded Koestler's call to choose Israel or leave Judaism. Instead, they are searching again, for other ways of defining themselves, other ways of being a Jew, only to find an endless maze of possibilities, an infinite number of new answers to the question what it means to be a Jew. One could perhaps see this as a natural and healthy pluralism, but the extremes of this spectrum of Jewish existences or cultures are now so distant from each other that not only does one extreme not recognise the other as Jewish, but it is virtually impossible to find anything in common between them, except that they are made up of people who insist on calling themselves Jewish.

So, fifty years after the establishment of a Jewish nation-state, the old questions crop up again – at the end of another road travelled. What is a Jewish nation? What is the purpose and character of a Jewish state? What does it mean to be a Jew? These questions have become even more burning as the national route has opened up into a maze of side alleys, dead ends, and crossroads. During this journey, the development of Jewish life in a nationalist context in Israel has heavily influenced the self-perception of Jews elsewhere, mainly resulting in a conspicuous ethnification of the Jewish Diaspora. Surveys in several Western European countries (the Netherlands, Sweden, and Britain), as well as in the U.S., affirm that a growing number of Jews define themselves in ethnic terms, as individuals linked more by a common national ancestry and heritage than by common values and lifestyles. Their Jewishness then becomes ever more eclectic, incorporating whatever elements that come to mind or seem proper, creating a diversity in beliefs and traditions that transcends all historic limits, united only by the purely coincidental bonds of family. As a religion Judaism is today perhaps becoming the most diverse of all major belief systems, historically lacking any common structure of authority.

This can of course be observed most clearly in the U.S.A., where American Jews nowadays assemble the most unlikely combinations of alleged Jewish ideas and traditions. Between 'Jews for Jesus' in San Francisco and the Chabad in Crown Heights there is a Jewish dish for every taste and caprice. If not content with the first, choose a second, or cook yourself a third. Or choose a non-Jewish identity. Most American Jews today live outside any kind of Jewish congregation, and the number of mixed marriages has increased from 9 to 50 percent over thirty years.

The number of people in America and Europe who see themselves as part of a Jewish community is shrinking rapidly. If present trends continue, writes Bernard Wasserstein in his study *Vanishing Diaspora*, 'the number of Jews in Europe by the year of 2000 would be less than a million – the lowest figure since the Middle Ages.' (Wasserstein 1996)

The situation, then, is rife with paradoxes. Some of the young Swedish Jews that I have met during frequent discussions of my book *Det förlorade landet. En personlig historia* [*The Lost Country: A Personal History*] (1996), almost defiantly demonstrate their Jewishness, but when I ask them what makes them Jewish, their answers fly apart. Many of them proudly claim to be secular and free to make of their Judaism whatever they like. Most of them proclaim an affinity with Israel and the Jewish people, but when asked with which Israel and with which Jewish people, they are confused.

In part this phenomenon of Jewish revival can be explained by a general search for identity in postmodern society. From this perspective, Jewish youngsters are often considered lucky to have an interesting identity waiting for them, a well-furnished tradition to settle into, a ready-made lifestyle to explore. The unexpected revival of Jewish music, literature and theatre, even in countries with few Jews, like Sweden, often involving people who are not Jewish, shows that this is a Jewishness of a new kind. Some Jewish intellectuals (Pinto 1996; Rejwan 1999; Vital 1990; Waterman 1999) have tried to make a virtue out of this new reality, arguing that a modern Jewish identity might be constructed from a practical tradition of multiple loyalties, from an ability to transcend national and cultural boundaries, the possibility of being many things at the same time, thus showing the way to a new era of European tolerance and coexistence. However desirable the development of such a postmodern individual identity in general might seem, it will in my opinion lead to the further trivialisation of whatever once made up a Jewish civilisation in Europe. In addition, this line of discourse tends to obscure the more fundamental and sombre aspects of the modern Jewish dilemma.

The hitherto most dramatic effect of the rise of Nationalism in Jewish existence has been the late emergence of a rampant, national-messianic interpretation of Judaism. The potential for such an interpretation was perhaps always there, but during almost two millennia it was well checked and balanced by strong internal and external forces. However, the currently ongoing fusion between the secular power of a modern state and the reawakened and unchecked fervour of a neo-messianic Judaism has brought the internal conflicts and tensions of Judaism to a breaking point. These are not minor differences about how the Jewish state should be run, or about the interpretative details of Jewish tradition, or about the proper rules of conversion, but a full-blown war about fundamental principles and beliefs, a war paradoxically brought about and aggravated by the very process of framing the Jewish dilemma in nationalist terms – which was supposed to put an end to the Jewish dilemma in the first place.

The dilemma of Judaism is then clearly not the dilemma of a single nation but of something larger – perhaps, as the Israeli sociologist Shmuel Eisenstadt (Eisenstadt 1992) has argued, of a small but distinct civilisation, basically facing the same challenges as it did two hundred years ago, when the walls of the ghetto came down. With the decisive difference that the national option, the long-nurtured dream of the return to Jerusalem being a panacea has now been tried, explored, and – for all real-life purposes – exhausted. The specifically Israeli–Jewish conflict regarding peace, Palestinians, and territories, will have to play itself out mainly on the national scene, leaving the Diaspora Jews as anxious but basically power-less spectators.

This does not necessarily mean that the option of discreetly fading into a growing postmodern mosaic of ethnic and cultural pebbles is a feasible one for the non-Israeli Jews of the world. First of all, the Jewish dilemma is clearly not an ethnic one. What made Judaism resilient and creative during so many centuries was a complicated dynamic involving several other important factors, especially the specific interplay between the outer civilisational conflict of Judaism with Christianity and the inner balance between Messianic promise and the pious fulfilment of daily duties (see also Rosenberg 1999: 65–8, 196–8). These factors are not at hand any more. Secondly, the unwritten post-war taboos of Auschwitz might very well once again yield to the revival of old, ingrained, anti-Jewish sentiments, sometimes treacherously linked to the Israeli–Palestinian issue. The blatant anti-Semitism of Le Pen in France is an ominous sign, the knee-jerk reactions in Switzerland to Jewish claims for economic compensation seem to be another. Even in Sweden, with few Jews, there appears to be a potential resonance for ideas, openly and skilfully propagated by small but well-organised groups, maintaining that powerful Jews run the country, that they are behind the 'sell-out' to Brussels and that they conspire to overturn the Swedish way of life. This might in turn provoke the Jews of Europe into a new cohesion and new defensive postures.

In a way, fifty years of Israel have brought us back to a point where old and difficult European questions must be asked again, on the one hand knowing that immediate answers might not be readily available this time, but on the other hand contributing to a timely and necessary discussion on the character and future of European civilisation.

There are very few contributions so far to this discussion; one, however, by Diana Pinto (1996), argues that European Jews can and should become the transnational avant-garde of an emerging European culture. The historically complex identity of the Jews, their unfathomable mixture of religion, nation, culture, and ethnicity, their tradition of 'multiple loyalties', are elements of exactly the kind of identity a democratic and pluralistic Europe must foster in its citizens.

But if that which is specifically Jewish can be reduced to a talent for flexible identities and multiple loyalties, then what we should rather expect is an accelerated *dissolution* of Jewish bonds and ties, and the increasing convergence with non-Jewish identities. Pinto seems unwilling to grade or evaluate different Jewish identities, but she nevertheless attributes to the ultra-orthodox Jews (of whose undemocratic disposition and general intolerance she disapproves) the important task of anchoring Judaism 'to a living Talmudic faith. Without them, Judaism as a whole would be immeasurably impoverished' (Pinto 1996: 8). Why would it?

What Pinto actually hopes to formulate is a new Jewish destiny (after the *Shoah* and the State of Israel). She energetically attempts to tie it to a secular European venture, but inevitably comes up against the Koestler dilemma: if living Talmudic faith is central to Judaism, should not most Jews somehow be defined by that? And if increasing numbers of the world's Jews do not allow themselves to be so defined, but on the contrary react with fury to the political and social utterances of 'living Talmudic faith', to what extent are they then Jews?

Naturally, there may be a thousand respectable reasons for wishing to define oneself as a Jew of a more ambivalent and compound variety, but it is reasonable that there should be some connection between being associated with a specific Jewish destiny and the content of such a destiny. At some degree of dilution of Jewishness, talk of a comprehensive Jewish fellowship and mission becomes either racist or meaningless. If 'Jew' can mean anything, logic demands that Jews cannot be expected to think and act in any particular way.

A common Jewish destiny demands a common Jewish view of the world. To what extent can and should the notion of a specific Jewish destiny be upheld, when the Jewish view of the world has cracked? Can Judaism then be something else than a mosaic of more or less Jewish sects? Or as a purely national–ethnic affiliation? After two hundred years, the question remains more open than ever.

There is a Chassidic story which goes like this: 'An old Chassid, profoundly absorbed in prayer and thought, lost his way in the forest. After a week of starvation and privation, he met a weatherbeaten, leather-clad man of the forest making his way through the undergrowth. Radiant with joy, the Chassid went over to him to ask him the way. "I have good news and bad news", the forester replied. "The bad news is that I am also a Chassid lost in the forest. The good news is that after ten years I know of a great many ways which do not lead home.'"

To conclude, although a good many wrong ways have been explored by now, there is no guarantee that the right one will eventually be found. And that perhaps we should settle for the joy of exploring forests.

Jewish existence was for hundreds of years a precarious balance between a moral-religious covenant and a national-ethnic mission, between the book and the people, between the hope for the advent of Messiah and the halachic demands of daily life (see also Rosenberg 1999: 193–4). This balance was thoroughly upset two hundred years ago, giving rise to that persistent question: 'What is a Jew?' This question can today be narrowed down to the following: is there room for a specific Jewish mission in the world of today? Do the Jews, as a living collective, have an internally coherent role to play in the world? Or are they at least bound together by the *belief* that they have one?

If the answers to these questions are mainly negative – and I believe they are – we will see a Jewish existence characterised by ever more division and arbitrariness, by the continued dissipation of common energy and vitality, by the reduction of what was once a resilient Jewish civilisation, to on the one hand the state of Israel and its project of mutating Judaism into a nationalist creed and on the other hand the continued secularisation, ethnification, and diversification of Diasporic Judaism and Jewishness into a myriad of lifestyles.

This means that the questions of Jewish cultural revival and survival cannot be disconnected from the question of what we mean by being Jewish, and from the question of whether the Jews of the world can have more in common than a common history and a not so common future.

Bibliography

Eisenstadt, Shmuel. 1992. *Jewish Civilization*. New York, State University of New York Press.

Koestler, Arthur. 1954. 'Judah at the Crossroads'. In *The Trail of the Dinosaur*, ed. A. Koestler. London, Hutchinson.

Pinto, Diana. 1996. *A New Jewish Identity for Post-1989 Europe, Policy Paper No. 1*, London, Institute for Jewish Policy Research.

Rejwan, Nissim. 1999. *Israel in Search of Identity*. Gainesville, FL, University Press of Florida.

Rosenberg, Göran. 1996. *Det förlorade landet. En personlig historia* [*The Lost Country: A Personal History*]. Stockholm, Bonniers. [German translation: 1999. *Das verlorene Land*. Frankfurt a. M., Suhrkamp. Also in Danish, Dutch, French, and Norwegian translations.]

Vital, David. 1990. *The Future of the Jews*. Cambridge, MA, Harvard University Press.

Waterman, Stanley. 1999. *Cultural Politics and European Jewry, Policy Paper No. 1*, London, Institute for Jewish Policy Research.

Wasserstein, Bernard. 1996. *Vanishing Diaspora. The Jews in Europe since 1945*. Cambridge, MA, Harvard University Press.

PART II
INNER-JEWISH CONCERNS:
REBUILDING AND CONTINUITY

Chapter 6

LEFT OVER – LIVING AFTER THE *SHOAH*: (RE-)BUILDING JEWISH LIFE IN EUROPE. A PANEL DISCUSSION

Chaired, edited, and translated by Sandra Lustig

This panel discussion took place in Berlin on 3 June 2001, at Bet Debora, the Second Conference of European Female Rabbis, Cantors, Jewish Activists, and Scholars.[1] The theme of the conference was 'The Jewish Family – Myth and Reality', and this panel discussion explored issues of rebuilding Jewish life in Europe after the Shoah, with the conference theme in mind.[2] Even though the Jewish experience in each European country is unique, several parallel situations have emerged, and Jews in the various countries have responded differently. A whole web of interlinking issues appeared: Do we feel safe, physically and emotionally? How does that affect what we do or refrain from doing? Has our capacity for spirituality been affected by the trauma in our families? How have small communities dealt with pluralism within the congregation? How open or how disapproving were the various communities to non-Orthodox practice? What effects have these attitudes had on Jewish life, especially for women? What obstacles do we face as women, and what opportunities do we have? Is the notion of Jewish identity as a political identity still current? How do we relate to our non-Jewish environment, and how do non-Jews relate to us? What are the benefits – and the dangers – of a Jewish education for young Jews growing up in Europe? How much or how little do we even know about the situation in other European countries? Do we really understand the situation for Jews in countries with or without direct experience of the Shoah, with or without experience of socialism? How are we going about rebuilding: within or outside the existing communities? In secular or religious ways? What are we seeking? What have we achieved?

The Panellists

Lynn Feinberg is a Norwegian-born Jew whose mother is English. She has been instrumental in forming two Rosh Chodesh groups in Oslo. She has represented the Jewish Community of Oslo in several cross-religious dialogue groups and also at Bet Debora. She recently completed her studies in the History of Religions with the thesis *The Prayer Quorum and Ritual Purity in Judaism. Trying to understand underlying causes related to the Jewish dichotomic understanding of gender.*

Dr Jael Geis was born in Zurich and holds an MA in Chinese and American Studies and a Ph.D. in Contemporary History. She is also a Registered Nurse. The title of her doctoral dissertation, *Übrig sein–Leben 'danach'. Juden deutscher Herkunft in der britischen und amerikanischen Zone Deutschlands 1945–1949* [*Left Over–Living after the Shoah. Jews of German Descent in the British and American Zones of Occupation in Germany, 1945–1949*] (Geis 2000) inspired the organisers of Bet Debora to conduct this panel. After having lived in Holland, France, and the United States, Dr Geis now lives in Berlin and works as a freelance historian. She was an active member of the Jüdische Gruppe from its inception.

Wanya F. Kruyer was born in Amsterdam and is a sociologist and historian. She is currently working as a journalist specialising in Jewish Thought. She is co-founder and past President of the progressive egalitarian congregation Beit ha'Chidush, which was founded in Amsterdam in 1995.

Dr Eleonore Lappin was born in Vienna, where she lives today. She holds a Ph.D. in Comparative Literature and Jewish History of Ideas. She works at the Institute for the History of Jews in Austria, and her research focuses on modern history and history of ideas of German-language Jewry, Hungarians as forced labourers in Austria, and policies of justice and memory in the Second Republic. Her publications are too numerous to list here. She has been active in the Jüdische Forum in Vienna, and is a co-founder of Or Chadash, Vienna. She offered a workshop on Jewish families after the *Shoah* at Bet Debora.

Dr Andrea Petö was born in Budapest, studied History and Sociology and holds a Ph.D. in Contemporary History. She was an Assistant Professor at the Central European University, Visiting Professor at ELTE Ethnic and Minority Studies in Budapest, and has lectured and conducted research at other universities as well. Her many areas of research include post-Second World War Central European history, oral history, women's history, history of Jewish women, theoretical problems of gender relations, transition, and the history of Communism. She has published widely. She serves as

President of the Feminist Section of the Hungarian Sociological Association and editor of *Esther's Bag*, the women's section in *Szombat* (Budapest).

Sandra Lustig (Berlin): Welcome to the panel discussion 'Left Over – Living after the *Shoah*: (Re-)building Jewish Life in Europe'. The *shiurim* yesterday and this afternoon provide opportunities to talk on a more personal level about the Jewish family. In this panel discussion, we would like to transcend the personal level, and bring the discussion to a societal level. We're interested in locating current issues concerning Jews and family in the particular historical and societal context of post-*Shoah* Europe.

When we speak about (re-)building Jewish life, we do not mean reconstructing exactly what was there before the *Shoah*. What was lost in the *Shoah* was destroyed forever. What we do mean is building up Jewish life in a manner appropriate for today. In doing so, of course it is important to remember what was lost, and to try to understand the effects of the *Shoah*, but it is equally important to look at the present and the future, and not to focus solely on the past.

For the first section of this discussion, I have asked the panellists to speak about their work in (re-)building Jewish life in Europe. They have been involved in (re-)building Jewish life mostly outside the mainstream in their communities. I've asked them to talk about their work in the context of a few questions: 'left over' from what? What was important about Jewish life in their communities before the *Shoah*? What effects did the *Shoah* have on their communities? What was the community like just after the *Shoah*, and how has it developed since? The answers to these questions – sketched out very briefly – should provide the backdrop to understanding their new activities.

Lynn Feinberg (Oslo): I'd like to talk briefly about Norwegian Jewish society, which I suppose not so many know about. According to the first Norwegian constitution of 1814, Jews and Jesuits were not allowed to enter the kingdom. That meant that there were no Jews in the kingdom until after 1853, when the law was changed. The first Jews to settle in Norway came in the 1890s, and the majority came from Lithuania and Poland at the beginning of the 1900s. When the war broke out on 9 April 1940, there were about eighteen hundred Jews all in all in Norway. There were two communities, one in the north in Trondheim with about four hundred people, and the largest community was in Oslo, and this is still so. Approximately 760 of the Norwegian Jews were deported to Auschwitz. The majority of the rest fled to Sweden. About 30 percent of the Jewish men who weren't deported joined the Allied forces. Of the 760 Jews deported, only twenty-five returned. Of those, my father was one. After the war, almost half of the Jewish population had disappeared. Almost everyone came back to their homes and places although this, of course, was difficult.

Jewish life after the war – I was born in 1955 – consisted of trying to reconstruct what was there before, trying to make things work. It was like a shell; to me there was no inner spirituality. I was not nourished as a Jew more than in a traditional way. I think that is a situation that probably many post-war Jews in Europe have experienced. We didn't have our own rabbi; the Danish rabbi was also our rabbi. We only got a rabbi in the 1970s, Rabbi Melchior, who is now a minister in the Israeli government, which is rather interesting. And when he came, things changed. The first thing he did was to found a Jewish kindergarten, a very important way of socialising Jewish children and their parents into the Jewish community, and actually giving the community new life.

The community calls itself Orthodox, which means services are kept according to Orthodox Jewish tradition, but I would say that 90 percent of its members have a liberal approach to their Judaism. Most Jews drive to shul on Shabbat, very few keep a strictly kosher home. They seem to identify with the tradition in a cultural rather than in a spiritual way. Increasingly over the years, many of the community's members are converted, and in this group you find the majority of those that keep kosher and walk to shul, since they have to live according to the standards of an Orthodox conversion. We've had some Russian immigrants. Straight after the war, in the late 1940s, five hundred refugees from D.P. [Displaced Persons] camps were invited by the Norwegian government to settle in Norway, so in this way it balanced out the numbers of the Jews in some way, but many went to Israel.

Today we're about 950 Jews in Oslo, about 250 or even less in Trondheim. In Trondheim, it's been so hard to get a minyan of men that they have started to count women, simply out of need. <laughter> But in Oslo, we still have the women's gallery, where I must sit during service. Since I grew up, the service has become much more lively. Everybody joins in the singing during *mussaf* on Shabbat. We also have a children's choir. Many attend the communal Kiddush that follows the Saturday morning service in the community centre.

The first Rosh Chodesh group was formed by one of the more established Jewish women in our community; I had inspired her through a talk I had given where I introduced this idea. This group was inspiring to be in since everyone was very open to learning and sharing experiences. For the first time, we made our own kiddushim and our own ceremonies, something we had previously only experienced men doing in our company. That in itself was great! But when it came to doing more experimental and experiential ceremonial work, I found there to be much more resistance. Generally, I believe there is a fear of straying too far away from the traditional Jewish path, connected with a fear of getting in touch with and sharing deep emotions. I think some of the reason behind this could be connected to an inherent fear of change brought on by World War II issues that still need to heal.

The second group, consisting of less established Jewish women, I found to be lacking in basic Jewish grounding, so that it was more difficult to get a dialogue based on Jewish experience going. It ended up becoming more of a group for Jewish women to meet socially.

Wanya F. Kruyer (Amsterdam): The story goes: the Jews in Holland were saved by the Dutch. When I grew up, this myth was reality. It was told over and over in stories about how the brave Dutch fought the Nazis, stopped the trains of deportation, sabotaged the German administrators, and how heroes took up weapons if needed. Long stories about how courageous men and women risked their lives to save as many Jews as possible, Jews like Anne Frank and her family.

However, no one reminded us of the end of the Anne Frank story, how the Frank family was betrayed by their Dutch neighbours. It took many decades before we realised that most people in Holland had accommodated the Nazi regime very well. Civil servants and police collaborated, trains ran on time, even those packed with Jewish families on their way to the Dutch transition camp Westerbork, the first stop to Auschwitz-Birkenau.

The end of the real story is that 76 percent of the Jewish population in Holland, among them over 90 percent of the Jews in Amsterdam, perished in the Holocaust. 102,000 Jews who lived in Holland in 1940 were killed in a well-organised process between 1942 and 1945. Amsterdam, once a Jewish city like Prague, Cracow, or New York, lost her Yiddishe heart.

When I grew up, the Jewish space in Amsterdam was a dark hole, the colour was brownish or black, the material was piles of stones. Ruins. Dark bricks, ruins overgrown by weeds, empty spaces of what once were community centres and synagogues.

In those days, in the 1950s, the 'Anne Frank myth' was constructed. A myth filled with courageous people, helping all the persecuted to hide in canal houses and on countryside farms. A myth spread everywhere, including in schoolbooks and at official memorial sites. Part of it presumed the survivors to be grateful to their rescuers, and be silent ('we all suffered in those days') about their sufferings. 'Let's face forwards and forget the past' was the adage that suppressed successfully that Dutch society was living with witnesses of less heroic deeds.

The survivors did indeed live as invisibly as possible. Only in the late 1960s did the first psychiatrist discover that some survivors could no longer cope with life. Slowly, awareness evolved that almost all survivors showed traces of underlying harm that made them act differently, that had changed them into fearful or emotionally 'dead' people, something later recognised as 'concentration camp trauma'.

How did the survivors deal with their Jewishness? Most felt above all shame or guilt. Their Jewishness was a remote landscape, a dark and painful place you didn't want to belong. For many the first association with the word 'Jew' was a black word on a yellow star you had to wear sewn on every garment.

No wonder the children they raised had a very confused concept of Judaism as well. When I began to live a more conscious Jewish life in the 1980s, I met men and women like me wrestling with their Jewishness. A complex, ambivalent heritage transmitted by small families, for whom the few memories of the riches of pre-war Jewish life were immensely overshadowed by unwanted memories. Small families living in a society where heroes, not victims, represented 'The War'.

Slowly I found Jewish friends in small secular groups, in support groups of Jewish Social Welfare, I met people at music events, exhibitions, and lectures of Jewish interest, all of them landmarks of a revival of Jewish life in Amsterdam and some other cities in Holland in the 1980s and 1990s.

During a few trips to the United States, I found another kind of Jewish life in *chavurot* (groups) and small congregations associated with denominations unknown in Europe, like Reconstructionism and Jewish Renewal. I fell in love with that kind of Judaism, a vibrant Jewishness, filled with creativity and passion for the future.

Thanks to my U.S. experiences, and to American Jews living in Amsterdam, I was able to be one of the founders of Beit ha'Chidush, House of Renewal, in 1995, a community inspired by our modern American counterparts. Founding a religious community in Amsterdam was not only a leap into unknown territory. Doing this in the hip capital of Western Europe looked like an anachronistic deed, particularly for someone like me, coming from an atheist and affluent family.

I simply missed something in my life, something that felt like the cement in my life, more profound and connected to tradition than what secular groups inside and outside Judaism could give. I missed a space where rituals, education, cultural events, would go together with the celebration of Shabbat, the High Holidays, and Pesach. Soon, this new house became a visible newcomer on the Jewish map in Holland. Nowadays, we are in many ways a congregation like others, only far less formal in structure, non-hierarchical in leadership, open to newcomers, and egalitarian: there are no specified gender roles, we use degenderised liturgy, and we don't distinguish between straight and gay relations. It's a kind of post-Halachic Judaism common in the U.S., and new in Europe.

Two years ago, at Bet Debora, I was delighted to discover that more *Beitim Chidushim* (Houses of Renewal) or other Jewish spaces had come into existence in the mid-1990s in various countries in continental Europe. As if, fifty years after the Holocaust, something new were in the air.

Eleonore Lappin (Vienna): It is not an easy task to provide an overview of the Viennese community before the war, so I'll stick to the figures. The Jewish population peaked at about 216,000 Jews shortly after the First World War, many of whom were refugees. In 1910 about 190,000 Jews lived in Vienna, in 1938 maybe 180,000. Today, the Jewish community (*israelitische Kultusgemeinde*) has about seven thousand members. However, not all of the people who call themselves Jews are members of the *Kultusgemeinde*; estimates of the total number of Jews in Vienna range from ten thousand to fifteen thousand. The Jewish community in Vienna developed very rapidly from the middle of the nineteenth century to its peak in 1910. It was never a very 'Viennese' community: it was always a community of immigrants and their children, from Poland, Galicia, Hungary, Bohemia, Moravia. And the post-war community exhibited roughly the same composition again. After the Second World War, Austria was a transit country, a transit country to the U.S., a transit country to Palestine/Israel, and some of the numerous Displaced Persons got stuck in Vienna, fewer in the provinces, and that, too, follows a tradition. That means that we have the same composition of people again: Poles, Hungarians, Romanians, but they are much, much fewer in number. And still – and this may differentiate the Viennese Jewish community from what I hear from Germany – this community is attempting to reconnect to pre-war traditions. That means that today's immigrant children can identify with the pre-war immigrant children. And I believe that this could be a strong point of the Viennese Jewish community: perhaps feeling not quite as alien as a Jew. I am not speaking here of permanent anti-Semitism in Austria, I am not speaking of the unwillingness of the Austrians to render even financial compensation in whatever way which would have enabled the community to recover financially. When we talk about patterns of identity within the community, the pre-war community still has a certain force. And this pre-war community was Orthodox. There simply were no liberal houses of worship in Vienna before the Second World War. We exported our Reform movement to Hungary where it developed into the Neolog movement. It got stuck in Vienna for political reasons.

When we founded Or Chadash eleven years ago, it was something completely new in Vienna, and it succeeded because there were people who had become familiar with non-Orthodox Judaism in Switzerland, in Israel, and in the United States. Nonetheless, when I look at our community today, I see that we have become a very Viennese community, in spite of considerable hostility on the part of the 'establishment'. That means that this imported idea of liberal Judaism attracts Viennese Jews most of all. Discontent with Orthodoxy, maybe also the expectation on the part of those who had been estranged from Judaism for years that certain fears of entering something new would be easier to overcome with us: that is our strong point. Praying in German is important, too. Since March 2001 we have had a woman rabbi – an idea completely alien to Vienna. Eveline Goodman-Thau is originally from Vienna, and we have brought her back to Vienna – I don't know for how long. And that, too, is very fitting for this Community that is in flux, in movement.

Andrea Pető (Budapest): A national census was conducted in Hungary in the first part of 2001, and that will explain to you a lot about the problems, questions, and the aspirations of the Jews in Hungary today. In this census, there were three questions about religion that might serve as identification or coming out for the Jews. The first one was about nationality. For Hungarian Jews, this was Hungarian. The second question concerned religion. This was a closed question, so there were several possible answers to check: Catholic, Protestant, Jewish, Other. And since 90 percent of the Hungarian Jews have no religious identification, most of them marked 'Atheist' or 'No Answer'. The third question was about cultural identity; that was an open-ended question, which means that most people did not understand what this was. The survey instructions suggested that it referred to the mother tongue, and that is Hungarian in most cases. There was a certain debate about the result: the present Hungarian government, which is a right-wing conservative government, certainly had motives to formulate the questions in this way, but it has been estimated that 70, 50, 90 percent – it depends whom you ask – of the Hungarian Jewish population became invisible due to the formulation of the questions in the census. But it does shed light on the cultural identification of the Jews in Hungary. In 1990, the Hungarian Jewish community made the decision that they would not define themselves as a nationality or an ethnic group but as a religion, and in a community that is 90 percent non-religious, this is pretty problematic.

I'd like to introduce the different journals available for Hungarian Jews. The most prestigious one, an academic journal, is called *Past and Future* (*Mult es Jovo*), a quarterly which is not that sensitive to women's issues. The second one is the *Shabbat* (*Szombat*), the journal of the Hungarian Jewish Cultural Association, which tells you about its orientation, and it was actually the first one to introduce women's issues in its section 'Esther's Bag'. Katalin Pecsi is one of the editors of that special women's section, and she has also edited a book on contemporary Hungarian Jewish writing. The other Jewish journal is called *Hope* (*Remeny*), a quarterly, not as academic as *Past and Future*. There is the community weekly called *New Life* (*Uj Elet*), there is the *Eretz*, the Zionist newsletter, and there are other newsletters as well.

In 1999, Katalin edited an issue of *Szombat* dedicated to exploring the place of women in the Hungarian Jewish community. This was the foundation of our group, Esther's Bag. We decided in the autumn of 2000 to start a different type of publication, partly a journal with news, partly academic writing, and also with literature (Katalin watches very carefully that we fulfil the quota in *Szombat*), which would reflect on gender issues. The editors, three men, were very receptive to the idea of starting a women's section. So far this is the only regularly published feminist intellectual product in the Hungarian press. We emphasise the democratic character of our work. We, seven women in our thirties, belong to different disciplines, such as history, law, literature, and psychology. There are always two editors of each issue, which ensures that we learn from each other. We have fun, and we love spending our time together reading the articles, and eating – we always make a big feast when we meet – but the issue is that we are doing two things: we are constructing a community for ourselves, and we are constructing an audience through our writing.

We have an imagined readership: we don't really know for whom we are writing these articles. We imagine and construct an audience, and have been able to test our assumptions. First, by the kinds of responses we receive through our e-mail address. Secondly, we had a live event at Shavout, at which we introduced ourselves at the House of the Hungarian Jewish Cultural Association. You might imagine some of the reactions we received, because we were reading the midrash written by Prof. Shalvi. We were accused by some members of the audience of attacking the religion. It should be noted that the number of issues of the journal *Szombat* sold increased after January 2001, when we started the so-called women's section – perhaps the most surprising development. Now we print 2,500 copies of each issue, which may seem nothing, but for an imagined Jewish community like the Hungarian one, it's a lot. The number of readers, not the copies sold, is around ten thousand. *Szombat* is financed by the Hungarian Jewish Cultural Association. We receive a fee for the three pages the women's section has in *Szombat*; and we are accumulating this fee to form a fund to serve a common purpose.

Jael Geis (Berlin): I will speak about the Jüdische Gruppe (Jewish Group), even though it no longer exists. In a sense, the Jüdische Gruppe paved the way for today's groups outside the mainstream. It was founded in protest against the invasion of Lebanon by Israeli troops in 1982, and also in protest against the policy of the Jewish Communities never to criticise Israeli policy in public, as if to say, 'my country, right or wrong'. The occasion says something about the interests of its members, who are about fifty to sixty-five years old today. Most of them considered themselves to be more or less secular, more or less leftist intellectuals who took a critical position on issues of social and cultural politics in Jewish and German society. For example, in 1988, on the fiftieth anniversary of the 9 November, the Jüdische Gruppe initiated a public demonstration against nationalism and discrimination against minorities. During the Nachmann affair,[3] the group demanded the immediate resignation of the Zentralrat (Central Council of Jews in Germany) and the installation of a Jewish committee of inquiry, but in vain. The group was active in the movement to boycott the last census in West Germany, supported the Israeli peace movement, and had a standing committee on the Middle East, which is still active today. The Jüdische Gruppe kept up contacts sporadically with analogous groups in Frankfurt am Main, in Zurich and in Vienna, and also with other minorities, for example Afro-Germans here in Berlin.

At first, the aversion between the Jüdische Gruppe and the Jewish Community was mutual. But even when the Jüdische Gruppe modified its negative stance, it was still impossible to convene meetings on the premises of the Jewish Community, let alone to realise any of the group's ideas during the Jewish Community's cultural festival, so that the Jüdische Gruppe staged its own cultural festival in parallel for several years, of course on a much smaller scale. At some point we were permitted to use the premises of the Jewish Community; that must be said for fairness's sake. The Jüdische Gruppe and other groups before and contemporary with it owe their existence and their polemic with the Jewish Communities to the Communities' rigid structures. And those structures are a product of Jewish post-war history in Germany. (Please excuse me for referring only to the Federal Republic of Germany and not to the German Democratic Republic as well.) Jewish life in West Germany since the end of the Second World War was distinguished (a) by being a political issue, (b) by rapid institutionalisation and very slow regeneration, with the preponderant problems of intellectual, religious, and cultural impoverishment, (c) by an extremely ambivalent attitude towards remaining in the 'land of the murderers', and (d) by substantial heterogeneity in relation to the small number of Jews. Into the 1990s, there were about thirty thousand registered Jews in Germany, compared with almost half a million before Hitler's assumption of power. Jews of German descent have been a tiny minority since 1945, the leftover of a once influential, innovative, and affluent group, which was abruptly marginalised and thrust into poverty. Polish and other Central European Jews were the majority of Jews in Germany after the end of the Second World War. This group was homogeneous insofar as they were all survivors. During every decade since 1945, Jews have settled in Germany and compensated for emigration to other countries, for example immigrants returning from Shanghai in 1947, Jewish refugees from the German Democratic Republic in 1953, refugees from Hungary in 1956/7 and from Czechoslovakia in 1968, immigrants returning from Latin America, immigrants from Israel who had gone there from Germany, and immigrants from Israel originally from other places, immigrants from the Soviet Union and after the end of the Soviet Union. The more or less latent feeling of being threatened and the resulting siege mentality favoured undemocratic structures within the Jewish Communities. As a consequence, Jews either felt that they had to put up a united front in public, or they retreated into invisibility. The invisibility of real Jews was coupled with a strong presence of dead Jews in the public arena. I say 'was', because changes have become noticeable in the last fifteen years.

Elisa Klapheck (Initiator of Bet Debora, Berlin): It struck me that Jael Geis set the starting point at 1982 with the founding of the Jüdische Gruppe, a political group. I remember that for a long time, Jewish life in Germany –

insofar as it was *lively* Jewish life, not a ruin, not an empty shell – was defined politically above all. People were leftists, or active against xenophobia and anti-Semitism in society. They were oriented towards Israel, be that in a supportive or a critical way. Israel was at the centre of Jewish self-understanding. For a long time, it seemed to me that one could live with defining Jewish life in a political way, until the moment came when a political identity was not enough. I became conscious of the fact that we have to return to tradition, to the sources, and study the religious or traditional content of Judaism. That is how I saw it here in Germany. I would be interested to hear if elsewhere in Europe, too, it was possible for decades to consider oneself a kind of political Jew in today's society, the problem being that this identity had petered out.

Eleonore Lappin: In Vienna, there was a similar phenomenon, yet it was different, too. The decisive moment was the election of Kurt Waldheim as president in 1986. In the run-up to the election, and afterwards, a public discourse critical of the Austrian way of dealing with the Nazi past developed for the first time, and influenced 'official' Austria, too. For the first time, an Austrian chancellor, Franz Vranitzky, had to apologise for the Nazi past. That really was something! It also strengthened Jewish self-confidence in Austria, especially around 1986/7. The Jüdische Forum (Jewish Forum) was founded, a group of Jews who deliberately defined themselves as non-religious, and the group sustained itself very well for several years. It was not all that easy during the Waldheim debate, when a lot happened in this sphere in Vienna. And these Jewish artists, writers, and musicians became active and came to the Forum; it was their Forum, too. Institutions like the Jewish Museum were founded. We had the first public discussion of all about it, and received information. However, this group petered out at some point. That must have been around 1992; I don't think I committed child abandonment when I changed over to Or Chadash, but interestingly, we didn't succeed in bringing the Forum people to Or Chadash, with a very few exceptions. On the whole these secular leftist Jews remained secular leftist Jews; they lost their framework, but they didn't come to Or Chadash, and they have no place in the *Einheitsgemeinde* (unified community), either.

Wanya F. Kruyer: I recognise a lot of her story. After Israel occupied 'the territories', there was a group of critical Zionists in Holland, people who supported dialogue with the Palestinians in several ways. Recently, they founded a group called 'The Other Jewish Voice', opposing the voice of the Jewish establishment, which is still very supportive of Israeli policy. I went to one of their meetings earlier this year, because I support their ideas. Most people in this group were older, sixty and over, once Zionist, who were very disappointed in Israel's policy. People who once believed in the founding myth of Israel: a people without a country, a country without a people. They were very, very disappointed when they discovered the reality, and learned about the lives of the Palestinian people. I have the feeling this new critical group serves above all the social needs of the disillusioned Zionists.

Lynn Feinberg: Most Norwegian Jews are first Norwegian, and then Jews, at least those who have lived in Norway for a longer period of time. The community in Norway, especially in Oslo, isn't as homogeneous as it was, so it's easier to be Jewish. The question of being religious has come more into the open. I think in Oslo you see a split: the assimilated Norwegian Jews are less connected to the community, and then you have a group that is more connected to the community, or interested in developing their spirituality. There is obviously also an interest in alternative ways, but we haven't yet found a form of doing this, except for the two Rosh Chodesh groups that I have been instrumental in forming. It was difficult to make a form of religious participation where there is no culture for it; there is nowhere to start. I recognised that situation.

Uri Hart (Berlin): I've spent quite a bit of time studying anti-Zionism, especially from the Jewish side. And I wonder to what extent leftist Jews may have contributed to leftist Germans' anti-Zionism. In particular, I have the leftist German students' movement in mind that was founded in the 1968 generation. I have in mind, for example, *Agit 883*, which used pictures from the *Stürmer*. Also people like Horst Mahler, who was on the left then and has changed into a rightist today. Didn't you have that creeping feeling: no, it can't go on like this, that we are so far to the left that we're making the leftist Germans so friendly towards the Palestinians that things could turn dangerous?

Jael Geis: I refuse to be held responsible for what has become of Horst Mahler or anyone else. It is undisputed that there was and is anti-Semitism in the Left. And that led to considerable estrangement between 'German leftists' and 'Jewish leftists' (I'll use these terms for now). But that has nothing to do with the fact – and one doesn't even have to be anti-Zionist to say this – that I criticise the Israeli government for things that I feel are flagrant injustices. And that is something that I learned from Jewish tradition: to stick with something, even if others make something else out of it. Unfortunately, you can never prevent that, but can only attempt to set it right again. I'd like to give just one example. That Israelis are settling in the areas that were given back to the Palestinians is simply unacceptable! Just one example, and I must be able to say that regardless of who says what about it or who makes what about it.

Nea Weissberg-Bob (Berlin): To my knowledge, Dan Diner and Susann Heenen-Wolff, both major figures in the criticism of Israel in those days, were never anti-Zionists.

I also think that it is simply normal to this day that – regardless of which Jews speak out – criticism is always exploited by non-Jews for their own purposes.

Eveline Goodman-Thau (Vienna/Berlin): About the Dutch issue: being one generation removed from what you are talking about, I must say that I totally understood the Anne Frank myth. I left Vienna as a 4-year-old on really the last train because the visa to Holland came on 31 December and that was the day that our Austrian passports expired. The Dutch took us in, so we were able to survive as a whole family in Holland. A couple of years ago, I wrote on Righteous Gentiles in Holland. I think that we shouldn't make the mistake of saying that all Dutchmen were bad. These Righteous Gentiles were a fantastic chapter in the history of war and peace, where single families risked their own lives to save Jewish people. So as somebody who doesn't call herself a survivor: I want to remind us of the famous Talmudic saying: 'Whoever saves one person, it is as if he has saved a whole world'. And that is what we should remember.

Wanya F. Kruyer: I know that a lot of Gentiles saved the Jews. But I have to make a remark that's a little bit cynical: all those Gentiles have at least three Yad Vashem medals by now to keep up the myth. I grew up with that myth, and still books are published about all those Gentiles who saved the Jews that were not around when I grew up.

Uri Hart: In the Netherlands, Catholics, Protestants, etc., each have their own television, their own schools, their own kindergartens, their own daily newspapers. Does that apply to the Jews, too?

Wanya F. Kruyer: The Dutch community had 140,000 people in 1940; of these, 102,000 lived in Amsterdam, meaning one out of five people in Amsterdam were Jewish. We would have had a development like in New York, where 20 percent of the people are Jewish. After the war in 1945, in the whole country, from deep down south to the north, only twenty-five thousand Jews were there. A very small group in Amsterdam.

Of course, it's logical: if you have so few people, only a few thousand, you can't have your own schools, you can't have your whole structure, that's why a lot of people moved to Israel after the war. Now, we have forty-five thousand Jews in Holland, and that's a miracle! Natural population growth was very low, there are the immigrants from Israel, and a little bit of irony of history: more than nine thousand immigrants have come from Israel to Holland in the last ten years, especially to Amsterdam; that's much more than all the Dutch Jews who ever made *aliyah* to Israel. Now we have a group of forty-five thousand Jews in the Netherlands, and of them only 27 percent are organised in the congregations.

Toby Axelrod (Berlin/New York): What were the effects of the *Shoah* in terms of the definition of who is a Jew in your communities after the war, and how is that issue handled in your various communities today?

Lynn Feinberg: There certainly was a difference between those who came back from the camps and those who came home from Sweden. You're talking about those who are not part of the community. Many, or I would say most, Norwegian Jews of my generation intermarry, although many of their spouses convert, so there are quite a lot of mixed marriages. Children can attend the kindergarten as long as one of the parents is Jewish, but both parents must commit to bringing their children up in a Jewish way. Children can even have bar mitzvahs/bat mitzvahs, as long as they convert before this age, regardless of whether the mother is Jewish or not. So we go a very long way in order to include non-Jews into the community. But obviously, with an Orthodox rabbi, who converts according to Halachic Israeli standards, this means that it's not easy to convert, either, so it's not necessarily the option for most Norwegians.

Wanya F. Kruyer: It's a complicated situation in the Netherlands, because more than half of the survivors had a mixed marriage background, simply because they had a better chance to survive. When the communities were rebuilt, this issue was not addressed, and there is still a lot of denial about mixed marriages.

Jael Geis: That issue in Germany is really too complicated for a brief answer here. There was a lot of chaos right after the war about exactly these questions, what to do with *'nichtarische Christen'*, *'Mischlinge 1. und 2. Grades'* ('non-Aryan Christians', 'first and second-degree half-breeds' [as they were called in Nazi terminology]), etc., etc. It's a topic for a paper.

Eleonore Lappin: In Vienna, after the war, if there was a Jewish man with a non-Jewish wife, there was no problem to get the child into the Community, which was Orthodox, and this openness remained right into the 1970s. It was easy to get in. We were also the transit country for immigration from the former Soviet Union, and even then a lot of conversions were made in Vienna very quickly. This was a mistake, because then the Israeli rabbis started to look a bit more closely at what was going on, and from then on, it was not that easy to become a member of the Jewish Community. Now we have a situation where people who were members of the Jewish Community but are without a Jewish mother, if they left the Community for one reason or another – they may have lived abroad – they're not taken in any more.

Jael Geis: I would just like to add briefly that in Germany, it was not at all so easy to get into the Jewish Community. The Jewish Communities certainly did try to prepare children of Jewish fathers via religious instruction, but one cannot speak of their simply being accepted into the Community, not in Germany.

Lori Klein (Santa Cruz, CA, U.S.A.): For those of you who have been involved in renewing things in a religious or spiritual way, could you give an example of a ritual or liturgy or something that your group has made relevant for this time period and for this society that you're in?

Jael Geis: I can't help you with new rituals. I feel most at home in a Conservative context. I think that the traditions are so rich that I would need my entire life just to take them in, let alone to try to adapt them for our times. One can tackle problems like women's rights using the tradition, too. It could also happen that one concludes that they are insufficient for dealing with a specific problem, or that one considers the results unacceptable and must then do something else. But generally speaking, I have no need for anything fundamentally new, which often isn't all that new, either.

Wanya F. Kruyer: If the Jewish traditions and the sources have a meaning for us as contemporary Jews, and I think they do, let's reclaim it!

Member of the audience (from Germany): I am a member of a Masorti community. We have so many possibilities, so many alternatives within our Judaism, only we aren't really familiar with them. We must first learn all about this Judaism that we have and use it, before we create something new on top of it. Because when we know it well, then we will see with our contemporary mentality that we have a wealth of possibilities.

Sandra Lustig: For the second part of this discussion, I've asked the panellists to speak about specific family-related topics. We'd like to focus on just a few selected themes, and each member of the panel has chosen one issue.

Eleorone Lappin: I mentioned earlier that the Viennese Jewish Community has only seven thousand members. Yet this small community has no fewer than three Jewish schools. It has one school that includes both primary and secondary school, a vocational school, and the Lubavitcher primary school. Very surprising, and for us Viennese Jews a fact that makes us proud. We have a school system; we are providing for our children's future. The first Jewish school was founded in 1980 and is today the Zwi Perez Chajes Secondary School, with an associated primary school and kindergarten.

The Zwi Perez Chajes Secondary School was first founded back in 1919. In those days it was a school for the children of *Ostjuden* immigrants and had a staunchly Zionist orientation, at least among the students, not quite as much among the teachers. Even critical students say today that this Zionist orientation saved their lives. After all, they emigrated, either to Palestine or to America. So there is this tradition now in the new Zwi Perez Chajes Secondary School, founded in 1980. The reason for founding it was that government subsidies were available, but also that suddenly children were there again, namely, from the immigration from Uzbekistan, Georgia, the Caucasus – at last, immigration with children, which had not occurred previously. There was also a changing of generations in Vienna. Suddenly, my generation came to the fore, also in the Jewish Community: not I, but my generation, and this generation had children, and there were also well-to-do families with children. The school was founded, and I enrolled my daughter there, too. After all, when I was I child, I really suffered through religious instruction: it was dreadful, one wasted afternoon per week, and at the end you couldn't even read Hebrew. It was awful. But at least one had a foothold in the Jewish kehillah, and that's why I went. I wanted something better for my daughter, and we really wanted to create Jewish life in Vienna. The school provides high-quality education. That was important: the Jewish school had to be somewhat elitist, at least as good as the Lycée Française, otherwise people wouldn't enrol their children, since the unofficial Jewish school was the Lycée Française. We were better, we had four foreign languages in the final exams, our children: lots of Jewish geniuses. No wonder that we needed the Chabad school very soon, for the normal children, <laughter> or for the children who immigrated; that is a change from the earlier tradition.

My daughter was in the first graduating class, and now I look and see what became of this class. The children are all highly intelligent, maybe they weren't such brilliant students, but intelligent children. Two-thirds of these children no longer live in Vienna. Exactly what other people told me when I decided to enrol my daughter in this Jewish school has happened: 'She will become too Jewish, don't send her back to the ghetto. How will she be able to make it here in Austria?' And I said, 'in order to live here, she needs a Jewish education'. The children don't live here any more. My daughter lives in Jerusalem. And I made the mistake to having her go to Hashomer Hazair (a leftist Zionist youth movement). It was probably too much. But the question really does arise: if we want to raise children with a Jewish consciousness, and maybe even with a little bit of Jewish education, then we have to send them back to the ghetto, in a way. And what about a Jewish renewal if these children leave? My daughter tells me,

'I won't marry a man whom I met when I was just ten'. And that's how most of them feel. If we keep our children in closed groups, then they have no perspective for the future.

What should be done? I'd like to put this issue up for discussion, because I believe that it is a very important issue of family policy. How can I use children's education to create Jewish renewal? It is not enough for me to renew myself in my kehillah. What do I do with my children?

Member of the audience (from the U.S.): I feel that one of the great failures of the Progressive and Renewal movements in the U.S. has been a failure to find ways to help parents and children together to reconnect with Judaism. I think it's very sad that that movement, for all that it's giving individuals in redefining and recapturing their sense of Jewishness, has not begun to find the right kinds of forums and institutions for connecting children to that movement. Perhaps you can find ways to do that so that we can then learn from you in America.

Andrea Pető: My purpose is to point out the changing structure of Jewish women's organisations in Hungary after the Second World War (see also Pető 1988 [in Hungarian] and Pető 2001 [in Bulgarian]). Before 1944, there were 152 Jewish women's organisations in Hungary; after 1945, sixteen were refounded. I found the detailed documentation of eight of them. The story of how I found the documents is an interesting one.

Four organisations have two dates of their dissolution. The first date – between 1945 and 1947 – is actually a very telling one, because the Jewish women's organisations were dissolved, or banned, together with the different conservative women's organisations, because there was a point in the Hungarian armistice saying that those civil organisations which hadn't renewed their activity after the war, or that did not submit a request to renew their activity up to a certain deadline, would be banned. So in that sense, the Jewish women's organisations were packed together with the right-wing organisations and were banned. Then, surprisingly, some Jews returned from the deportation and wanted to continue their activity. The second date of dissolution is 1950. When 1950 came, the secret police came to the offices of the Jewish women's organisations, they put what they found into boxes, and they took it away to the Ministry of Home Affairs to a secret archive which was opened up in 1993, and that was the moment when I got to these boxes for my research.

The reason why I think this is interesting, as far as the reconstruction of Jewish life is concerned, is that if you look at the demographic data of women who took part in this active Jewish life, you see that they are non-professional women in their forties and fifties, with no career as working women. They were mostly active in charity and redistributing aid from the Joint and UNRA and other organisations. I would say that their aim and their perspective in participating in this renewal of Jewish life was related to somehow reintegrating themselves, to constructing something that had been lost, to networking, to making themselves acceptable again in Hungarian life. They were members of at least three organisations: (1) a political party, Communist or Social democratic, (2) the Jewish women's organisation and (3) the mass women's organisation or the Zionists.

Why was this world eliminated by 1950? The first factor was the Communist takeover. They destroyed the Jewish women's organisations for two reasons. The first is religion: they identified these organisations as religious organisations and banned them, together with the Catholic, Protestant, and other organisations. The other reason is related to the anti-capitalist tendencies of the Communists, because it was the affluent upper middle-class Jewish women who took part in the Jewish women's organisations; consequently they were labelled as 'class enemies'. So after they returned from the concentration camps, they were deported within Hungary to other internment camps. This destroyed the network that they had constructed with such care and effort after 1945.

The second factor contributing to the loss of these organisations was Zionism. This was the very brief period in the history of Hungarian Jews when Zionism had certain deeper roots. We have police reports from 1950 saying that they did not find anybody who had been previously active in these women's organisations, because they had all left for Israel. Between the two forces of Communism and Zionism, Jewish feminist associations disappeared, although they hoped to reconstruct the social networks that were so important to them for reintegration into Hungarian society.

Wanya F. Kruyer: Since this section is about families, I will start with my own family. My family consists of an American student who comes to study at the University of Amsterdam in a programme called Gender, Identity, and Sexuality for one semester, and I am her host family. It's a programme of the School of International Training in Vermont, U.S.A. They always find a nice Jewish girl for me. In the past two years, my Shabbat evenings are joined by a young man of thirty who lives in Amsterdam. He came into my life thanks to his mother, whom I met two years ago here at Bet Debora. So this conference has been instrumental in making my family. My own home-made little family, with two different stepdaughters a year, and a mishmash of regulars at my shabbes table.

I was born in 1954, I have never been married, and I have never carried a child. I am not the only one in my Jewish peer group: the vast majority of my Jewish friends have no children themselves. I said earlier that 27 percent of the Jewish population is organised in the two major congrega-tions, the Reform and the Orthodox. There are two Orthodox schools in the Netherlands, one Chabadnik style which has grown from five children in the 1960s to 250 children today. So among them, there is population growth. However, among all other sections of the community the birth rate is very low, even lower than the general population. But something else is happening. We're getting a population influx from other parts of the world, some from Russia, mainly from Israel. So the overall Jewish population in Holland is growing, despite the low birth rate, a development that nobody could have predicted some years ago.

Lynn Feinberg: I'll talk a little bit about spiritual life and my experience as a Jew and my quest for a place in it. One argument for keeping our community Orthodox is so that any Jew can participate ... anywhere, all over the world. I should say: any man, that is. Yet the most active women in our community are those who have converted. Many are married to Israelis, and others to Norwegian Jews. There seems to be a tendency among Norwegian-born and raised Jews to assimilate and feel alienated from the synagogue and community life. I, too, shunned the synagogue for many years. I had to seek my spiritual home elsewhere, something I have found to be the case for many Jews, especially women, of my generation. Somehow, I insisted on finding a bridge between Judaism and spiritual life as I experienced it through other channels, and that is what I think my work in the future is going to be about. I studied psychological astrology, and through astrology I came to kabbalah. I realised that kabbalah could answer some of my questions, could give me a framework, yet spurred other questions related to inherent gender dichotomies. Kabbalah led me more deeply into Judaism. These insights are also what made me want to do something different, and led to the idea of forming Rosh Chodesh groups as a forum to share and explore Judaism both from a woman's and from a more spiritual perspective.

Being a single mother of two Jewish boys, I think my Jewish quest started when I chose to give them a *brit milah*. I was married at the time to a non-Jew, and he was against circumcision. Later, after choosing to raise my sons alone and then send them to the Jewish community kindergarten, I started to re-socialise with the Jewish community. I now became what you may call a Jew of choice. I was choosing my Jewishness back. I think this is a totally different situation from that ten years earlier, when I left Norway – and left Judaism: I didn't want to have anything to do with it. I did, however, spend two years in Israel after leaving home. This gave me the experience of how I could be both Jewish and live a secular life in a Jewish environment. Later, when I started to look into my Jewish roots, I still needed to identify with a Judaism that wasn't Orthodox and that was not imposing fixed roles on me. I believe a less defined approach to Judaism might be easier to do in my community in Oslo than in Israel, where concepts of what it is to be a religious Jew seem to be far more fixed. Being so few Jews in Oslo, everyone is needed. I am not pushed out when I introduce new ideas, but actually welcomed in.

There have been suggestions as to how to make our community more liberal, but I think many of our community's members find the thought threatening. Many oppose this idea out of fear that reform is the first step towards assimilation, and they don't know of any other alternatives. We have now an Orthodox British-born rabbi, educated in Israel, and my communication with him is fairly open. His opinion is somewhere along the lines of 'There is nothing halachically against having a women's minyan, but if you do this be aware of the inherent danger of splitting the community. Women are very much a part of the service, only not a part of the minyan.' So being such a small community, that is also a problem. We cannot make two communities in Oslo with only 950 members, we have to make our way together somehow.

My idea is that I have to start with small groups of women, and first of all make these groups feel safe and thereby transform from within. My next idea is to begin with a women's prayer group, maybe once a month, where women can experience how it feels to participate actively in a service. This must not necessarily be a full service, but consist of singing and understanding the liturgy that already is a part of the traditional service, with songs and tunes that many already know. This idea came to me after I had attended services as they are practised within Jewish Renewal in the U.S. My aim is not to change Orthodox Judaism, but to ask questions and to begin by practising and sharing a Judaism that I can relate to. Hopefully this may inspire others.

Being so few means that Norwegian Jews are very visible in society. There has been a lot of cross-religious activity in the last years, and I have been participating in several such groups, representing the Jewish community. Although my father was the leader of the community for many years, I have in many ways also broken with the tradition. I'm a single mother, I have studied astrology and esotericism, and done lots of things that are very contradictory to the Jewish traditional ways; yet I am used as a representative here at Bet Debora, and also in these cross-religious dialogues. The first one was on 'Ecology and Religion' (which was a bit far out for most, so that's where I was put), and there was one on 'Religion and Peace'. Norway must be the first country to have a coalition of representatives from the different religious communities. There is government support to work on political issues that are related to religion, and in these forums, Muslims and Jews cooperate quite well. And that's one of the things that's interesting about living in small communities: that such diversity happens.

Jael Geis: I would like to call to mind the context in which I believe the question of the family after the *Shoah* must be discussed. The Nazis' attempt at extermination did not aim at Jewish individuals, but at the Jews as a people; it included both history and the future, that is, the children and the potential to reproduce. All potential parents after the *Shoah* were faced with re-establishing parenthood both physically and emotionally, even if individual people did not see themselves confronted by this question in this way. Dina Wardi quotes survivor and Israeli writer Aharon

Appelfeld: 'We are dry, withered seeds, continuity will no longer come from us'. (Wardi 1992: 20) The veritable baby boom in the DP camps in the first post-war years stands in stark contrast to this statement. They had the highest birth rate in the world at that time. Children were material proof for one's own survival and generally played a role in their parents' desires for undoing what had happened, replacement, continuity, and refutation of Nazi doctrine. Every child born after Hitler was a triumph over the persecutors. We – and using the word 'we' I mean all Jewish men and women of every age – should not be surprised if today, we still have to deal with the consequences of this not entirely successful attempt at annihilation. The trauma of annihilation was collective, and so are the consequences.

What did the post-war communities have to do with the post-war families? Jewish communities in post-war Germany were concerned to a great degree with social welfare responsibilities, taking care of survivors and their families as well as orphans and refugees. It was demanded of them – and this was surely often more than they could do – to compensate for what these mostly incomplete and/or torn-apart families, often 'second families', could not achieve, for instance, responding to the children's needs, or leading a *Jewish* life, which people were still emotionally connected to, in light of repeatedly broken traditions. The communities, however, were not in a position to satisfy all these needs; after all, they were themselves affected by the devastation and, like the families, had to be reconstructed in adverse circumstances. I do not agree with the concept that societal institutions are an extended continuation of family. But the question arises as to whether post-war Jewish communities did not actually become 'extended family' in the function described above and also became a link between the community member and the state. For example, many Jews in the post-war years were reluctant to approach government agencies, even when they were entitled to specific goods or services. Instead, they contacted agencies of the Jewish communities that dealt with the government on their behalf.

Member of the audience (from Germany): In Germany after the *Shoah*, there was the problematic task of integrating and working with the Jews who came back from the concentration camps and the remaining Jews that were here. Today we have a second problematic task, and that is the enormous immigration wave from the Commonwealth of Independent States. We are having terrible problems with that, we have to build things up now, we have to teach and learn an enormous amount, because the generation that we lost in the *Shoah* is missing. We must now try to, not replace that generation, that would be the wrong word, but we must take on what they would have given us.

Wanya F. Kruyer: I don't know what will happen in continental Europe, if prosperity grows: whether we will feel safe, as I feel safe in Amsterdam, being out there as a Jew and a community representative. I don't know what will happen if more Jews come from Israel and Eastern Europe to this part of the world. This morning at breakfast, I was reading the newspaper, and I was crying, seeing the news from Tel Aviv. For those who don't know: a bomb exploded in front of a discotheque in Tel Aviv, and twenty-two people were killed. Here in Berlin, in the breakfast room, I saw Dr Alice Shalvi nearby, having breakfast on her own. She was surrounded by groups of German Protestant Christians, because it is a Christian place where we have breakfast. Tall, healthy and wealthy-looking, soft-spoken Germans. Dr Shalvi was sitting there, safe and calm. I was crying over my newspaper. When I saw her, I had to suppress a weird thought. I thought, 'Where are we safe in 2001, where are the Jews safe?' I don't know what will happen if this situation continues. Maybe we will see a kind of redistribution of the Jewish community.

Lynn Feinberg: I think there's so much work to be done in making Jews feel safe. I mean, it's not as if we don't feel safe here: in Norway, I don't think Jews feel threatened in being Jews. Of course, it's difficult today, with the many left-wingers in Norway who are all pro-PLO. The press is influenced very much by this, and it's not *comme il faut* in Norway to say that you're pro-Israel.

Eveline Goodman-Thau: I feel that the reason why Jews don't feel really at home in Austria or in Germany is that the peoples of Europe have not done their homework concerning the meaning of this *Zivilisationsbruch*.

Jael Geis: I would like to pose a question to the audience which I would not like to be understood as an appeal: why is there no organisation of survivor's children in Germany of all places? An organisation in which this generation *itself* is active, and does not only receive support. These two things do not necessarily contradict each other. For me, that is an open question.

Esther Kontarsky (Berlin): It was mentioned earlier that the situation of the Jewish Community in Germany after 1945 was like being under siege, and that that had a lot to do with mistrust. Spirituality in particular has a very strong connection to trust. The treacherous issue of Jewish identity after 1945: having survived the *Shoah* isn't enough to define Jewish identity. In defining it, what could be a counterweight to having survived the *Shoah*? Whatever that might be would require trust. How can we develop that trust?

Jael Geis: Do you mean trust in the environment? That the others have done their homework?

Esther Kontarsky: Trust in oneself, simply basic trust, trust in life itself and in what surrounds us. There's no question that our environment is a very important factor.

Why do I sometimes feel somewhat strange around people who have converted? I know that it's entirely unfair and that I'm putting my foot in my mouth. But I think that this uneasiness really does come from the fact that they tend to have this kind of trust that I lack entirely. And I don't know how it will develop over time.

About the question of Second Generation organisations. It's also a question of whether we demand something like that. If we really did demand them, and massively, then it probably wouldn't be so difficult. After all, there is ESRA,[4] for example Rabbi Jonathan Magonet pointed out recently that it's his impression that people in Holland are working on just this issue much much more. So the question arises: what is the difference between the work in Holland and the work in Germany? Both are communities of survivors. I'd like to describe my impression of a psychotherapeutic workshop in Holland and the same workshop in Germany. In Holland it was evident that people could articulate much more precisely what they need, that they are suffering, that they feel terrible, and so on, whereas here in Germany, things are sublimated much much more.

Lidia Drozdzynski (Cologne): In Cologne there was already a Second Generation group that was founded in 1994, I think, probably the first one in Germany. I was in it. We worked with one another for four years, with a therapist, because we knew that if we got involved with this topic, that we couldn't do it without professional help. We didn't do this in a particularly official way. I think that it was the first step. ESRA in Berlin helped us a lot.

The reason that the Second Generation issue is not a public one may be because it is a taboo, even in the Jewish Communities, in the First Generation. This means that when the Second Generation comes out and breaks this taboo, it should receive support. This is about processes that need support. It isn't really political work, it's psychological work. In my view it's very personal.

The concept of trust touched me deeply. I think it's very courageous, because I'm grappling with a similar problem. Collective trauma and collective consequences were mentioned earlier. Precisely this trauma, that my parents were robbed of their fundamental trust, and that that was transmitted to me in the Second Generation, means that I am not capable of finding spirituality, because I don't have this trust. I need tangible things: I'm floating in an intermediate space and can find my place only with great difficulty.

Another point that is very important for me: I live in Germany, and I consider Germany a very special place. It cannot be compared with London, Amsterdam, New York, or with any other country. It is extremely difficult for me to connect with the outside world right here, in this country, to have this trust that is a prerequisite for living in contact with my environment. That means that I'm always tense: am I safe? Am I not safe? It this my friend or is this my foe? The psychological situation is very difficult.

Lara Dämmig (initiator of Bet Debora, Berlin): We belong to the Second Generation, too, but we reject the term when applied to ourselves. We consider ourselves First Generation, the First Generation thereafter. We want to build up something new here, but based on the traditions. That is the reason for this conference in this venue, on the women's gallery of the largest Berlin synagogue, the place where Rabbi Regina Jonas served, the first woman rabbi in the world.

Elisa Klapheck: Strictly speaking, Bet Debora is a Second Generation organisation that is trying not to remain trapped in the trauma of the *Shoah*, but is setting off towards new horizons as a first generation.

Jael Geis: I will attempt to answer the question I asked, in light of all that I've heard. We don't have enough trust to form an organisation of children of survivors. I think that that is something different from what you, Lara and Elisa, are doing with Bet Debora. I think that if one calls oneself Second Generation, one does in fact create that connection.

Lori Klein: In the U.S., there is also this echo of having a lot of immigration at the beginning of the twentieth century, of people fleeing the pogroms, and also survivors of the Holocaust and those who lost people in their family. There also has been a period when there was a real sense of loss, where to find a spiritual home. For a while, the real renewal and life was in the intellectual and political realms. It seems to me that the point at which people felt capable again of renewing the spiritual realms was when there had been some emotional healing.

Andrea Pető: I think the quest for spirituality is important, but when in September 2000, I had a lot of time accidentally at my disposal, I went to the Chabad ...

Elizabeth Tikvah Sarah (Brighton, U.K.): On this whole notion of reconstructing Jewish life: I think we have to do it with the materials of who we are *now* and we start with ourselves. I'm addressing both the issue of spirituality, and also that comment about 'We send our children to Jewish schools, and then they get terribly Jewish and don't want to live with us any more'. The Zionist dream is gone, and we don't want our children to all run off to Israel. And I'm not saying we don't want Israel. We don't want our children to run off to Israel, we want our children to find a way and a path, whoever they are, wherever they are, as Germans, as Hungarians, whatever: it's a real task.

Alice Shalvi (Jerusalem): I wanted to relate to the children 'running away' to Israel: I was one such child, fifty-one years ago, who 'ran away' from Europe to Israel. Israel may be the only place where a young (or older) Jew can now live fully as a *secular* Jew. And I'm very pleased that people are running away to Israel because if nine thousand Israelis have gone to Amsterdam, I would like to have at least nine thousand to replace them, maybe an interesting exchange of population. Don't be afraid of your children running away to Israel!

The second point I wanted to make was about Andrea's telling us that when she went to synagogue, she went to Chabad. I was appalled, I must say. Because this is an indication of what's happening with many people who are 'returning' to Judaism: they believe that Chabad is the only genuine form of Judaism, and I would have thought that as a feminist, you would have tried to search out someplace where as a woman you had status which one does not find behind the *mechiza* in an Orthodox synagogue. There are a variety of ways of living as a Jew, having a spiritual life as a Jew, and I think we have to ensure that all of them are available, though I know it is difficult where you have only nine hundred Jews altogether. We as women, as feminists, have to ensure that there is as wide a range of options as possible from which to choose.

Andrea Pető: I don't want to be considered an undercover agent of the Lubavitchers here. <laughter> You have to understand that there is a very special characteristic of Eastern Europe: the difference between *Dichtung* and *Wahrheit*. Even for myself, who considers herself a poststructuralist feminist, *Wahrheit* as a concept is a little bit problematic. I was looking for a spiritual place, I was exploring possibilities, I found the women's meeting organised by the Lubavitchers in Budapest to be a good site for formulating an opinion of my own. I wanted to look for a source of knowledge to be in a position to make judgements myself. You might say this is an opportunist point of view to have, but in reality, it is a very individualistic one.

Sylvia Rothschild (Bromley, Kent, U.K.): I was boiling inside listening to some of the things I've heard! The question really is: What does it take – I don't know if it's just the women – for the Jews of Europe, post-*Shoah*, to actually claim their own authenticity? Because I'm hearing people talk about the 'real' community in which 'we' are all invisible. And the 'official' community, and 'we can't split them'. And so on, and so on. It seems to me ridiculous! Jewish communities have always been plural, it is traditional to have many different kinds of Jewish community. And yet, the whole time I've been here, I've heard about a 'lack of authenticity' in anything we're building, because the 'real' community is somehow out there, it's official, it's traditional …

Andrea Petö: It's rich!

Sylvia Rothschild: … it's rich. So what?! You can set up a community in somebody's kitchen! You don't have to wait for the money to come in to you. You don't have to worry what the Germans think about the Jews in Germany. You don't have to worry about what the *Einheitsgemeinde* thinks in Norway, or whatever. If most of the community are outside the official community, that tells you something. The word 'author' – somebody who writes something – is connected to the word 'authentic'. Actually, you write your own authenticity.

Elizabeth Tikvah Sarah: What I think we've got to do is: to be honest, bring all the different elements together, about where we live in our situation, whether it's in Vienna, or it's Budapest, or it's Berlin, or it's Norway, wherever we are. We must be honest about where we are, and living with that and *owning* it, together with exploring our Jewishness, which is to me not living through the past, but recognising our own journey as a Jewish journey, and finding a way of connecting with the symbols and the ideas and the stories.

Elisa Klapheck: We of Bet Debora think that what Rabbi Rothschild said is very important. We *are* authentic! We're doing Bet Debora *within* the Community, here in Berlin. We, too, travelled to America and Israel to get oriented there. But at some point we thought: we have to be able to be authentic here, in our own place. And isn't it great that such an international Jewish conference can take place here and now, in Berlin, the place where the annihilation originated? We don't see Bet Debora as outside the Community, on the contrary. We received financial support from the Community, from Jewish institutions as well as non-Jewish organisations. And by the way, we do want friction. We're doing something different from what has existed so far – there must be renewal, always. We want to trigger a discourse within the Community, but also outside it, in non-Jewish society. We seek out our discussion partners. We see us as *within* society, not in a niche outside.

Lara Dämmig: Not everybody in the Community loves us, but we have to deal with that. It's important to create a consciousness for the fact that there is diversity in our Community and that everyone should have the opportunity to do things their way.

Lynn Feinberg: I think that in Oslo, the community is very diverse and there is room for everybody. Even though we do have an Orthodox synagogue, the services are extremely lively, many come, we have very lively Kiddushim every Shabbat after the service, so even in an Orthodox community it is possible to make room for all. That is very important to stress.

Wanya F. Kruyer: I agree totally with Elisa: Beit ha'Chidush, the new community I represent, is fully part of the Jewish community in Holland, and if others don't recognise us as such, *they* have a problem.

Alice Shalvi: One of the most interesting developments in Israel recently has been 'reclaiming the Jewish bookcase'. People who are not in any way religiously observant, who feel that they have been denied their heritage because they went to the state school system and not the state religious school system, are now setting up numerous *batey midrash* to study Judaism, Jewish texts and customs. I find this a wonderfully encouraging development.

Wanya F. Kruyer: When I spoke about rediscovering Jewish life in Amsterdam, I was exactly talking about this reclaiming of our bookcases, from the mid-1980s on. And not only about our bookshelves, but also Jewish culture as a whole. Much later this concept developed in Tel Aviv, so I'm proud that Jews in Western Europe were in the vanguard of this movement of reclaiming our bookshelves, rather than walking behind! Some of them, very dedicated ones, are also busy reclaiming our rituals and our spirituality, and not only reclaiming it, but also renewing and reconstructing it so that it fits contemporary needs. So, by reclaiming our bookcases, we have a very open and inclusive Jewish cultural life.

Sandra Lustig: This has been a very rich discussion; thank you all, on the panel and in the audience, for your thoughts and insights. It is my duty – and privilege – as chair to sum up this discussion, but that is no mean feat! We have heard today that almost sixty years after the *Shoah*, which was committed here in Europe, we *are* on the path to reclaiming our bookcases, our authenticity, our Jewishness, our culture, our traditions, our com-munities of different kinds, and we're doing so *in Europe*. We are conscious of how difficult it is to rebuild, since the losses were so immense: the losses of people, families, whole generations, losses of communities, libraries, synagogues, organisations, material resources, and, very importantly, a loss of Jewish self-confidence. This place we call Europe is a kaleidoscope of different Jewish experiences, both historically and today. We hope that the result of our rebuilding efforts will be a cornucopia of flourishing Jewish life in Europe.

Notes

1. The panel discussion was held in English and German with simultaneous interpretation.
2. Excerpts of this panel discussion have been published in Dämmig and Klapheck 2001.
3. Werner Nachmann, president of the Zentralrat der Juden in Deutschland from 1965 to 1988, was accused of financial irregularities in connection with *Wiedergutmachung* (compensation) monies. The details have not been resolved to this day.
4. Esra (Hebrew): help. 'esra e.V., Beratungszentrum für NS-Verfolgte und ihre Familien' (esra, Counselling Centre for Victims of Nazi Persecution and their Families) offered individual counselling and self-help groups for the people mentioned in its name. After its dissolution in 1998, the group 'ESRA-Treffen für Schoah-Überlebende und deren Nachkommen e.V.' (ESRA–Meetings for *Shoah* Survivors and their Descendants) was founded.

Bibliography

Dämmig, Lara, and Elisa Klapheck, eds. 2001. *Bet Debora Journal 2: The Jewish Family–Myth and Reality*. Berlin, Edition Granat.

Geis, Jael. 2000. *Übrig sein–Leben 'danach'. Juden deutscher Herkunft in der britischen und amerikanischen Zone Deutschlands 1945–1949* [*Left Over–Living after the Shoah. Jews of German descent in the British and American zones of occupation in Germany, 1945–1949*]. Berlin/Vienna, Philo-Verlag.

Petö, Andrea. 1988. *Nõhistóriák. A politizáló magyar nõk története (1945–1951)* [*Women's Stories. History of Hungarian Women in Politics (1945–1951)*]. Budapest, Seneca.

Petö, Andrea. 2001. 'Ungarszkie jevreiki mezsdu Holokaustza i sztalinizma, Organizacii na ungarszki jevreiki b Ungarija cleg Vtorota svetovna viona 1945–1951' ['Hungarian Jewish Women between Holocaust and Stalinism. Hungarian Jewish Women's Organisations after the Second World War']. In *Granicci na grazsdansztvoto: evropeiski zseni mezsdu tradicijata i modernocta* [*Borders of Citizenship: European Women between Tradition and Modernity*], eds Kracimira Daskalova and Raina Gavrolova. Sofia, Bulgarszkaya Grupa za izledovania po ictoria na zsenite i pola.

Wardi, Dina. 1992. *Memorial Candles: Children of the Holocaust*. London, Routledge.

Chapter 7

DEBORA'S DISCIPLES: A WOMEN'S MOVEMENT AS AN EXPRESSION OF RENEWING JEWISH LIFE IN EUROPE

Lara Dämmig and Elisa Klapheck

In 1999 we hosted a conference of European women rabbis, women cantors, rabbinically educated, and interested Jewish women and men. This was the first time in Europe after the Shoah that the renewal of Jewish life was discussed from a Jewish women's perspective.

Why women?

Put differently: did history pass by us Jewish women in Germany, in Europe, and are we just catching up with what happened in the U.S. a long time ago? *There*, a Jewish women's movement has existed since the 1970s; *there*, Rosh Chodesh groups had come into being where women experimented with their spirituality; *there*, a Jewish feminist theology had been developed; and *there*, the first women rabbis had been ordained.

So, were we German, European Jewish women just lagging behind this development, and were we just bridging a gap with our first Bet Debora conference in 1999, a gap that separated us from the rest of Jewry after the decades-long paralysis of Jewish life because of the *Shoah*?

Of course, we, too, had read the works of American feminists like Judith Plaskow or Susannah Heschel when we founded our Rosh Chodesh group in Berlin in the early 1990s. In the beginning, we often used American feminists' models to get our bearings. In our Egalitarian Minyan that was founded at the same time – one of the first in Germany in which women and men had equal positions from the beginning – we experimented with liturgies and exegeses that we had brought back from trips to the U.S. But one Shabbat, when one of us unexpectedly read a prayer by Bertha Pappenheim from the year 1935 instead of one of the usual psalms, it touched a special nerve in all of us.

Appeal

My God, you are not a god of softness,
of the word and of incense, not a god of the past.
A god of the omnipresent you are.
A demanding god you are to me.
You bless me with your 'thou shalt';
you expect me to choose between good and evil;
you demand that I prove to be strength of your strength,
to strive upwards to you,
to inspire others, to help with all that I can.

Demand, demand, that I feel
in every breath of my life in my conscience:
there is a God.

Bertha Pappenheim, 14 November 1935[1]

Suddenly we realised the fact that we had a tradition *of our own* – that we were standing on our own turf and could make further steps on it. Little by little we discovered the works of many great Jewish women in Germany before the *Shoah*.

Bertha Pappenheim, founder of the Jewish women's movement in Germany, had created the Jüdischer Frauenbund (JFB, Jewish Women's League) in 1904.[2] Together with other women who shared her beliefs, she fought for equal rights for women in the Jewish communities, for the right to vote and to be elected, and for the right of women to professionalise their skills. For Pappenheim, all this did not imply opting out of Jewish tradition. It was because of her deep religiosity that she developed entirely new thoughts on the societal dimensions of femininity. While Pappenheim did hold onto the traditional ideal of the woman as 'keeper of the family', she liberated this ideal from the isolated sphere of private life by defining the Jewish community and the state as 'family'. From this, she derived a claim for women to be active in the public sphere as their 'natural domain' (Konz 2001).[3] The domain she had in mind primarily was a social welfare system that she and thousands of other women built up in the Jewish communities of Germany at a high professional level.

Bertha Pappenheim was not the only Jewish woman before the *Shoah* who opened up a new dimension in Judaism with feminist ideas. Regina Jonas, the first woman rabbi in the world, completed her studies at the Hochschule für die Wissenschaft des Judentums (Academy for the Science of Judaism) in Berlin in 1930 with a halachic thesis entitled, 'Can Women Serve as Rabbis?'[4] In this thesis she determined that woman was by nature particularly qualified to be a rabbi, because it was especially she who had social skills such as love of people, tact, empathy, and access to young people, which were essential prerequisites for the rabbinical profession and for passing on Judaism (Klapheck 2004: 34). Jonas used the grammatically feminine form '*Rabbinerin*' (Klapheck 2004: 111).[5] According to her argument, women were not only to be permitted to carry out the same tasks as men, but should also be able to give the rabbinate a specifically feminine identity. Jonas went so far as to say that a woman as rabbi must take on the role of a leader in her congregation as a matter of course.

Both women, Bertha Pappenheim and Regina Jonas, expressed in their own way what many Jewish women in Germany before and after the First World War were ready to do: to authorise themselves to be carriers of Judaism that they intended to continue developing on their own responsibility and from a women's perspective. Pappenheim and Jonas are only the most famous women religious thinkers of that time. In the *Blätter des Jüdischen Frauenbundes* (*Papers of the Jewish Women's League*) a multitude of women authors formulated a new profile of women and thereby placed Jewish tradition in a broadened or even new context.

The *Shoah*, however, suffocated the uninhibited spirit of this new departure. After 1945, Jewish self-confidence was shaken to such a degree that the survivors rigidly clung to handed down clichés of an ideal world *à la* Orthodox *shtetl*. They felt any impetus towards renewal to be a threat and fended off such attempts reflexively.[6] While the Jüdischer Frauenbund (JFB) was indeed founded anew in 1953, only a few women of note of the pre-war generation were actively involved (Schwermer 2001). For example, Jeanette Wolff (Lamm 1981; Lange 1988) – one of the re-founders of the JFB – brought Jewish women's perspectives to bear in her political work both in the Representatives' Assembly (parliament) of the Berlin Jewish Community and as a politician with the Social Democratic Party. The welfare activities of the JFB, however, were directed foremost towards caring for the survivors. In the 1960s, enthusiasm waned little by little, and interest focused on Israel instead. The younger women joined organisations like WIZO to raise money for the Jewish state with annual bazaars and other events. For decades, the self-identification of Jewish women who chose to live in Diaspora was no longer a theme for discussion.

Indeed, there were several women who took Jewish feminist positions – but only as individual voices and outside the communities. For example, Pnina Navè Levinson (1921–1998) obtained a professorship at Heidelberg University as early as the 1970s, but she taught a largely Christian theological audience. Her books were the first Jewish feminist publications written in German after the *Shoah* (Levinson 1989, 1992 and 1993, for example). Non-Jewish women readers did attempt to acknowledge the historical achievements of Jewish women, but were more enthusiastic about 'dropouts' like Rahel Varnhagen (1771–1833) or Dorothea Schlegel (1764–1839, daughter of Moses Mendelssohn), who had left Judaism, than they were about women who tried to change things within Judaism. The few Jewish women who were interested in Jewish women's history followed these preferences for a long time. The *Shoah* had not only cut off many from their own history: for a long time, no one considered it necessary to continue developing the traditions as living ones. Not a few were content with a kind of museum Judaism and seemed to believe that this could last forever. Many secular Jews even felt uncomfortable about topics concerning religion.

When Daniela Thau completed her rabbinical studies – the first woman from Germany since Regina Jonas – at Leo Baeck College in London in the 1980s, not only did she have no prospect of a position as a community rabbi: it is particularly painful in hindsight that hardly a Jewish woman in Germany took note of Thau's ordination, let alone supported her being hired as a community rabbi (Thau 2000).

For a long time, the only imaginable starting point for Jewish self-identification for women in Germany seemed to be the *Shoah* – that is, first of all identification with the victims of the *Shoah*, or dealing with new forms of anti-Semitism. In the 1980s, Jessica Jacoby succeeded in persuading Jewish women to express themselves as Jewish women in German society. A Jewish feminist, Jacoby was active in the women's movement and founded the Shabbes-Kreis (Shabbes Circle) in Berlin, perhaps the first Jewish feminist initiative in Germany after the *Shoah*. Above all, this circle criticised latent and open anti-Jewish sentiment in parts of the German women's movement as well as its repression of Germany's Nazi past. We have Jacoby to thank for the first book on Jewish women's self-identification in Germany after the *Shoah* (Jacoby et al. 1994). Most of the contributions to this book are characterised by the ambivalence of living as a Jewish woman in the 'land of the perpetrators' – whether as survivors or as members of the so-called Second Generation. For some women, this ambivalence was overlaid by another one: ever since the invasion of Lebanon in 1982, more and more Jews began to criticise Israeli policy. What remained of Jewish self-definition often consisted only of a reserved position – be it reserved about Germany or reserved about Israel – and did not build upon positive personal approaches.

In East Germany, too, Jewish life was focused on preserving handed-down tradition. In the shrinking communities with small congregations composed mostly of survivors and returning emigrés, simply maintaining a minimum of Jewishness proved to be a major effort. They were more or less cut off from the rest of the Jewish world.[7] Nonetheless, it is worth mentioning that the returning emigrés remained closer to the intellectual German–Jewish heritage than did the Jews in West Germany.

Although most Jews responded to the changes in November 1989 and the beginning of the process of unifying Germany with reserve, the fall of the Berlin Wall did also mark a change in Jewish life. Not only did tens of thousands of Jewish immigrants from the former Soviet Union flock to Germany and change the face of the communities over night. At the same time, history returned. In Berlin, the historic Jewish sites became visible again. Most of them are located in Mitte district, formerly downtown East Berlin, such as the ruins of the New Synagogue, which has housed the Centrum Judaicum since restoration in 1995, or the building of the

Hochschule für die Wissenschaft des Judentums, where Regina Jonas had studied, or the head office of the JFB on Monbijou Square.

In 1993, several Jewish women in Berlin founded a Rosh Chodesh group that met regularly at the beginning of the Jewish month, following a tradition in the Talmud, and that discussed Jewish traditions from a women's perspective. At the same time, the Egalitarian Minyan came into being. But a new departure with a new quality was perceptible not only among Jewish men and women in Berlin. In almost all the larger cities of Germany, liberal Jewish groups and egalitarian minyanim were founded independently of each other – some as private initiatives, others as new liberal communities, for example Kehilla Chadascha in Frankfurt/Main, the Jewish Forum in Cologne, a liberal community in Göttingen or a Reform Jewish community, Beth Shalom in Munich. All of them criticised the dominant religious paralysis of Judaism and sought opportunities for a contemporary renewal. Even if the intellectual stimuli initially often came from the Anglo-Saxon countries, these activities followed on from the tradition of liberal German Jewry, which was hardly known about any more and which was thought to have come to an end. One fundamental feature common to all of them was equal rights for women and men. A signature image of this new movement was a woman standing on the *bima*, wearing a head covering and *tallit*, reading from the Torah and carrying out all the other ritual functions of the service. And, indeed, it was a majority of women who took the initiative. From the beginning, their stronger presence in comparison to the men was noticeable in the new minyanim: it was not uncommon for them to outnumber men two to one. Many taught themselves *leining* and how to conduct services, and studied the liturgy critically. For example, in Berlin, a new *siddur* was developed that experimented with variations of the prayers, named God in masculine and feminine images, contained a coming out prayer, introduced new elements, and rediscovered old ones in doing so.

Since the mid-1990s, this innovative movement has established itself as a new, but stable, component of Jewish life. Even though the official establishment is to this day mostly reserved towards this development, a number of political successes have been achieved. A meeting of the Berlin Rosh Chodesh group at Shavuot in 1995 led to a first political action within the community. The Berlin women protested against the recently intro-duced election rules for the boards of the synagogues. According to the new rules, only male candidates would be eligible to be elected as *gabbaim*. By collecting signatures, it was possible to show a broad consensus against the archaic opinions of most of the elected representatives of the community. Women demanded their right to carry out ritual functions in the synagogues. They referred to discussions that had taken place in the 1920s. Already in 1930, Martha Ehrlich had officiated as the first *gabbait* in Germany in Berlin's Rykestrasse synagogue. The action led to the election rules being changed two years later, so that from then on, the synagogues could determine themselves whether to admit women to their boards. In 1998, after a tenacious struggle, the community officially permitted the Egalitarian Minyan and the Equal Rights Services (Gleichberechtigter Gottesdienst), a more traditional group that had been founded in the meantime, to use the synagogue in Oranienburger Strasse. From the beginning, *gabbayiot* were active there.

Meanwhile, Bea Wyler had taken a position as first woman community rabbi since the Second World War in Oldenburg, Braunschweig, and Delmenhorst, which still amounted to breaking a taboo. Since 1995, there was an annual meeting in Arnoldshain of the Vereinigung liberaler und reformjüdischer Gruppierungen und Gemeinden (Association of Liberal and Reform Jewish Groups and Communities), which turned into the Union progressiver Juden (Union of Progressive Jews) two years later. The development has called into question the one-sided orthodox-influenced view of the Zentralrat der Juden in Deutschland (Central Council of Jews in Germany). The main point of contention was always whether women were permitted to actively carry out ritual functions during the service – put bluntly: whether the Torah would be soiled by being touched by a woman.[8]

But reality had long since moved beyond this question. If they liked, women stood on the *bima* as equals of the men – and not only in Berlin and other German cities: a similar development seemed to have occurred across Europe. Whether in Minsk or Paris, Budapest or Oldenburg, Vienna or Oslo, groups or communities had been founded everywhere, and women had been at the helm, at times even as rabbis and cantors. Great Britain, of course, was a forerunner, where Jacqueline Tabick had been ordained as the first woman rabbi at Leo Baeck College in London as early as 1976.

In the other European countries, Jewish women had begun to rediscover and unearth their history, just like we Jewish women in Germany had done. But in contrast to the U.S., for example, consciousness of the discontinuity of Jewish history in one's own country is an essential part of European Jewish feminism. Not only does this make it difficult to create links from pre-*Shoah* Judaism to today, but Jewish experience since the *Shoah* seems to prohibit creating such links. In many countries in Europe, women often stand alone and need to struggle against the opposition of the community establishment. From this loneliness stemmed the desire to exchange experiences and create a network. That is how Bet Debora was born.

In contrast to many panel discussion on the status of woman in Judaism that we had experienced, we no longer asked whether women were permitted to enter into mens' territories in Judaism. We went straight ahead to the next step and asked: what effects does it have on Jewish tradition if women have an equal say? What does this mean in particular in the European context after the *Shoah*? Which themes and challenges are coming to the fore? Are the new women activists even changing the coordinates of Jewish self-identification as a driving force in renewing Jewish life in Europe, like their predecessors before and after the First World War? We had these questions in mind when we, the initiative group 'Bet Debora Berlin' hosted a conference of European women rabbis, women cantors, rabbinically trained and interested Jewish women and men in May 1999 – the first of this kind in Europe.[9]

Above all, we wanted to take stock: what are women rabbis and Jewish women activists doing? What are their themes, their successes, their concerns? What did they experience *as women* in these positions? Before the conference, we had long discussions about what to name it. We agreed on the name 'Debora' quickly, since the biblical Debora, as a judge, a prophet, and a politician was a suitable leading figure. Just as quickly, we rejected the idea of regarding ourselves as Debora's 'sisters' or 'daughters' – titles of many feminist publications. In contrast to the attributes usually associated with femininity, and which the women's movement, too, uses at times, we made a point of not using biological metaphors to define ourselves. Instead, we wanted to create room for spiritual and intellectual analysis – a place of encounter and exchange. When the Talmud differentiates between the traditions of exegesis, it calls them 'houses', houses of learning of great scholars, for example, the 'School of Hillel', 'Bet Hillel'. Did we not also want to found a 'house' with a tradition of exegesis of its own? That is how the name 'Bet Debora', House of Debora, came into being.

From the beginning, Bet Debora defined itself as European and pointed out the autonomy of European Jewry, which had begun to rediscover its own culture and tradition after decades of dominance by American and Israeli Jewry. In the beginning, we feared that there may not be enough qualified women speakers for the conference, but even as we began our research, those fears turned out to be unfounded. Indeed, at first we were ridiculed again and again. After all, people thought there were women rabbis only in Great Britain, and then Bea Wyler in Oldenburg, too. We ourselves were surprised at how many we found. In the end, Bet Debora invited no less that twenty speakers from Eastern and Western Europe, among them:[10]

- Katalin Keleman, who had just become a rabbi in Budapest and led the Reform community *Szim Salom* there.

- Nelly Shulman (née Kogan), the youngest woman rabbi in Europe, who was born in Leningrad (St Petersburg) and who is in charge of no less than eighteen Reform communities in Minsk and other places in the former Soviet Union.

- Bea Wyler, who from 1995 to 2004 worked in Oldenburg as the first woman rabbi since the Second World War in Germany, as well as Daniela Thau, who lives in Bedford, England and who, as the first

German woman rabbi since the *Shoah*, had not been able to gain a foothold in a German community a decade before.

- Eveline Goodman-Thau, who, a year later, was the first woman in Europe to gain an Orthodox *smicha*.

- Rabbis Sylvia Rothschild, Elizabeth Tikvah Sarah, and Sybil Sheridan, who were already the second generation of women rabbis and had established a women's tradition in British Judaism.

- Historian Diana Pinto from Paris, who used the slogan 'voluntary Judaism' for a new concept of Jewish identity in the new political circumstances in Europe.

- Religious scholar and feminist theorist Judith Frishman from Amsterdam, who spoke on the concept of a 'usable past' for Jewish women.

- Cantors like Avitall Gerstetter and Mimi Sheffer from Berlin, who were not even known in their own communities and were hired after performing at Bet Debora.[11]

- Many women activists from different countries, such as Marine Solomonishvili, who had built up a Jewish women's organisation in Georgia; Valérie Rhein, co-founder of the egalitarian minyan 'Ofek' in Basle; and Wanya Kruyer, who founded the Renewal Community 'Beit Ha'Chidush' in Amsterdam.

Many did not know each other before the conference, exchanged views for the first time and found they were part of a pan-European development. Bet Debora created a network. Since it was the purpose of Bet Debora to show Jewish women's perspectives with which women and men alike could participate in renewing Jewish life in Europe, the conference was open to men, too. Several men took advantage of this opportunity.

The conference apparently struck a chord. None of us had counted on such overwhelming resonance, especially since the conference took place in Berlin, the place where the *Shoah* was planned and which was bound to trigger strong reservations. But two hundred Jewish women and men from sixteen countries – both Eastern and Western Europe – came to Berlin for this event. And it was precisely the conference venue – the former women's gallery in the Neue Synagoge, once the largest synagogue in Germany, now a lecture hall – that was to develop special symbolic power. Regina Jonas, too, had preached in the Neue Synagoge in the 1930s. In one of the services, Rabbi Katalin Kelemen expressed the feelings of many. The daughter of a concentration camp survivor and an atheist communist, she could hardly have imagined herself becoming a rabbi, even just a few years before. But it was even less fathomable for her to be standing on a *bima* in Berlin, of all places, at to speak to an audience that was living proof of the beginning of a new Jewish era in Europe.

Again and again, women participants emphasised how important it was for them to experience being part of a pan-European development. For much too long, they had believed that the were individuals fighting for a lost cause, acknowledged by no one, in the shadow of a diffuse inferiority complex which made modern Jewish life after the *Shoah* in Europe seem to be illusory.

While rebuilding was still at the centre of the continental European women's efforts (Fruchtman 2000a; Fruchtman 2000b, for example; Rhein 2000; Wyler 2000), the British women displayed greater ease in forging new paths, for example developing new rituals for women's life cycles or rewriting existing liturgies (Rothschild 2000; Sarah 2000, for example). At the same time, however, several participants questioned whether religion and liturgy were actually the field for renewal or just a starting point (Klapheck 2000, for example).

Looking forward also implied taking up the heritage of our mothers' generation. Bet Debora invited three guests of honour who had taken an active part in Jewish religious life in the 1920s and 1930s: Shoshana Ronen (née Elbogen) and Ilse Perlman (née Selier) studied at the Hochschule für die Wissenschaft des Judentums (Academy for the Science of Judaism) a few years after Regina Jonas. Hanna Hochmann (née Gerson) headed services for young people in a liberal synagogue in Berlin. Their contributions to the discussions during the conference showed that the older generation had not only opened new horizons at the time, but indeed did have something to say to the younger generation (Dämmig 2000; Ronen 2000; Seidel 2000, for example; Weiss 2000). For example, Hanna Hochmann felt today's Jewish feminists' strong interest in liturgical questions to be 'nostalgic affected piety' and held that the women of her day had been more modern and more courageous. The *Bet Debora Journal*,[12] which documents the conference, showed up an area of controversy between two poles. Many contributions were founded on the hypothesis that women have a spirituality of their own (Herweg 2000, for example), while a number of articles pointed to the fact that going back to the biblical sources and rabbinic writings led one to the insight that defining Judaism as a religion did not provide all the answers, maybe even only the least of them.

This and other realisations found an expression in the theme of the second conference in Berlin, attended by two hundred participants from all over Europe. Bet Debora picked up an issue that is not primarily defined in a religious sense, but that is of immense importance both for the continuity of Judaism and for each individual's way of living: does the Jewish family still have a future? The classic nuclear family is still seen as the foundation of Jewish tradition, and the women's roles seem to be clear-cut. But in fact, the Jewish family of one's dreams is no longer necessarily the norm. Today, Jewish women and men live also as singles, as single parents, in 'mixed' partnerships, as lesbians and gays – in short, in a multitude of lifestyles. This is also an expression of a general societal development. Bet Debora examined these realities of life from a Jewish women's perspective in June 2001, at a second conference entitled 'The Jewish Family – Myth and Reality'.

This second conference dispensed with clichés in a radical way. Themes such as single womens' loneliness, interreligious partnerships, gay and lesbian weddings, single mothers, the status of children of Jewish fathers, as well as such taboos as abandoned wives (*agunot*), the dogma of motherhood, and violence in Jewish families (Allebes 2001; Axelrod 2001; Egger-Rollig 2001; Feinberg 2001; Hall 2001; Jacoby 2001; Rheinz 2001; Sarah 2001a; Shalvi 2001a; Shalvi 2001b) were put up for discussion. At the same time, the participants discussed alternative models of the family that extend beyond biological relations, and the responsibility that the Jewish community has to integrate them as well. The second conference brought to the fore that historically speaking, Judaism is by no means exclusively family-oriented: institutions such as the minyan or the seder demand that one feels responsible for the entire community. Rabbi Elizabeth Tikvah Sarah made it clear in her keynote speech that a community seder especially can accommodate the range of today's lifestyles, because not everyone has a place at a family seder (Sarah 2001b). In this respect, living Judaism is not restricted to the private sphere at home, but requires that public space which Bertha Pappenheim claimed for the women of her day.

There were controversies about the 'Second Generation' issue time and again during the conference. They illuminated to what extent the renewal of Jewish life is still in its beginnings. Many participants explicitly viewed themselves as 'Second Generation' and linked their identities with the trauma of persecution that they felt their parents had passed on to them. But others, like us, the initiators of Bet Debora, objected to an identity that focuses first of all on being a victim and paralyses itself in this way (Furedi). It is because of our respect for the survivors that we refuse to equate ourselves with them. Instead, we regard ourselves as 'First Generation "after"', that does not define itself in terms of the *Shoah*, but that desires to build up something new that is founded on the old traditions. This position was quickly misunderstood as disrespect for the survivors. However, the fierce controversy that followed showed that some members of the current generation are standing at the threshold of stepping out of the shadow of the *Shoah*. This position is also a prerequisite for a fruitful inner-Jewish debate.

The conference and the *Bet Debora Journal* 2, published subsequently, bore witness to another point of contention concerning the self-identification of today's Jewish feminists. Do we view ourselves as outsiders and accordingly withdraw into a niche? Or do we want to work within the existing Jewish institutions and communities, in defiance of all the resistance there? Bet Debora makes a clear plea for the latter option.

But this leads to the question of whether coalitions between Jewish women with different cultural, political, and familial backgrounds are possible and may bring forth new structures of solidarity within the communities.

The third conference of Bet Debora, in May 2003, was thus dedicated to a more political approach: In what ways, and how much, do Jewish women engage in the power structures of their communities? What are the historical and social implications of their engagement? What do Jewish scripture and tradition have to offer to support women's engagement in the power structures? What could the definitions of 'power' and 'responsibility' in Judaism be with regard to women's activities? How does this interact with the rise of a new European Jewry, as well as with regard to the general European unification process? What are the differences between East and West? What are the responsibilities of Jewish women with regard to general developments in their respective societies, for example, Jewish–Christian–Muslim dialogue, multicultural society, and combating racism and xenophobia?

Between 150 and 200 Jewish women and some men from Eastern and Western Europe responded to this invitation. The conference itself was designed as an open forum for the exchange of thoughts. The fifty-six (*sic*) speakers included many Jewish community presidents from all over Europe, directors of Jewish institutions, spiritual leaders (rabbis and lay leaders), activists operating on various community levels, scholars who added historical and Judaic perspectives, and artists who provided cultural contributions to the conference theme.

Among the speakers were:

- Gabriele Brenner, President of the Jewish Community of the southern German town Weiden.

- Rabbi Gesa Schira Ederberg, Principal of the Masorti centre in Berlin and Congregational Rabbi in Weiden.

- Liliana Furman, Program Director for social and pedagogic projects of the American Jewish Joint Distribution Committee (JOINT) in Germany.

- Rabbi Prof. Dr Eveline Goodman-Thau, Director of the Hermann Cohen Academy in Buchen (Germany).

- Prof. Bente Groth, Professor of the History of Religions at the University of Oslo.

- Katerina Jelinkova, Editor of the monthly magazine *Maskil* in Prague.

- Anetta Kahane, Managing Director of the Amadeo Antonio Foundation in Berlin, which combats racism and neo-Nazism.

- Cynthia Kain, Vice-President of the Jewish Community in Berlin.[13]

- Dr Susanna Keval, Editor of the Jewish Community journal of Frankfort am Main.

- Prof. Dr Rita Kleiman, Head of the Academic Judaica Department and Chairwoman of the Jewish Community of Kishinev (Moldavia).

- Charlotte Knobloch, Vice-President of the Central Council of Jews in Germany, and President of the Jewish Community in Munich.

- Wanya Kruyer, journalist and founder of Beit Ha'Chidush in Amsterdam.

- Becca Lazarova, Vice-President of the Jewish Community of Sofia (Bulgaria).

- Dr Katalin Pesci and Andrea Deak, Editors of the Jewish women's page 'Esther's Bag' in *Szombat*, Budapest.[14]

- Prof. Dr Tania Reytan-Marincheshka, university professor and human rights activist in Sofia (Bulgaria).

- Prof. Dr Alice Shalvi, until recently Rector of the Solomon Schechter Institute of Jewish Studies in Jerusalem, founder of the Israel Women's Network.

- Rabbi Sheila Shulman, Congregational Rabbi at Beit Klal Yisrael in London.

- Bella Szwarcman-Czarnota, Editor of the Jewish-Polish magazine *Midrasz*.

- Carola de Vries, founder and co-ordinator of Jewish Renewal activities in Amsterdam.

- Sylvie Wittmannova, founder of Prague's first liberal Jewish community, Bejt Simcha.

- Rabbi Bea Wyler, Congregational Rabbi in Oldenburg.

- Svetlana Yakimenko, founder of Kesher, a Jewish women's network in the former Soviet Union.

- Prof. Dr Nira Yuval-Davis, Professor of Gender, Sexualities, and Ethnic Studies at the University of East London.

Some highlights of the numerous panel discussions, workshops, and lectures were:

- Charlotte Knobloch's opening speech, 'Experiences of Power in Jewish Institutions'.

- Politics for the Kehillah – Politics for Women? – Jewish Women in Positions of Leadership.

- Reality in Synagogues: 'Women as Decisors of Halachah'; 'The Relationship between Learning Women and the Established Orthodox or Traditional Community Structures'; 'Contemporary Rabbinic Responses to the 'Liberation' of Women'.

- Jewish Feminism – a Perspective for Everyone?: 'The Religious Life of Jewish Women in Poland'; 'The Contribution of Jewish Women as Rebbe, Rabbi, and Rebbezin to the History of Women in Prague'; 'Projects of Jewish Women in the former Soviet Union'.

- The 'Fourth' Power? Journalists and Editors in Jewish Media.

- Queens: 'Female Regents in Biblical Times'; 'Power and Female Sovereignty in the Talmud'.

- Ageing and Authority: 'Spiritual Ageing'; 'The Responsibility of the Young towards the Old'; 'Honour Father and Mother'.

- Opportunities and Obstacles of Women's Networking.

- Female Authority – Male Perspectives: 'Men who Follow in the Footsteps of Women'; 'New Impulses for Male Academics'.

- Jewish Women and their Responsibility for Politics and Society.

This third conference proved to be especially successful. The emergence of a European-wide network could be observed clearly. Many participants had come to the previous conferences and now their contacts were deepened. Quite a number of participants have started to co-operate in various projects on a professional level. Ties between different Jewish communities and groups have been strengthened. The willingness of the 'establishment' of Jewish communities and members of grassroots movements to cooperate with each other was affirmed several times during the conference. This was expressed especially by Charlotte Knobloch (Vice-President of the Central Council of Jews in Germany) in her opening speech, as well as by some other representatives of Jewish organisations in Europe. Such an alliance might in the future be a key to the revival and renewal of Jewish life in Europe. Knobloch said that the renewal of Jewish life depends on initiatives such as Bet Debora, which at first sight seem marginal but prove to be the motor for central new developments.

In addition, there was a much stronger presence of Eastern European women, and Bet Debora took special efforts to include them. The fact that, next to English and German, simultaneous translation into Russian was provided, enabled women from the former Soviet Union to speak in public with much more ease. However, it wasn't only them – all Eastern European women showed remarkable self-confidence this time, to step up and let the others hear about their experiences and points of view. As a consequence, Western women did not dominate with their views, or assign Eastern women the role of pupils. This time, Western women clearly learned a lot from their Eastern counterparts, and vice versa: both sides met on equal terms.

Another indicator of the success of this conference was the dynamic that the theme itself unfolded among the participants. At the beginning, many participants, including community politicians, confessed ambivalence regarding the word 'power'. In the course of the conference this ambivalence faded. The necessity of participating in power structures was seen more clearly – and pragmatically. The question shifted from whether Jewish women should want to attain power, to how they might express their power in a responsible way. What are the criteria of responsibility? What are the fields in which participants should strive for their share of power and in which they can best contribute to the continuation of Jewish life in Europe?

Of course there is not just a single answer to this question. Every participant had her special situation in her country. But it seemed that all of them brought new ideas and inspiration back home, to be applied there in concrete ways.

The conference closed with two panel discussions showing future perspectives for Bet Debora, derived from the experiences and interests of all three conferences and their participants.

The first was titled 'Think Tank and Platform for European Jewish Women'. After three conferences in the city of Berlin, which of course has its own symbolism sixty years after the *Shoah*, the Bet Debora conference will travel to different European cities in the future. Participants from Amsterdam, Baku, Kishinev, and Vienna at the 2003 conference expressed interest in hosting Bet Debora in their cities in the future, and the initiators of Bet Debora would be happy to support them. They hope that Bet Debora will give a special impulse to Jewish life in the host cities. The academic conference 'Jewish intellectual women in Europe: gendering history, politics and culture' that Professors Andrea Pető and Marina Calloni are planning to hold in Budapest in 2006 is also an outcome of the Bet Debora process.

The final panel discussion 'Religion is Political – Creating Forums for Socio-Political and Multicultural Debates', was organised in co-operation with 'Sarah – Hagar: Religion, Politics, Gender', a Berlin project that initiated a debate between representatives of political and religious spheres, incorporating a Jewish–Christian–Muslim trialogue. The purpose of this panel discussion was to go beyond the solely Jewish approach of the conference and to see possibilities of interaction with other sectors of society.

One of Bet Debora's concerns is to introduce Jewish women's points of view not only into the internal Jewish debate, but also into predominantly non-Jewish society. In doing so, Bet Debora is challenging the current community establishment in many countries in Europe, which to a large extent is still clinging to the 'fence around the Torah' and which cannot imagine a Jewish dynamic that has a productive influence on the predominantly non-Jewish society beyond admonishing appeals against anti-Semitism and the repression of history.

It is particularly the women who will not be able to avoid this challenge within and outside Judaism, since Judaism is in their hands more and more. Even today, the majority of students at liberal rabbinical seminaries are women. In Jewish education, women teachers are in the majority. In countless Jewish organisations, armies of women are doing indispensable volunteer work. In fact, they are challenging the classic role of the Jewish woman and are working to realise a Judaism in which patriarchal structures are increasingly being dissolved.

Translated by Sandra Lustig

Notes

1. Elisa Klapheck and Lara Dämmig, eds. 2003. *Bertha Pappenheim. Gebete/Prayers*. Teetz: Hentrich & Hentrich. A new edition of *Gebete (Prayers)*. Düsseldorf, Verlag Allgemeine Wochenzeitung der Juden in Deutschland 1954, reprint from 1936. This prayer translated by Sandra Lustig.
2. See Kaplan 1979.
3. As Pappenheim wrote to Martin Buber in 1935, she considered woman to be 'creator' or 'shaper of life' who brings forth the 'neighbour' (or 'next one') in the pain of labour and childbirth and must lead, admonish, and consciously develop the seeds of the divine in him in unending love (Konz 2001).
4. Regina Jonas was ordained by the liberal rabbi Max Dienemann in 1935. However, there remained only a few years for her to work as a rabbi in Berlin: in 1944, she was murdered in Auschwitz. See Klapheck 2004.
5. The term '*Rabbinerin*' (woman rabbi) is controversial today, too. For example, Bea Wyler would like to be called '*Rabbiner*' ((grammatically male) rabbi). *Translator's note:* In German, the feminine form of professions usually has the suffix *-in*. Traditionally, the masculine form has been used also for women, and some argue that it is gender-neutral. Many feminists argue that the masculine form is indeed *not* gender-neutral and insist on the feminine form when speaking about women.
6. See Jael Geis's contribution to the panel discussion in Chapter 6 above; also Geis 2000.
7. There were eight communities in East Germany. The largest was the East Berlin community with 209 members. Next in size were Dresden with sixty-one and Leipzig with fifty-three members. The smallest community was in Schwerin, with two members (statistics from 1990).
8. According to a Jewish superstition that seems impossible to stamp out, the Torah becomes 'unclean' if touched by a woman during her menstruation. However, this concept lacks any basis at all in the rabbinic writings. Rather, tractate Megilla 23a of the Babylonian Talmud states explicitly that women are permitted to read from the Torah just like men.
9. At that time, the initiative group Bet Debora Berlin consisted of the authors of this chapter as well as Dr Rachel Monika Herweg.
10. All of the women rabbis named here were ordained at Leo Baeck College in London, with the exceptions of Bea Wyler and Eveline Goodman-Thau. Wyler studied at the Conservative Jewish Theological Seminary in New York. Goodman-Thau received a private *smicha* from an Israeli rabbi.

11. In the mean time, the Jewish Community Berlin has dismissed both of them.
12. Journals 1, 2, and 3 can be read on the internet at www.bet-debora.de. The German and Russian editions of Journals 1 and 2 are out of print; the English edition can be ordered at bet-debora@hagalil.com for a small donation.
13. Cynthia Kain was not re-elected to the Repräsentantenversammlung, the Community Council, in the 2003 elections. Since those elections, only three of the twenty-one representatives are women, and none of them is on the Executive Committee.
14. In the mean time, the women's page has been discontinued.

Bibliography

Allebes, Rochelle. 2001. 'Violence in the Jewish Family'. *Bet Debora Journal 2: The Jewish Family – Myth and Reality*: 37–8.

Axelrod, Toby. 2001. 'Being Fruitful: On Forms of Creation'. *Bet Debora Journal 2: The Jewish Family – Myth and Reality*: 26–7.

Dämmig, Lara. 2000. 'Community Activists'. *Bet Debora Journal 1*: 14.

Egger-Rollig, Esther. 2001. 'Intergenerational Consequences'. *Bet Debora Journal 2: The Jewish Family – Myth and Reality*: 34–5.

Feinberg, Lynn. 2001. 'Single Mother in an Orthodox Community'. *Bet Debora Journal 2: The Jewish Family – Myth and Reality*: 28–9.

Fruchtman, Ruth. 2000a. 'Debora in Eastern Europe'. *Bet Debora Journal 1*: 35–6.

Fruchtman, Ruth. 2000b. 'Rabbi in Minsk'. *Bet Debora Journal 1*: 39–40.

Furedi, Frank. 'The "Second Generation" of Holocaust Survivors'. *Spiked*. www.spiked-online.com/articles/00000000545B.htm.

Geis, Jael. 2000. *Übrig Sein–leben 'danach'. Juden deutscher Herkunft in der britischen und amerikanischen Zone Deutschlands 1945–1949* [*Left Over–Living After the Shoah–Jews of German Descent in the British and American Zones in Germany 1945–1949*]. Berlin, Philo-Verlagsgesellschaft.

Hall, Guy. 2001. 'Mixed-Faith Couples'. *Bet Debora Journal 2: The Jewish Family – Myth and Reality*: 31–2.

Herweg, Rachel. 2000. 'Do Women Pray Differently?' *Bet Debora Journal 1*: 28–9.

Jacoby, Jessica. 2001. 'Children of Jewish Fathers'. *Bet Debora Journal 2. The Jewish Family – Myth and Reality*: 33–4.

Jacoby, Jessica, Claudia Schoppmann and Wendy Zena-Henry, eds. 1994. *Nach der Shoa geboren. Jüdische Frauen in Deutschland* [*Born after the Shoah. Jewish Women in Germany*]. Berlin, Elefanten-Press.

Kaplan, Marion A. 1979. *The Jewish Feminist Movement in Germany: The Campaigns of the Jüdischer Frauenbund 1904–1938*. Westport, CT, Greenwood Press.

Klapheck, Elisa. 2000. 'Do We Need Liturgy?' *Bet Debora Journal 1*: 30–1.

Klapheck, Elisa, ed. 2004. *Fräulein Rabbiner Jonas. The Story of the First Woman Rabbi*. San Francisco, Jossey Bass. (English translation of Klapheck, Elisa, ed. 1999. *Fräulein Rabbiner Jonas. Kann die Frau das rabbinische Amt bekleiden?* Teetz, Hentrich & Hentrich).

Konz, Britta. 2001. 'Bertha Pappenheim: A New Look at the Concept of the Family.' *Bet Debora Journal 2. The Jewish Family – Myth and Reality*: 20–1.

Lamm, Hans, ed. 1981. *Jeanette Wolff: 'Mit Bibel und Bebel. Ein Gedenkbuch'* [*With the Bible and Bebel. A Memorial Book*]. 2nd, corrected ed. Bonn-Bad Godesberg, Verlag Neue Gesellschaft.

Lange, Gunter. 1988. *Jeanette Wolff. 1888 bis 1976. Eine Biographie* [*Jeanette Wolff. 1888 to 1976. A Biography*]. Bonn, Verlag Neue Gesellschaft.

Levinson, Pnina Navè. 1989. *Was wurde aus Saras Töchtern? Frauen im Judentum* [*What Became of Sarah's Daughters? Women in Judaism*]. Gütersloh, Gütersloher Verlagshaus Mohn.

Levinson, Pnina Navè. 1992. *Eva und ihre Schwestern. Perspektiven einer jüdisch-feministischen Theologie* [*Eve and her Sisters. Perspectives of a Jewish Feminist Theology*]. Gütersloh, Gütersloher Verlagshaus Mohn.

Levinson, Pnina Navè. 1993. *Esther erhebt ihre Stimme. Jüdische Frauen beten* [*Esther Speaks Out. Jewish Women Pray*]. Gütersloh, Gütersloher Verlagshaus Mohn.

Rhein, Valérie. 2000. 'Exotic from Switzerland'. *Bet Debora Journal* 1: 42.

Rheinz, Hanna. 2001. 'A Cassandra Call'. *Bet Debora Journal* 2. *The Jewish Family – Myth and Reality*: 57–8.

Ronen, Shoshana. 2000. 'We Didn't Aspire to the Rabbinate'. *Bet Debora Journal* 1: 16.

Rothschild, Sylvia. 2000. 'Creating New Rituals'. *Bet Debora Journal* 1: 24–5.

Sarah, Elizabeth Tikvah. 2000. 'Keva and Kavvanah'. *Bet Debora Journal* 1: 21–2.

Sarah, Elizabeth Tikvah. 2001a. 'Gay-Lesbian Kiddushin'. *Bet Debora Journal* 2. *The Jewish Family – Myth and Reality*: 30–1.

Sarah, Elizabeth Tikvah. 2001b. 'Long Live Jewish Families!' *Bet Debora Journal* 2. *The Jewish Family – Myth and Reality*: 6–8.

Schwermer, Dagmar. 2001. 'No Trace of a Salon'. *Bet Debora Journal* 2. *The Jewish Family – Myth and Reality*: 22–3.

Seidel, Esther. 2000. 'German-Jewish Legacy?' *Bet Debora Journal* 1: 19.

Shalvi, Alice. 2001a. 'Agunah–the Abandoned'. *Bet Debora Journal* 2. *The Jewish Family – Myth and Reality*: 55–6.

Shalvi, Alice. 2001b. 'The Maternal Imperative'. *Bet Debora Journal* 2. *The Jewish Family – Myth and Reality*: 49–50.

Thau, Daniela. 2000. 'Rabbi on the Margin'. *Bet Debora Journal* 1: 9–10.

Weiss, Iris. 2000. 'A Young Lay Preacher'. *Bet Debora Journal* 1: 15.

Wyler, Bea. 2000. 'Reconstruction Work'. *Bet Debora Journal* 1: 13.

Chapter 8

A JEWISH CULTURAL RENASCENCE IN GERMANY?

Y. Michal Bodemann

No social constituency in Germany today is as much subject to distortive representations as the Jews, representations fed in part by old-fashioned anti-Semitism, but to a far greater degree by the Jews' ideological labour within the German national narrative and their ascribed role as labourers of memory within that narrative. The distortive imaginations of the Jew undoubtedly have put their mark on contemporary Jewry in Germany and have shaped much that is being written on this topic; there are, however, also internal developments, relatively independent of the Jews' role for the German state, that have shaped its overall character. It is this second aspect that I will address in the following pages without, however, losing sight of the first.

Within a given community, demographic fluctuations alone might sometimes reveal changes in its character and its sociocultural, economic, and political structure. This certainly seems to be the case in relation to Jewry in post-war Germany. For nearly forty years, following the great fluctuations of the post-war period due to the Jewish Displaced Persons, the Jewish population in West Germany had been stagnating at around twenty-five to thirty thousand members, and of these, little more than five to six thousand had settled in West Berlin. Indeed, this stagnation did not consist in the figures alone; the entire structure of the community, its religious orientations, and the role of Jews in German society itself seemed rigidly cemented, and the community controlled through authoritarian leadership and bureaucratic patronage.

Critical voices of particular individuals and of entire groups such as the Jüdische Gruppen in several German cities, mostly inspired by the student movement, partly in reaction to it, were savagely attacked or, at best, ignored. In the German Democratic Republic, despite the minute Jewish population of about four hundred in the late 1980s, the situation developed on quite similar, even more accentuated tracks, with no possibilities for experience of cultural diversity. In both East and West, this stagnation slowly began to break up in the 1980s, but only after German unification was that cast really broken. Since 1989, total community membership in Germany has more than tripled, from less than thirty thousand to over one hundred thousand, and in Berlin from under six thousand to more than eleven thousand today. To these figures, we should add an estimated ten thousand Jews or individuals of partly Jewish origin not registered with the Berlin community; for all of Germany, we would, accordingly, arrive at a figure of well over a hundred thousand Jews which, after all, is already one-fifth of the figure of 1933 – totally unimaginable only a few years ago.

In East and West Germany, then, the Jewish Community stagnated demographically for almost forty years, and it also stagnated in its entire structure. Its institutions were immobilised and turned into an empty shell of mere political representation, and the Jews let themselves be instrumentalised for political goals, in East Germany to the point of abject self-renunciation. Mario Offenberg, secretary of the small orthodox Congregation Adass Jisroel in Berlin, has characterised this leadership poignantly as 'state and memorial-site Jewry'. The explanation for this development is quite straightforward. When Robert Weltsch, the German Zionist leader, returned to Berlin in 1946 for a visit, he wrote back to Palestine: 'It smells of corpses here, of gas chambers and torture chambers. The remnant of Jewish settlements in Germany must be liquidated as quickly as possible. Germany is no soil for Jews.' The communities at the time saw themselves largely as temporary structures, *Liquidationsgemeinden*, communities set up for the sole purpose of temporarily harbouring and caring for individuals who were to leave Germany shortly thereafter, preferably for Palestine.

As a consequence, and even when that 'liquidation' did not come to pass, the Jews in Germany were bound up inside their communities in a corset of bureaucratic patronage, having to contend with, or accepting, an ageing and monolithic leadership and a diminishing number of people in the younger generation. The community questioned and rejected its own legitimacy, and many thought of themselves as living with 'packed suit-cases'; these suitcases were often very literally packed, even where, after some time, they were put behind a staircase and were collecting dust. Into the 1980s, Jewish authors published books such as *This Is not My Country* (Fleischmann 1980), *In the Home of the Henchman* (Heenen-Wolff 1992), *Stranger in One's Own Land* (Broder and Lang 1979), and a magazine of these imaginary exiles called itself *Babylon*. These Jews imagined themselves, and sometimes, in fact, might have been, exiles in the classical sense: they were sojourners, the type of strangers whom at the turn of the century,

Berlin sociologist par excellence Georg Simmel, would have termed as those who come today and leave again tomorrow, expressed here in the very metaphor of the packed suitcase.

Yet ironically, during the long and lonely journey of these Jews through post-war Germany, from the founding of the two German states and the Cold War, rearmament and the economic miracle, from the student movement and *Ostpolitik* to the memory wars of the late 1970s and 1980s and to unification, a second development remained largely unnoticed: soon, the Jews in Germany, and the Jewish Displaced Persons in particular, had begun to form an armoured cocoon shielding themselves against an alien and hostile world, the world of their murderers and tormentors, a world that they rejected and that, initially at least, rejected them. Within that cocoon, Jews married and raised children, established nursing homes and schools and a large web of personal, social, and economic relations, and more complex communal structures. It is my contention that this armoured cocoon was the precondition for a renascence of communal Jewish life in Germany; when the cocoon began to burst in the mid-1980s, it had created the preconditions for a new vitality of Jewish life beyond the stagnation of the previous forty years.

There have therefore been marked changes in the past fifteen years. Although we cannot know today whether the wheel could not be reversed tomorrow, and some of my own lingering doubt notwithstanding, I would venture the prediction that today, German Jewry is the most dynamic Jewish Diaspora in Europe and worldwide. Apart from the dramatic growth of the communities, the change is apparent, for example, in the fact that the Berlin Community, whose past two leaders were well over seventy years of age, is now being chaired by a man twenty years younger, and that half of the twenty-one members of the Repräsentanz, the community council, are under fifty years of age, and only three over sixty. This youthfulness, of course, and a jump over an entire generation and in particular the sparse or decimated birth cohorts between about 1930 and 1946, is directly due to the *Shoah*.

This abrupt generational change has also produced entirely new interpretations of one's own life and identity that, only a few years ago, would have been sharply rejected by the previous gerontocracy. These include statements such as the following, made by a university student and candidate at the 1997 council elections:

> as a Jewish community we [are at] a point where we have to look straight forward into the future, and where we can no longer look into the past. With the enormous Jewish immigration ... great opportunities have opened up for the Jewish community of Berlin ... Judaism cannot be lived in humility, but [should be lived] in joy – not in order to defend our Jewish identity, but in order to celebrate it. (Jüdische Gemeinde zu Berlin 1997)

Only a small number of Jews in Berlin would go that far today, and turn away so radically from their past; and yet, the rupture between Jews and Germans, based upon that past, is ever more clearly being suspended, as in this statement of a younger candidate:

> The community must open itself. The fact that Berlin has changed fundamentally cannot pass us by without leaving a trace. The community cannot place itself at the margins. It must participate fully in the life of this city. It is part of this society and also has to be part of it. (Jüdische Gemeinde zu Berlin 1997)

We must remember here that only about fifteen years ago, members of even this community council were vigorously opposed to the immigration of Jews from the former Soviet Union to Germany. Today, on the other hand, this affirmation of Jewish life in Germany goes so far as in the case of this elderly candidate, who reminded her readers of her own fate as a former emigré, who had to live 'so many years abroad ... in a foreign country', and who is therefore concerned about a 'warm acceptance of the new community members'. In earlier years, it was an outright embarrassment to many Jews having to live in the land of the perpetrators; today, however, Norma Drimmer, until recently member of the council executive, wishes that the 'Jewish community may become a lively centre which could take on a key function for the Jewish communities of Europe'. Within these interpretations and in contrast to the priorities of previous years, the *Shoah* and Israel have lost some of their significance, while still being critically important.

This change has become noticeable even in the way the community officially presents itself. In the post-war period, the Berlin Jewish Community still had its own monthly paper, *Der Weg*, which went out of existence in the early 1950s, with the beginning of the years of stagnation – although it then still appeared *pro forma* for some time as a page in the *Allgemeine Wochenzeitung der Juden in Deutschland*, published in Düsseldorf. Only in 1984 was a small monthly bulletin published once again: the *Kulturspiegel*. Five years later, this was turned into the *Berlin-Umschau*, and at the beginning of 1998, a glossy and colourful new magazine appeared: *jüdisches berlin*. Within fifteen years, then, the community first looked at itself in a 'mirror', relating back unto itself; as the *Umschau*, it began 'looking around', more clearly taking note of its environment, and now with the new name it sees itself, in the affirmative, as a part of Berlin, and presents itself as such to its environment.

In one of *jüdisches berlin*'s first issues, we find on the cover a suitcase from Russia on a street in Berlin – a direct reversal of the metaphor of the packed suitcase of the earlier years: it is an arriving Jewish suitcase, not one that is about to leave the country. A few issues later, the cover features a shofar blown by a young man, far above Berlin – an image inconceivable only a few years earlier. Originally, the *Kulturspiegel*'s masthead was dominated by a large sketch of the community centre, as an emblem of the

Figure 8.1   Jüdische Gemeinde zu Berlin Kulturspiegel Nr. 19, October 1987

Credit: Der Vorstand der Jüdischen Gemeinde zu Berlin

administration and of the Jewish social life hidden inside; later, in the *Berlin-Umschau* this emblem was shrunk substantially, and now in the new *jüdisches berlin* it has moved entirely into the background, as a tiny icon. Clearly, a community that sees itself firmly as a part of Berlin stands in contradiction to a fortress, as it saw itself in earlier years.

In this last decade, not only the representation of the community towards the public, but especially its inner life, has been intensified in dimensions that were entirely unimaginable before. For example, a look at the calendar of events of autumn 1997 compared to just ten years earlier indicates that community events had quadrupled, concurrent with a doubling of the membership. Theatre, art, and computer groups have shot up, new egalitarian forms of the religious service, folklore and tradition groups have emerged, and notably, thanks to the Russian immigrants, a club of veterans of the Great Patriotic War has been set up. This development, often described as a 'renaissance' is due especially to three elements.

The most obvious one, first, is indubitably demographic, the immigration of East European Jews to Berlin and to the rest of the Republic. Even if it is too early to tell today whether this is a long-term development or merely a short reflorescence that will wither without its necessary nutrients, this intensification of Jewish life is due unquestionably to a very high degree to this new immigration of largely highly trained, highly educated and motivated immigrants. The new vitality due to this immigration, of course, has not only revitalised the Jewish Community alone, but is also an immense contribution to the cultural and economic life of Berlin and Germany as a whole. Indeed, the German authorities were unwise not to have encouraged the emigration of Russian Jews to a much greater degree and much earlier; the immense benefits of this immigration and especially its potential in the younger generation, with its highly trained and motivated individuals are palpable in Germany today as is the case, albeit in entirely different dimensions, in Israel and even North America. Here was, and still is, an opportunity which the German authorities have missed.

Another reason for this renascence that should not be overlooked is the continuous public financial and, within specific limits, political support given to the Jewish Community. Of its twenty-four million Euro budget, the community receives from the City Senate and from other public sources twenty-two million. These funds are earmarked for schools and kindergartens, money that, however, would also be made available to non-Jewish institutions; approximately one and a half million Euros are raised through the Community's own membership taxes. There can be no doubt, furthermore, that the Jewish Community, from questions of immigration and building permits to cultural programming such as street festivals, has been enjoying the special sympathy of the Berlin Senate; even recent conflicts such as that concerning curatorial and financial autonomy for the Jewish Museum cannot hide that fact. The well over a hundred thousand

Figure 8.2   Berlin-Umschau: Nachrichten aus der Jüdischen Gemeinde Nr. 8, November 1997

Credit: Der Vorstand der Jüdischen Gemeinde zu Berlin

Muslims in Berlin have not received any comparable concessions. This political support is closely connected to the fact that in Germany Judeophile milieus have developed together with a wide-ranging interest in Jewish culture and Judaism. How else can we explain the fact that in 1992, an exhibition on this small ethno-religious minority – *Jüdische Lebenswelten* – drew over 300,000 visitors?

A third and very important reason for this new dynamism is the structural changes within the community – on the one hand, what historian Michael Brenner has termed the emergence of a secular, Jewishly educated stratum and on the other hand, within this stratum, the new role of women. Women are pushing for reforms in the area of ritual practice, they have been developing, jointly with like-minded men, egalitarian forms of religious service, and have become involved ever more visibly in the various organisational spheres of the community. Here as well, today's Jewish community is markedly different from its years of stagnation when only older males determined its politics and public life. Next to the Russian immigration, nothing will affect the Jewish Community as much, and enrich it as much, as this advancement of women and of the new intellectual stratum in its public terrain.

What could the contours be of this astonishing re-emergence of Berlin Jewry and of the German Jewish Community at large – contours that as little as a dozen years ago were still unimaginable? Internally, the monolithic, asphyxiating control of community affairs, largely within a culturally conservative, if not religiously Orthodox environment, has disappeared. The diverse interests and orientations, the new plurality, can no longer be joined under one roof in the same way as in the past. The authoritarian role of former Jewish leaders such as Werner Nachmann, Heinz Galinski, or even the late Ignatz Bubis has long become anachronistic. There is a movement away from authoritarian structures towards a spectrum of leadership that is located somewhere between oligarchical and democratic rule. No doubt, in Berlin, Andreas Nachama was until recently the principal elected representative of the community. Yet who could deny that inside and outside the community today, there are also other authoritative Jewish voices? The voices, in Berlin for example, of Mario Offenberg of Adass Jisroel, György Konrad of the Akademie der Künste, Julius Schoeps of the Moses Mendelssohn Zentrum in Potsdam, Gary Smith of the American Academy, Michael Blumenthal of the Jewish Museum, and now even the voice of the American Jewish Committee in Berlin are being listened to in Jewish affairs. As a natural consequence of this new Jewish multipolarity in Germany, internal conflicts will increase – but what would a vibrant Jewish community be without internal conflicts?

Externally, in relation to the Berlin public, the political strength of the community, paradoxically, has been weakened on account of its current resurgence, and for two reasons. For one, by virtue of the plural differentiations

Figure 8.3   Jüdisches Berlin Nr. 1, February 1998

Credit: Margit Schmidt; layout, Kurt Blank-Markard; logo, Adam Blank-Markard

and the newly competing political poles in the Jewish community, the monolithic core has disappeared: with this new institutional diversity, the various Jewish representatives simply do not always have identical interests and perspectives, and for this reason as well, Jewish interests are not as effectively advocated as in the previous decades. The controversy concerning the Jewish Museum, where the community could not obtain satisfaction in its very own affairs, is an example for this loss of power. In the time of Heinz Galinski, the community's former long-term leader, these machinations would hardly have been imaginable. The second reason has to do with the increasing distance from the *Shoah*. The cynical remark from within the Berlin Senate that Andreas Nachama's problem is that he does not have a tattoo on his arm is quite to the point: the current generation of German politicians is no longer impressed by references to the German past. This disappearance of a monolithic Jewish politics, however, the diffusion of power, surely does not mean that in the future, the relations of German politicians to the Jewish Community will become easier. Since from now on, there is no longer just one representative for the Jewish Community with whom it is possible to negotiate, it will also be more difficult to reach political agreements.

What consequences does Berlin as the new capital have for the Jewish community? It is remarkable, first of all, that the Russian–Jewish influx to Berlin coincides with the decision to move the capital from Bonn to Berlin. A Western capital without ethnic diversity, as has been the case with Bonn, was still conceivable, but a capital that also wants to be a European metropolis and be cosmopolitan, will not be able to function without ethnocultural division of labour. This means, for countries in the West, that a Jewish presence here is a *sine qua non*.

Up until 1989, the Jewish political centres were Düsseldorf, Frankfurt, and initially Munich as well; for the small Jewish community in East Germany, it was of course Berlin; with unification, the particular identity of the East Berlin community was extinguished. The Jewish leadership in the times of the Bonn Republic came, as a rule, from West Germany; Galinski remained the fly in the ointment from Berlin. All of this has now changed. Jewish institutions, most notably the offices of the Zentralrat der Juden in Deutschland (Central Council of Jews in Germany), have returned to the historic Jewish sites in the centre of Berlin and have occupied the *lieux de mémoire* which had been the locales of the small East Berlin community. With that return, however, a historically unprecedented centralisation has set in that will profoundly transform Jewish life in Germany at large.

It has often been argued that the memory of the *Shoah* in Germany is slowly coming to an end and that, in particular, the concrete that has been poured for the construction of the Memorial for the Murdered Jews of Europe will bury this memory forever. Yet Jewish history is irrevocably inscribed in German society and into the memorial landscape of this city.

This memory, with or without artificial memorials, will be perpetuated and even strengthened as long as Berlin is capital, and as long as German national identity retains any social relevance.

What about the distortions and myths concerning the Jewish Community on the part of German society? With today's renascence of German Jewry and its emergence out of its cocoon, Jewish life in Germany might at some point again be taken as a matter of course, by both Jews and Germans. Once this point has been reached, the distortive imaginations of the Jew may be corrected in favour of real-existing German Jewry; and only then will the dominant Jewish self-perception, that of being a stranger in one's own land, finally have become a thing of the past.

Postscript, July 2005

Since I presented this essay at the *Galut 2000* conference in 1998, there have of course been a number of new developments in Jewish affairs in Germany. Paul Spiegel is the established successor to Ignatz Bubis and has developed his own style as national community leader, Andreas Nachama as leader of the Berlin *Gemeinde* has been replaced – an anomaly here – first by the older Alexander Brenner, and then by Albert Meyer from an old Berlin Jewish family, the Jewish Museum in Berlin has opened, the Liberal Rabbinical College in Potsdam has been established, the Memorial for the Murdered Jews of Europe has been built, the *Jüdische Allgemeine* has changed its format and broadened its scope, and the immigration from Russia continues, albeit at a slower pace.

Yet my principal observations from the time of the conference have only been confirmed: Jewry in Germany has moved further away from being the monolithic and closed community with its authoritarian leadership that it had been from the post-war period all the way through the 1980s; an ever wider range of small alternative synagogues and minyanim have formed, together with a range of often smaller circles of artists, musicians, and others in the cultural Jewish sphere. Indeed, today we can see ever more clearly what I would call the *proliferation of the Jewish fringe*, and this fringe, this periphery, is, among other things, a meeting-ground of Jews with non-Jewish Germans from what I had previously described (Bodemann 1996a; Bodemann 1996b; Bodemann 2002) as the 'Judaising milieus'.

Other recent observers have detected that development of hybrid milieus as well – a development which is not confined to Germany, but is apparent all over Europe and typically includes both Jews and non-Jews, albeit in different proportions and varying constellations. It is a fluctuating and fragile public space which Diana Pinto describes as 'the Jewish Space' (Chapter 9). It is, in turn, not entirely dissimilar to what, more ambiguously, Ruth Ellen Gruber calls 'virtual Jewishness' (Gruber 2002). More for Germany, Michael Brenner has aptly described these margins as 'non-Jewish Jewish culture' (Brenner 2002: 58). These hybrid milieus include both Jews and non-Jews – witness such institutions as the new Jewish Museum in Berlin and other Jewish museums elsewhere, such as the one in Frankfurt which are never staffed by either Jews or non-Jews alone. Indeed, at these Jewish fringes – and at these fringes alone – the cultural expressions and the thinking of Jews and non-Jews about Jewish matter are sometimes 'virtually' identical; witness the irony that the *Aufbau*, originally the paper of Jewish emigrés published in New York, was subsequently published by non-Jewish Germans in Berlin, with Jewish and non-Jewish writers; not to speak of the non-Jewish klezmer groups that are perceived in concerts abroad as more authentic than the American klezmer bands. In this respect as least, the 'rift' or the 'negative symbiosis' in the Jewish–German relation is a thing of the past. But to which degree and in which ways do distortive imaginations of Jews still play a role? It is both a disconcerting and a positive development at the same time.

Bibliography

Babylon. Beiträge zur jüdischen Gegenwart. [*Babylon. Contributions to the Jewish present*]. Frankfurt am Main.

Bodemann, Y. Michal. 1996a. *Gedächtnistheater. Die jüdische Gemeinschaft und ihre deutsche Erfindung.* [*Memory theatre. The Jewish community and its invention by Germans*]. Hamburg, Rotbuch Verlag.

Bodemann, Y. Michal. 1996b. *Jews, Germans, Memory. Reconstructions of Jewish Life in Germany.* Ann Arbor, University of Michigan Press.

Bodemann, Y. Michal. 2002. *In den Wogen der Erinnerung. Jüdisches Leben in Deutschland.* [*In the waves of memory. Jewish life in Germany*]. Munich, DTV.

Brenner, Michael. 2002. 'The Transformation of the German-Jewish Community'. In *Unlikely History. The Changing German-Jewish Symbiosis*, eds L. Morris and J. Zipes. New York, Palgrave.

Broder, Henryk M. and Michel R. Lang. 1979. *Fremd im eigenen Land. Juden in der Bundesrepublik* [*Foreign in one's own land. Jews in the Federal Republic*]. Frankfurt am Main, Fischer Taschenbuchverlag.

Fleischmann, Lea. 1980. *Dies ist nicht mein Land. Eine Jüdin verläßt die Bundesrepublik* [*This is not my country. A Jewish woman leaves the Federal Republic*]. Hamburg, Hoffmann und Campe.

Gruber, Ruth Ellen. 2002. *Virtually Jewish. Reinventing Jewish Culture in Europe.* Berkeley, University of California Press.

Heenen-Wolff, Susann. 1992. *Im Haus des Henkers. Gespräche in Deutschland* [*In the House of the Henchman. Conversations in Germany*]. Frankfurt am Main, Dvorah-Verlag.

Jüdische Gemeinde zu Berlin. 1997. *Wahlbroschüre* [*Electoral Bulletin*].

PART III:
THE JEWISH SPACE IN EUROPE

Chapter 9

THE JEWISH SPACE IN EUROPE

Diana Pinto

Sixty years after post-war Europe relegated the *Shoah* to the realm of private Jewish suffering, or buried it publicly in a sea of anti-fascist rhetoric, Jewish themes, references, and life now occupy centre stage in ways that seemed unimaginable even twenty years ago. Across Europe, it has become impossible to open a newspaper without reading about some aspect either of the Jewish past or increasingly of the Jewish present. This interest goes well beyond the recent controversies over dormant Swiss bank accounts, Nazi gold, unpaid insurance claims, art spoliations, slave labour, or the last trials of Nazi collaborators. It transcends by far the polemics about Jewish monuments and memorials, especially about Berlin's *Denkmal für die ermordeten Juden Europas* (Memorial for the Murdered Jews of Europe).

Interest in Jewish themes is increasingly focused on each country's Jewish life, be it bimillennial as in Italy or 'merely' two centuries old as in Sweden. Jewish museums are mushrooming across Europe. Jewish Studies is becoming a rapidly expanding university field, while Jewish history and culture are taught increasingly even in secondary schools. Publishing houses are churning out books on Jewish themes ranging from Jewish humour to philosophy and mysticism, and above all Jewish 'culture', a catch-all word that can encompass cooking as well as religious tradition. Jews are increasingly the subject of literary, poetic, cinemato-graphic, and even television bestsellers written by non-Jews. All cities that think of themselves as living cosmopolitan centres (and who would refute such a claim in our day and age?) now have Jewish itineraries on their maps, while even the smallest towns bring out their long forgotten or newly discovered signs of past Jewish life, whether in Bath, Rouen, Oviedo, or Pitigliano, or now in the East, Tarnow, Kaunas, and Saratov. Jewish music has become marketable, and not only to Jews. Not just the old klezmer music of the *shtetls* which has now become a German staple, but the music of the Spanish Sephardim as well as Jewish medieval music and the until recently unknown productions of concentration camp victims, such as Viktor Ullmann's *Der Kaiser von Atlantis*. The Jewish reference even in universal works of art is increasingly spelled out, examined and pursued, when in the past it had merely been interpreted as a vague 'background'.

In brief, 'Jews' have become interesting, fashionable, indeed popular. Jewish themes are even becoming a rewarding object to invest in professionally, not just for Jews but for non-Jews as well. Of course this does not spell the end of anti-Semitism even in our most opulent societies, not to mention the resurgence of anti-Semitism in societies deep in an identity turmoil such as Russia. But the nature of this anti-Semitism has been transformed: it is no longer culturally as acceptable as it was in the past. Furthermore, Jewish life, opinions and feelings are now out in the open. Jewish themes are neither secret nor taboo. The Jewish Space is a result of this transformation. Everywhere in Europe there are now non-Jews who perceive the Jewish past and present, Jewish culture and traditions as inherently positive parts of their own cultural life, and, most importantly, relevant for their own collective futures.

It would be an error to assume that this centrality of Jewish themes means that they are finally 'back' in Europe after the cataclysm of the *Shoah*. The Jewish Space constitutes a new phenomenon which marks a sea change in the map of Europe's own consciousness and identity. One must not forget just how marginal even the most prominent Jews (who often had to convert to play a central role) and Jewish life were in pre-*Shoah* Europe. Jewishness belonged at most to one's own family or extended family circle, and one's institutional religious life. It was, as defined in the French Jacobin tradition, a 'private' matter whose content was not relevant in the public sphere. Such a stance was widespread throughout the Continent because the different peoples of Europe did not consider Judaism as a living presence that needed to be incorporated into their respective cultures.

If we have growing Jewish spaces throughout Europe today, it is because we have a new and growing pluralist democratic context. Judaism no longer belongs just to the sphere of private life, nor does it owe, as in the past, its external legitimacy to the State. It is slowly but surely conquering its own space inside civil society as the expression of a collectivity, but also as a lifestyle produced by democratic individualism.

One can probably trace the 'birth' of the Jewish Space in Europe to the early 1980s, beginning with the series of fiftieth anniversary memorial events concerning the Nazis' seizing power, and the *Shoah*, a series of events which reached its peak in 1995, commemorating the liberation of Auschwitz and the end of the Second World War. *Shoah* exhibits throughout Europe, museums and memorials, as well as the cortège of autobiographies of the survivors, diaries of the victims, and general histories of the period may have been the starting-point of the Jewish Space, but it rapidly expanded to cover not just Jewish death but, more importantly, Jewish life. In a context of Jewish 'upmanship', every country in Europe that understood the importance of Jews as a sign of its own historical pluralist wealth actively pursued and presented the traces of its Jewish past dating as far back as possible. Cynics will say that such a search was often prodded, especially in Eastern Europe in the wake of the collapse of the Communist system, by the desire of countries to ingratiate themselves to hegemonic America and what was perceived as its all-powerful 'Jewish lobby'. Reality, fortunately, is much richer and more rewarding to contemplate. What is developing exponentially before our very eyes, both in Eastern and Western Europe, is the combination of a resurgent Jewish life, nations coming to terms with the past, enlightened global culture and simple trendy fashion. But the latter, rather than being the essence of the Jewish Space, is merely an epiphenomenon – even in Germany, where the 'trendiness' of the Jewish fashion is particularly visible.

In the beginning the Jewish Space was strongest in those countries which once possessed a powerful Jewish presence and which came to measure only now the power of its absence. Spain, Poland, and Germany are the prime contenders for this distinction, for they incarnated three very different and numerically important Jewish civilisations, which all came to a tragic end. Of the three, Germany has the greatest Jewish Space of all, for two reasons: the historical proximity of the brilliant Jewish past and its destruction, and the strength of civil society with its wealth, cultural means and increasing openness to Jewish themes. Spain and Portugal are making major strides in this direction, even though the period in question is further removed in time. One can only speak of symbolic Jewish 'survivors' (the Marranos of Belmonte in northern Portugal, or 'recycled' Jews who returned to Spain from the post-1492 Diaspora in north Africa or the Ottoman Empire, and who had lost living ties to modern Spain) and symbolic cultural traces (such as synagogues turned into churches, and Jewish quarters without Jews). Poland's Jewish Space is growing, but for it to truly blossom the country needs to come to terms with its own tragic national past and reinforce its own civil society. An important step in this direction occurred in 2001–2002 during the national debates that surrounded the publication of Jan Gross's book *Neighbors* (2001) about the wartime murders of the Jews of Jedwabne by their own village neighbours.

The Jewish Space in all three countries in reality is a dialectical concept. By remembering the Jewish past that was lost, such countries pay homage to a purported golden epoch of tolerant pluralism exemplified by the presence of Jews in their midst. But the tragic end of the Jewish presence belied the putative virtues of that epoch. It is today's pluralism and tolerance that are being celebrated with the Jewish Space. This is what makes the concept so important for the future – not the past – of our pluralist democracies. Judaism is becoming an important element of Europe's own contemporary national cultural debates over democratic consolidation and national identity.

On this count, the Jewish Space is now also growing in countries with sizeable living Jewish communities and with more 'moderate' horrors vis-à-vis the Jews in their past, either because Jewish expulsion took place earlier than in Spain (in the cases of Britain or France), or because the countries were not on the wrong side in the Second World War. The best example is France. The rethinking of its Vichy years in a Jewish light began in the early 1970s and came to a climax when Jacques Chirac, newly elected as President, acknowledged the responsibility of 'France' and its administration (even though the country was occupied) in the deportation of Jews. The Space was further strengthened by the Papon trial in which a senior civil servant with a prestigious post-war career was held accountable for his role in the deportation of the Jews of Bordeaux. This historical reassessment of the past with the Jewish factor at the centre rather than at the periphery is taking place throughout Europe, whether the countries in question were victorious, neutral or even vanquished during the Second World War. One can cite Sweden, the Netherlands and Italy in particular.

The Jewish Space may have begun as a place in which to commemorate the Jewish 'absence', but it is increasingly evolving into a space in which to celebrate a Jewish presence. It is for this reason that it takes on its future importance for Jewish life inside Europe. For if such a space is inhabited only by non-Jews, mourning 'their' Jews, it is destined to become little more than an open-air pedagogical museum, homage to a dead past with no future – the equivalent of so many menorahs on a shelf. If such a space were to be populated only by Jews, that is, restricted to the needs of the Jewish communities, it could become only an anaemic and sterile mini-Israel, without its collective numerical strength, cultural vitality, and sovereignty. The Jewish Space in America, thanks to the number of Jews living there, is a cultural and religious galaxy essentially populated by Jews who coexist with America's 'others' in a societal entente which has multicultural connotations. The Jewish Space in Europe instead stands out precisely as a space in which Jewish themes do not interact with the outside world in a sociological jockeying for cultural power as in America (where the Jews are very much 'on top'), nor in a hegemonical situation as in Israel, but in a context of Jewish and non-Jewish tension, interpenetration, dialogue, conflict, and even symbiosis.

These differences are important. They play a major role in the current debate over the possible revival or apparent end of Jewish life across Europe. Bernard Wasserstein in his *Vanishing Diaspora* (1996) claims that Jewish life in Europe is inevitably coming to an end for the simple reason that there will no longer be any Jews around to pursue it. For him, Jews in Europe were practically destroyed, at first physically at the hands of the Nazis, later culturally (and also to some degree physically) at the hands of the Communists; but now they are responsible for their own destruction through the sheer power of demography. Jewish couples (like their other European counterparts) are not even reproducing themselves numerically. Worst of all, because of intermarriage, many of the children born with one Jewish parent will not even be halachically Jewish, and many of the few who are raised as Jews are succumbing to indifference to an active Jewish identity. For pessimists such as Wasserstein, all references to the renewed Jewish cultural presence in Europe thus constitute a giant screen and cultural bubble full of colourful but insignificant anecdotes, which mask the effective 'end' of Jewish life in Europe. In this view we are inexorably heading towards a culture of Jewish *Ersatz*, and to pursue my analogy, to a Jewish museum space in Europe.

I could not disagree more. The issue is not to count the number of Jews around and to wring one's hands at their relative decline. Rather, it is to understand the new role that active and voluntary Jews are playing and should be playing inside Europe at its very heart (rather than on its fringes as in the past). In this context the Jewish Space is destined to hold a central function not only for non-Jewish 'consumers' of Jewish themes but, perhaps above all, for Europe's own Jews (however they choose to define themselves) as they take on a stronger identity and more self-confident roles. I would even contend that the Jewish Space is precisely what is most specific about any future Jewish life in Europe compared to Jewish life elsewhere.

Sceptics will laugh – or wince – at the innumerable klezmer bands in Germany and Sweden without any Jewish musicians who play in front of '*judenrein*' audiences, because the concerts are often held in such improbable places as Bari in Italy, or Coutances, a small town in Normandy, or Göteborg in Sweden (where, incidentally, there *are* Jews). I see nothing wrong with this trend: a piece of Jewish folklore music lives on and moves people, thus bringing back to life a spark of the world of Yiddishkeit. We cannot blame others if klezmer music has attained such an emblematic centrality as 'the' Jewish quintessence in the non-Jewish world. For those Jews who launched the klezmer revival in the first place believed it was so. If we disagree with this reading of Jewish culture, then it is up to us to show the world that there is much more to Judaism and Jewish music than klezmer. We are the keepers of our own cultural treasures, and the time has come to reveal them.

Future Jewish creativity must, however, have a living Jewish content that can be produced only by living Jews. One does not need numerical 'masses' to produce such Jewish activists and creators. Moreover, in their enrichment of the Jewish world, they can be inspired by non-Jews reproducing or reinterpreting in more universal terms that very Jewish past. Historically, Judaism thrived by exposing its inner core to outside influences. Many of the new adepts of ultra-Orthodoxy think that Judaism is an unchangeable rock, but they are wrong, for 'Orthodoxy' itself is a response to the outside forces of emancipation. Judaism survived for millennia precisely because it grew organically by confronting the challenges of the outside world. Jewish culture was produced in dialogue with or in opposition to other more dominant cultures. The novelty is that now in our global culture, non-Jews, by taking on pieces of the Jewish past for themselves, may become *even for Jews* vehicles for future Jewish creativity.

It is in Europe more than in Israel or in America (where Jews are sufficiently strong numerically to produce their own internal culture) that the dialectics of dialogue between Jews and non-Jews will probably produce their strongest effects. For it is in Europe that Jews as a numerically insignificant but culturally central minority must encounter historically laden 'others' on their turf. In the Jewish Studies departments of Europe's universities non-Jews will dominate, both as students, but above all as professors and researchers. In interreligious dialogue, Jews will confront 'others' whose religious mindcast still shapes European culture and whose institutions played a role in the *Shoah*. In historical research, Jews in Europe will be dealing, unlike their Israeli or American equivalents, no longer with national pasts that concern them deeply but ultimately only symbolically or professionally, but with pasts that must be reinterpreted to fashion collective national futures in which they will be directly involved as citizens. In terms of democratic debates, Jewish citizens will play a major role in strengthening pluralist democracy from within rather than as critics from without. The same will be true in the arts or in literature, in music or in cinema, and in any other walk of life.

Jewish religious life is not and should not be defined by the Jewish Space. It has its own internal rigour and constraints. Jewish community life, while being focused on activities run by and for Jews, is increasingly dealing with the interface with the outside world, if only because of the issues linked to non-Jewish spouses and conversions. As for Jewish cultural life, it will blossom essentially in the open market of ideas and symbols. We should not (and cannot) recreate a Jewish culture of the ghetto. Furthermore, even the ultra-Orthodox Jews have become masters of the Jewish Space. They no longer work and live in their own self-imposed 'ghettoes'. They know how to obtain public monies and to market themselves in the public agora, as the 'original' and 'true' Judaism, which presupposes that they are aware of other varieties. Above all, they have understood how to win back Jews to Orthodoxy by looking for them in the non-Jewish wilderness.

Yet the idea of the Jewish Space continues to fill many Jews with fear. Most Jews do not know how to react to the sudden surge of interest in and passion for Jewish themes among non-Jews who are not specialists. Suspicions based on often justified millennial fears that non-Jews had hidden agendas or impure motives (the desire to convert or the search for more refined techniques of repression) behind their proclaimed desire to approach Jews or Jewish life still prevail and will take time to disappear.

We still tend to consider our Jewish life as our own individual or collectively intimate space into which non-Jewish 'others' should be invited selectively, if at all. We live in a latent fear that if Judaism were to become transparent, even blurred with the Jewish Space, we would lose control over it. Judaism would be denatured, misinterpreted, dominated or even symbolically 'owned' by others who roam in the Jewish Space like wolves in sheep's clothing. This is particularly true in Germany, where those who want to come closer to Judaism today are the grandchildren of the *Täter* seeking out the grandchildren of the *Opfer* for a combination of conscious and unconscious reasons, ranging from a need to alleviate a feeling of collective guilt, to a desire to adopt 'things Jewish' as an existential statement, or to change identities through conversion … when not simply having a Jewish 'moment' as a life-enriching experience.

The overwhelming non-Jewish presence in the Jewish Space in Germany complicates matters for the tiny German Jewish community that sometimes feels 'harassed' by so much self-absorbed interest and attention coming from Germans who often expect Jews to solve their historical identity problems for them. But one should not lose sight of the essential: the fact that we are in the middle of a major transition in the relations between Jews and non-Jews, and this transition is the same in Germany as throughout Europe. We Jews continue to think of ourselves as still emerging out of historical and post-*Shoah*-induced victimhood with its attendant condition of cultural weakness. We are instead perceived by non-Jews as possessing an inherent moral and cultural strength precisely because of our historical suffering. (This attributed strength, by the way, bears no relation to the old anti-Semitic beliefs in our putative hidden and malefic power.) In a perfect illustration of Hegel's Master/Slave relationship, we are still trying to liberate ourselves while we are perceived by non-Jews as moral masters strong enough already to enlighten and even 'liberate' others. Such differences and even misunderstandings will eventually be aired in the Jewish Space when more egalitarian and self-confident relations (on both sides) have been established between the Jewish and non-Jewish protagonists of a Jewish culture, increasingly perceived as an integral part of Europe's own patrimony. Hence the critical importance for Jews to accept open-ended dialogue with interested 'others' rather than advocating autarchic cultural pride per se. This of course in no way excludes the purely intra-Jewish deepening of religious identity and knowledge. When our medieval ancestors engaged in unwinnable *Disputaciones*, they spoke from highly controlled and censored Jewish 'niches' in a Christian Space. When our grandparents partook of pre-war European culture, they did so in a purportedly universal Humanistic Space that was just as deaf to any specifically Jewish 'voice'. The emerging Jewish Space in Europe today is the fruit of a new Western pluralistic modesty. We should welcome this fundamental democratic transformation. But it entails a correlate on our part. We Jews must now overcome our self-defensive barriers based on a latent fear of not being able to hold our own in the global market of identity and spirituality – not because Judaism is wanting – but because we ourselves are too ignorant of our own creative and open Jewish traditions. We must therefore demolish ignorance and false certitudes on Jewish matters as much among Jews as among non-Jews. This is why the Jewish Space can become one of our greatest challenges. Not because we as Jews will confront enemies 'out there', but because we will be confronting ourselves in all our complex religious, lay, particularistic, and universalist identities, while rubbing shoulders with equally complex and fragile 'others'.

As non-Jews appropriate the Jewish past and present for their own historical, cultural and creative needs (think of Benigni's *La vita è bella*), Jews in Europe will have a crucial role to play, not as censors but as sounding boards. For only they can respond 'as Jews' to an ongoing creative dialogue with a living European culture. Only they can correct misperceptions; but above all, only with their presence can there be newly erected bridges between worlds that in reality often ignored each other before the *Shoah*, when it was almost exclusively Jews who performed the 'crossing over'. Most importantly, in an age of global references and universal ideals, I am convinced that Europe's more 'borderline' Jews, the ones that are going to disappear, according to the pessimists, will also plunge with pride into their often semi-forgotten Jewish traditions and roots precisely because the non-Jewish world around them will stimulate them to do so. The Jewish Space, rather than impoverishing or diluting Jewish life in Europe, may very well strengthen it.

Bibliography

Gross, Jan Tomasz. 2001. *Neighbors: The Destruction of the Jewish Community in Jedwabne, Poland*. Princeton, NJ, Princeton University Press.

Wasserstein, Bernard. 1996. *Vanishing Diaspora. The Jews in Europe since 1945*. Cambridge, MA, Harvard University Press.

Chapter 10

CAUGHT BETWEEN CIVIL SOCIETY AND THE CULTURAL MARKET: JEWRY AND THE JEWISH SPACE IN EUROPE. A RESPONSE TO DIANA PINTO

Ian Leveson and Sandra Lustig

'The Jewish Space' has come to be an accepted term in the discourse about Jewish life in Europe today. We refer, of course, to Diana Pinto's chapters 'The Jewish Space in Europe' and 'A New Role for Jews in Europe: Challenges and Responsibilities', both in this volume. Gruber (1996: 1) wrote about 'Filling the Jewish Space in Europe' in 1996, and Pinto has been using the term at least since the conference on *Planning for the Future of European Jewry* in Prague in 1995. In 1994, Bodemann wrote of a 'Judaizing terrain' (Bodemann 1994: 57).

While Pinto sees the Jewish Space primarily in the realm of civil society, we contend that its cultural and commercial aspects are equally important, and that the complex nature of the relationships between Jews and non-Jews colour what happens in the Jewish Space in Europe, whether in the political, the cultural, or the commercial realms (and of course they overlap). The relationship between Jewry and the Jewish Space is of interest as well: while Jewry and Judaism affect what happens in the Jewish Space, the Jewish Space may also affect developments in Jewry and Judaism.

Our observations and analysis have their roots in our experience of having lived in Germany for many years. In Germany, issues between Jews and non-Jews that may not be as apparent in other places stand out in stark relief. We discuss many of those issues in the introduction to this book. In chapter 1, Pinto writes of a '"greying" of Europe, one which is replacing the previous classifications of countries as "resistant" (France), "neutral" (Switzerland), or "victims" (Austria) with respect to the Nazis.'

This 'greying' is occurring with respect to the *Shoah* as well, for example, France dealing with its role in deporting Jews, and also – we think – with respect to Europeans' attitudes towards Jews. Therefore, we believe that the phenomena we observe so clearly in Germany exist elsewhere in Europe as well, albeit with national variations. Wanya F. Kruyer illustrates this for the Netherlands, for example, speaking about the 'Anne Frank myth' in the discussion in Chapter 6. Countries with relaxed or strained relations between Jews and non-Jews, countries with or without a recent history of persecuting Jews, countries with large or tiny Jewish populations, countries with more or less openness towards the 'other' all provide different backdrops for the Jewish Space.

That the term 'Jewish Space' has caught on, although it has not been defined precisely, indicates that it resonates. It seems to denote the space in society where Jewish themes – in the widest sense, far transcending the religious – are embraced. It includes everything from Jewish websites to debates about the incorporation of Jews and Jewish life into national identity, from Gentile klezmer bands to memorial name-readings of *Shoah* victims, from inter-faith dialogue to Israeli folk dancing courses, from Jewish Studies programmes at universities to bagels. The Jewish Space seems to be thought of as a recent phenomenon no more than a couple of decades old. It is not populated solely by Jews; indeed, it may exist even without any Jews at all. Depending on one's perception of the boundaries of the Jewish Space, Jewish religious life may or may not be a part of it. Of course, Judaism has existed independently of a 'Jewish Space' for millennia, and continues to do so. In any case, they are two different entities in terms of their contents, purposes, and forms of social organisation.

The Jewish Space serves diverse functions, for both Jews and non-Jews. It is a new place for outreach to unaffiliated Jews and a setting where Jews unfamiliar with tradition and religion can explore at their own pace what might be or become their own Jewishness, without having to make a commitment in advance to joining a particular synagogue or a particular movement within Judaism. It provides an arena for Jews to interact and communicate with each other – and also with non-Jews – about Jewish themes and issues. Jewish entertainment is performed in the Jewish Space; Jewish knowledge is imparted and obtained there. It is where the general public's interest in things Jewish is concentrated, and this helps to provide an audience large enough to make events feasible, even where the Jewish population is small (Institute for Jewish Policy Research 2000).

The Jewish Space in Europe is populated by both Jews and Gentiles. Both can initiate activities and thereby provide the content that fills it, and both can form the audience. Given that the Jewish Space is not entirely a Jewish affair (or not necessarily a Jewish affair at all), the nature of the relationships between Jews and Gentiles in it is of utmost importance. Indeed, the Jewish Space serves as both a magnifying glass (where the complexities of Jewish/non-Jewish relationships become visible) and a burning glass (where conflicts flare up) for those relationships, although these may not be its intended purposes. Jews' and Gentiles' roles and interests in the Jewish Space, their perceptions and expectations of it, may differ. Many questions arise (Waterman 1999). On what terms do they interact? Who defines the Jewish Space? What constitutes it, and where do its boundaries lie? Who owns it? Who develops the content, and for whom? Whose interests does it serve? Who profits financially? What are Jews' and especially Gentiles' motivations for participating in the Jewish Space? Is there sufficient respect for the Jews' opinions, even when they constitute a minority of the participants? Who arbitrates, and how, when it comes to resolving differences? What effects on Judaism might the Jewish Space have? Do Gentiles acknowledge that Jews consider some areas of Jewish life intimate – to the religious congregation, the family, or for internal Jewish debate – and do they respect that intimacy? Or is the Jewish Space at times turned into something of a 'Jewish zoo'?

Civil Society

Pinto locates the Jewish Space in Europe within the context of civil society and tolerant democratic pluralism. We agree with her that the Jewish Space is – and should be – a part of civil society; Jews and their interests have a right to be represented, Jews' many voices deserve to be heard. Our view of the Jewish Space as a part of civil society, and as a place for promoting tolerant democratic pluralism, is less optimistic than Pinto's, however. We illustrate our position with the example of *Shoah* commemoration.

Pinto seems more concerned with the incorporation of the *Shoah* into national identity formation, state ideology, and its institutional recognition than with the way in which individuals deal with the *Shoah* in their family's, and by extension, their country's history. This is reflected in her view of the Jewish Space. Yet these two levels are linked: only when many individuals have worked through the *Shoah*, in relation to their own, their family's, their nation's histories can appropriate national identity formation occur. Only if there is sufficient support by many individuals can state ideology meaningfully incorporate the *Shoah*. Conversely, of course, state ideology does have an influence on how people feel about themselves and their national identity.

In Chapter 1, Pinto writes of the time when all compensation will have been paid, all schoolbooks will have been changed, when societal institutions will have set right – to the degree possible – their past crimes against Jews or apologised formally for them. Yet when she writes of the Jewish Space, she is not as clear in stating that these prerequisites must be in place before it can flourish. We believe that this applies to it both in civil society and in the cultural market. Non-Jewish society is still grappling with these issues, and not entirely successfully. The last few years have shown how much work still remains, for example: the *Historikerstreit*,[1] the Walser-Bubis debate (see Chapter 11), the debate about the Memorial for the Murdered Jews of Europe in Berlin, and the problems in setting up, stocking, and paying out money from the fund compensating forced labourers of German firms during the Nazi era.[2] Solutions to these problems are essential conditions for civil society to develop fully, and it is important to remember that they are not yet firmly in place. Without these prerequisites, we think that Jews and non-Jews cannot come together in civil society as though it were a level playing field, and this hinders using the Jewish Space to further tolerant democratic pluralism.

Again and again, there are miscommunications and more fundamental misunderstandings between Jews and non-Jews in political discussions in the Jewish Space. These are due to the complex and often difficult relationships between them (which we analyse in the Introduction to this book). Some of these difficulties derive from the fact that certain elements of civil society have not yet been developed fully. While the *legal* prerequisites for equal treatment of Jews may be largely in place, the *cultural* mindset that does not discriminate, that respects different cultural backgrounds, permits them to flourish and even cherishes them may not be.[3]

Above and beyond official and institutional actions, the cultural mindset of the dominant culture still needs to accept minorities' rights and particularities, not just in the legal sense, but also in the sense of everyday interaction, of what is in people's hearts and minds. Equality as a legal principle must be brought to life by actual implementation in society on a day-to-day basis. This cultural mindset, too, is a prerequisite for the Jewish Space to be able to play a constructive role in civil society. Two important parts of it are empathy and respect: empathy and respect for the 'other', whoever he or she may be, and his or her cultural and historical background. Living in respect of others requires that one is willing – and psychologically able – to put oneself in the other's position and imagine which issues are most salient. In the case of Jews, one part of this is recognising the Jewish historical narrative as autonomous (but linked to other historical narratives, of course), and as a valid and valued way of interpreting history.[4] It is doubtless difficult to be respectful of all people at all times and in all situations. Essential, however, is an *awareness* of the centrality of respect, and a sensitivity to where one might breach it, in speech or in action, intentionally or inadvertently, and an attempt to set right breaches of respect when they do occur. Such respect on the part of the non-Jewish majority for the Jewish minority is not always present, nor is the awareness of the importance of respect.[5]

Pinto defines the Jewish Space as the societal space where non-Jews acknowledge Jewish history and thought as part of their own European legacy and identity. A central part of this, unfortunately, must be commemoration of the *Shoah*. In Chapter 1 she argues that over time, 'the

Shoah will no longer function as an abyss separating Jews from non-Jews but will slowly become a bridge between them in the name of pluralist democratic values' (p. 35).

The key reason why we must disagree with Pinto on this issue – at least for the present and the near future – is that Jews and non-Jews commemorate different things. Jews commemorate their own concrete persecution and that of their own families, relatives, and communities, and the annihilation of Jewish institutions. Non-Jews, at least the perpetrators and their descendants, commemorate their responsibility for the crimes they or their forebears committed, as well as their own suffering and losses. These are entirely different things to commemorate. Jews and non-Jews live in separate *'Erinnerungswelten'* ('worlds of memory') (Bodemann 1997: 10). This distinction is of fundamental importance.

We question whether it is possible to commemorate such different things *together*, with both groups at diametrically opposed starting points, and looking at the event to be commemorated from opposite perspectives. As long as the perpetrators' side has not come to terms with its responsibility for the crimes, or the younger generations' legacy of responsibility for them, and has not transformed that responsibility into appropriate compensation and restitution for the victims wherever possible, it is doubtful whether commemorating together can work. How sincere can one believe a symbolic act (and commemoration is symbolic) to be when the factual basis for such acts is still so shaky, when credibility – literally putting one's money where one's mouth is – is still an issue, when debates occurring at other times, outside of commemoration events, reveal sentiments that even border on anti-Semitism?

With the examples of the Walser-Bubis debate, the *Historikerstreit*, the rise in recent years of physical attacks on foreigners, Jews, and Jewish cemeteries, some Jews (for example, Ignatz Bubis shortly before his death) have begun to doubt whether progress is being made. After all, there have been a multitude of attempts to bridge the gap between Jews and non-Jews, many, many *Shoah* commemoration events, a seemingly unending string of television films documenting particular aspects of the *Shoah* and the Second World War, and so on. Yet anti-Semitic and xenophobic sentiments continue to exist in broad strata of society. It appears as though the ways in which non-Jewish Germans have tried to deal with the *Shoah* have not had the desired effects; the efforts to change their attitudes may have been misconceived. Tackling the complex cognitive and psychological issues of anti-Semitism, guilt, trauma of the war, ignorance, and denial is doubtless a difficult task, all the more for parents and educators who may have trouble with these topics themselves. Here, too, it is important to remember that the task facing non-Jewish Germans in dealing with the *Shoah* is very different from the one facing Jews.

When Jews and non-Jews attempt to commemorate the *Shoah* together, close examination of the form and content of such events and the motivations for them is warranted. Bodemann observes that official Germany has over time appropriated such common commemoration, even to the point of excluding Jews, as in the official fiftieth anniversary commemoration of the November pogrom (*'Kristallnacht'* in Nazi terminology) in 1988: 'Commemorations construct identity, and national commemorations construct national identity ... These commemorations moreover have to do with fantasies about Jews and with the problems of loss and of guilt. They need Jewish actors; not lead actors, however, but extras' (Bodemann 1996b: 196). In the 1990s, commemoration of the 1938 November pogrom was combined with opposition to xenophobia and racism, seen as analogous current-day phenomena that were to be opposed. Some of the commemorative events featured upbeat entertainment appropriate for getting people excited about opposing racism, but inappropriate for mourning the *Shoah*. In other words, where common commemoration has been attempted, Jewish themes and Jewish protagonists have sometimes been pushed aside. Where this occurs, the *Shoah* seems to provide merely the backdrop before which commemorative events take place, events whose thrust is in the direction of national identity formation or opposition to xenophobic violence – not primarily commemoration of the crime of the *Shoah*. Linking current neo-Nazism to the *Shoah* is legitimate, of course; it is a matter of emphasis, of whether the focus on current issues clouds the painful commemoration of the *Shoah*. At other times, Jewish leaders do play a prominent role in public commemoration events. In these situations, it is particularly the Jews who take on – and are given – the responsibility for keeping memory of the *Shoah* alive and exhorting the public not to commit such a crime again. In these cases, Bodemann calls the role ascribed to Jews 'labourers of memory' (p. 164 above).

He points out a third mechanism that leads attempts at joint commemoration to failure. 'In this new commemoration, Auschwitz and Kristallnacht turn into a romanticised horror suffered jointly by Germans and Jews; a commemoration of Jews and the decent new Germany against the evil forces in society. The lines of confrontation, therefore, are being blurred' (Bodemann 1996a: 42). An example for this is the national memorial at the Neue Wache on Unter den Linden in Berlin, which was newly dedicated in 1993 to the military and civilian victims of the Second World War, the *Shoah*, and Stalinist persecution in East Germany all at once, without differentiation.

What might the motivation be for this blurring of lines? Many Germans feel victimised themselves. And they feel that their own or their families' – very real – suffering during the Second World War and in the post-war years (in bombings, on the battlefield, as refugees, as prisoners of war, as children growing up without fathers, and so on.) is ignored. In addition, commemorating one's own crimes raises feelings of guilt. Rightly so, for the perpetrators. Their descendants, however, those uninvolved in the Nazi crimes, feel victimised because of the commemoration rites; they feel blamed for something they did not do, even if no one is burdening them personally with the responsibility for the crimes. The side of the victims seems morally advantageous when crimes are commemorated, so it is understandable if people would prefer to be on that side.

If the *Shoah* is to become a bridge across which its victims and their descendants join hands with its perpetrators and their descendants, as Pinto argues, then there must be honesty and clarity on each side about one's own position. When people attempt to blur the lines, they show a lack of such honesty and clarity. Use of unclear and/or coded language can also be telling in this context. Clarity of what one expects of the other side is essential. Sometimes, it seems as though the perpetrators' side were expecting Jews to say, 'okay, it wasn't so bad after all', and they resent that Jews still will not say so. They would like Jews to lift the burden of commemoration from their shoulders. Yet if Jews take on that burden – and why should they? – it relieves the perpetrators' side from working through the painful issues involved.[6]

The example of the *Shoah* commemoration illustrates the problems present in that part of the Jewish Space with civil society functions. It shows that, at least in Germany, society at large does not yet, as a matter of course, accord Jews *as Jews* appropriate standing in societal discourse. This is true not only of commemorative events, but also of what is said in politics, in the cultural realm, in the workplace, and in informal settings. It relates to Jewish contemporary life, Jewish experience and Jewish history, sensitivity to Jews' religious requirements, and to the positions Jews take on current events. All of these matter. Despite some people's and institutions' considerable efforts, others have yet to do their homework. Given the 'greying' (Pinto) of Europe concerning countries' guilt or innocence relating to the *Shoah*, we posit that this problem is not solely a German one, albeit it being particularly visible in Germany.

The Cultural Market

We see the Jewish Space as within the cultural market, in addition to being part of civil society, and we think this aspect is integral to the concept of the Jewish Space and not just an 'epiphenomenon', as Pinto writes. Our concern is that the cultural market aspect seems to be based on the erroneous assumption that the Jewish Space is a neutral space where Jews and non-Jews can interact at ease. Yet to date, unfortunately, that is not the case. Some of what happens in the cultural market is neutral or positive for Jews and Jewry, but the difficult relationship between Jews and non-Jews plays out in the cultural market as well, with stereotyping, misrepresentation, and miscommunication. Given the difficulties in the civil society aspect of the Jewish Space, what happens in it as part of the cultural market is all the more important.

Prior to its incorporation into the market, Jewish culture was within the Jewish sphere, and of little interest to others. In the Jewish Space, though, the cultural market has adopted Jewish culture as though it were a product line, and market forces influence its production and consumption. Culture in general – not just Jewish culture – has come to be provided within the domain of the market. Cultural products are produced and distributed by industries which operate in a market setting, so that the rules of the market apply just as they do in any other market.

In some ways, the products for sale in the cultural market – such as CDs, food and recipes, clothing, concerts, ritual items, books, theatre, visual arts, cinema, organised trips and tours for tourists, language and folk-dancing courses, and experiential events such as meditation retreats – are commodities like any other product in any other market. However, what differentiates products in the cultural market from products in other markets is that they are artefacts intended to convey certain cultural or religious meanings.

Such products are often of significance for some people, but not necessarily for all those who may be involved in producing or consuming them. For people belonging to a particular culture, ethnicity, or religion, they carry (sometimes deep) cultural or religious significance. For the producers and marketers, they are a vehicle for doing business. For mainstream consumers, they are this year's fad, or a way of showing interest in the culture in question, or simply decorative objects, or are fascinating, for whatever reason, without conveying to the mainstream consumer any of the meaning that they do for people of the culture concerned. For the latter, such consumption by others may be offensive or disrespectful, and they may view it as another form of discrimination or stereotyping. The mainstream producers and consumers may not even be aware of this, they may not be knowledgeable enough about it to ensure that the changes they make during product development are respectful to that culture, or they may find nothing wrong with using other cultures as a fad.

In order to market cultural meanings via cultural artefacts, it must be possible to isolate and package them as reproducible products or commodities. In the case of minority and ethnic cultures, what is made into a commodity for the market is not the entire culture, but only those parts which can be consumed easily by the majority, either because they are not too different from the majority culture or because they seem exotic, but still accessible. Those products are the ones which can be sold successfully to the largest possible market segment. For many cultures, this includes food and music, but only rarely ethics, for example, or intellectual traditions, or the religious and social significance of the cultural commodities that are consumed.[7] As a result, what is marketed as a culture may be a mere caricature, at times a jumbled mass of easy-to-digest bits and pieces that cannot represent what a culture actually is (or was). Packaging and selling a culture as a commodity may be akin to taking a 'still photo' of it and then moving it out of its societal context. It would be a fallacy to assume that this type of marketing would never have a negative effect on the original culture in its contemporary context. At worst, stereotypes – both positive and negative – may be reproduced, since they are what the public recognises easily and associates with a particular culture, and in this way, stereotypes and prejudices may be perpetuated. An example is the rough-hewn wooden dolls for sale in Poland which depict a stereotypical Jew with a long beard, hooked nose, kipah, and caftan, clutching a bag marked '$'.[8]

Marketing and trading cultures *as commodities* is based on the assumptions (conscious or not) that they are saleable, compatible, and universally accessible for all, and that buyer and seller have equal standing in the exchange transaction. These assumptions apply to anything traded as a commodity. In the case of cultures as commodities, they are also about the relationships between the mainstream culture and the culture being marketed. However, neither these assumptions nor the relationships between the cultures are made explicit. The assumptions necessary for the market setting omit the historical experiences that determine the quality of these relationships, be they peaceful coexistence or symbiosis, or persecution, slavery, or colonisation. This is particularly obvious in the case of Jews and non-Jews in Europe. Pretending that one can legitimately ignore such historical circumstances is an illusion, or even suppression (in the psychological sense of the word). The illusion of compatibility and exchangeability at will of different cultures reduces one's cultural identity to the equivalent of wearing a particular party hat: it is decorative, maybe stylish, maybe quaint, but has no deeper meaning. In the extreme, then, the cultural market robs a culture of its identity, reducing it to a fashion statement.

The potential for exploiting Judaism and Jewish culture as commodities depends on what they are considered to be. If they are considered a set of rituals, food and music, they may be packaged and marketed easily, just like any other commodity. But if they are considered to be a way of being, thinking, acting; a discursive process; a rich and sometimes contradictory culture, with many distinct traditions, and with a spiritual purpose, they would not lend themselves to being marketed, as there would be no fixed object to sell. Indeed, the Jewish concept of canon works against a simple standardisation process: 'The Talmud … is at once canonical and also the site for a remarkable polyphony of contradictory opinions. … a canon need not reflect a monolithic set of doctrines but might instead involve an ever expanding and transforming culture composed of creative contradictions' (Biale et al. 1998: 10). In Jewish settings, such creative contradictions are the basis for a multitude of local traditions as well as for intellectual debate, an important – if not defining – part of Jewish tradition. But this tradition of debate is not carried over into the market setting; just the menorahs, the bagels, and the klezmer.

The cultural market has taken on other cultures besides Jewish culture, of course. One may see the Jewish Space as just one booth in the multicultural marketplace, side by side with a Cuban Space, a Celtic Space and so on. What is presented in such spaces may have been reduced to a fashion: Tibetan or pseudo-Tibetan culture as last season's fad, Jewish or pseudo-Jewish culture may be trendy now, next year it might be Native American or pseudo-Native American. Whichever cultural fad becomes fashionable is initiated by lifestyle-setters, whether designers or subculture figures, as well as by the fashion scouts and marketing divisions of the entertainment and media industries.

After a minority's cultural goods have been adapted for the mass market, they may well end up being sold back to the original ethnic consumers (the niche market) by producers who do not belong to that culture and who normally meet the demand of the mass market. People who buy cultural accessories which they use in practising their own culture may thus become only a small fraction of consumers relative to those who buy such accessories for entertainment. The purchasing power exercised by the members of the minority culture may over time have less and less influence on producers' decisions about the cultural products in question. Thus the minority may lose control (to a certain degree) over the production of their own culture. An example of this is non-kosher food with no connection to any Jewish culinary tradition marketed as 'Jewish cuisine'.

Another example is the fashion for klezmer. Indeed, the klezmer craze itself can be placed in the context of representing Judaism as Yiddishkeit and *shtetl* romance, particularly problematic in countries where these images have never had much to do with reality. Once klezmer, Yiddishkeit, and *shtetl* romance have been perceived as the totality of Jewish music and culture (which they certainly are not), they are defined as such and then projected back onto Judaism, Jewry, and individual Jews. An example for this is the use of klezmer as background music in virtually every non-Jewish German-made documentary about Jews in Germany, past or present. Using these images serves – consciously or not – to put Jews and Judaism in a particular 'box', one that is 'alien', 'non-German', premodern, and religious, a world apart from current-day Germany, a world that no longer exists. Once Jews and Judaism have been placed in such a 'box', one may more easily believe that one understands them, since the rich complexity that is Judaism has been reduced to a few images. In addition, it is easier to deal with issues that are not too close to home, issues that one can distance oneself from at least a little bit. In defining Jews and Judaism as 'foreign', as a world apart, one can create that distance. Then, dealing with things Jewish and particularly with one's own relationship to Jews and to the *Shoah* seems 'safer'. [9]

Buying (into) a Jewish Identity

Consuming cultural goods from cultures other than one's own can have many different meanings and may spring from a variety of motivations: the enjoyment of eating exotic food, a genuine interest in learning about a particular culture, the intellectual stimulation involved in acquiring a new language or understanding a different world-view, or simply entertainment. Consumption of exotic cultural goods is often merely a superficial addition to one's existing lifestyle, but it can be more than that.

Since consumption is a part of Western culture, the products people consume have become markers of who they are, or who they would like to be. One's particular combination of cultural accessories characterises one's identity as an individual, but it is also an indicator of one's communal cultural affiliation. One buys certain things in order to belong to a group, but also to differentiate oneself from others.

It used to be that one was born into a culture and lived in that culture without the choice of leaving it. In the Western world in recent decades, many people's affiliations with the cultures they were born into appear to have become less important; indeed, people seem freer to loosen ties with their cultures of origin without being socially ostracised. (Of course, this is true only in certain respects; one cannot leave one's culture entirely.) One reason for this is an individualist ethos. A second one is the extension of the market into additional areas of life, for example, cultural life. A third is the growth of mass media, especially television, as well as cheap travel and communications providing people with the opportunity to see and experience other cultures. One's identity is thus increasingly becoming what one chooses it to be, and no longer wholly predetermined by the culture one grew up with. This development has definite benefits for personal freedom: people are now freer to live their own identities without being limited to whatever culture they happened to be born into. This is of value particularly for people who have trouble identifying with their own cultures and perceive (parts of) other cultures as more attractive than their own.

In the context of the cultural market, however, identity and cultural affiliation appear to be based on the consumption of certain cultural products and experiences, a notion that replaces – to a certain degree – ascribed communal cultural identity and what one learned during one's formative years. If one consumes cultural products of a certain variety, one might assume that one is practising that culture, or at least partaking of it. With cultures being represented by objects, indeed cultures being sold as if they were merely an assemblage of objects, cultural identity seems to be something which a person can change: one needs only to exchange one set of cultural accessories for another. The very existence of the cultural marketplace seems to imply that one can simply buy and adopt a cultural identity like any other commodity, or even mix and match pieces of different ones.

The distinctiveness of cultures which are associated with particular groups, whether defined by ethnicity, nationality, religion, class, or other traits, is often historical, complex, and multifaceted, and may be characterised by being born into a particular group, specific behaviour, language, or other features. None of these can be adopted simply and easily; moreover, their distinctiveness is often reinforced by entry to cultures being restricted. Full acceptance into a culture often involves a long period of probation until one's adaptation, loyalty, and commitment are assured. This exclusivity is not true of all cultures, of course, and even those which actively seek new members and make it easy for people to join, for instance Christian churches by proselytising, or the fleeting youth subcultures of each new generation, retain their distinctiveness.

The way to join another culture or religion traditionally does not go via the market. The cultural market may, however, lead one to believe that it is possible to adopt a new identity by means of the market, that is, by consuming certain cultural goods and services offered there. That illusion arises because the cultural market – in contrast to cultures themselves – is universal, in that its products are available to all who can pay for them (and some products are made available for free), and not restricted to people already belonging to a particular culture. The market does not inherently respect socially defined barriers to participation or entry, either for consumers or for producers.

Nonetheless, which parts of a culture are public and open to everyone and which are private and intimate to members, or even restricted to the initiated, is an important issue. Members of a culture or religion may resent it if boundaries are crossed and that intimacy is not respected. This question determines the limitations of that which is legitimately accessible to aficionados wandering in from the cultural marketplace. Such boundaries may be difficult to determine. For example, there is nothing wrong with eating 'ethnic' food, except that in some circumstances some foods have a special meaning, such as a religious one, and may thus be out of bounds. Offering a Passover-style dinner complete with seder plate in a restaurant year-round would be questionable, as would using communion wafers outside of a Christian service. There are even instances where a non-Jew says Kaddish or carries the Torah scroll in a Jewish service, as witnessed in Amsterdam (Kruyer 2002: 68). A central issue in such cases is whether people who do not belong to the culture in question treat that culture with due respect, whether as producers, as marketers, as consumers, as participants, or as observers.

When trying to understand people searching for meaning, and especially searching for a new identity, in another culture, three things are very important: (1) their attitudes towards their own culture; (2) the factual historical relationships between the two cultures; and (3) their perceptions of, knowledge about, and attitudes towards the new culture and the relationships between the two cultures. We illustrate this using as an example the situation of *some* non-Jewish Germans in the Jewish Space in Germany. We would like to emphasise that this certainly does not apply to all German Gentiles. The phenomenon is common enough, however, to cause Jews in Germany to be acutely aware of non-Jews in the Jewish Space, and of what they say and do.

Many non-Jewish Germans are uneasy with their identity as Germans because of their country's or their family's history. The main reason for this is, of course, Germany's killing so many Jews in the *Shoah*. Living with a postwar German identity is thus problematic, and many are unsure of their own identity or unhappy with it. People have different ways of dealing with this uneasiness, of which they may or may not be conscious. Some German Gentiles attempt to deal with their ambivalence towards being German by taking an extraordinary interest in things Jewish, sometimes to the extent of identifying with Judaism, or with that which they perceive as being Judaism because it is presented in the Jewish Space. In short, they hope to identify with the 'good guys' as 'good goys'. Some go so far as to convert, and of those, a few even take up rabbinical training. Others try – sometimes successfully – to pose as Jewish without converting, even though they know that to become Jewish one must convert.[10] One example of someone who may be posing as a Jew is the author of *Fragments: Memories of a Wartime Childhood* (Wilkomirski 1995; Wilkomirski 1996), a man in Switzerland calling himself Binjamin Wilkomirski and claiming to be a child concentration camp survivor, about whom a massive public debate occurred. Some others, too, claim to be Jewish, although they do so with less commotion.

Most non-Jewish Germans who take an interest in things Jewish know – at least in general terms, some even in minute detail – about Nazi Germany's persecution of the Jews, but they may or may not be aware of their own family's involvement. Many lack even the most basic knowledge of Judaism, even if they may know about the *Shoah* in intricate detail. Since they typically learn next to nothing about Judaism in school, and generally have had at most negligible personal contacts with Jews (given the small Jewish population in Germany), they have no basis with which to judge what is presented as Jewish in the Jewish Space. What they do know about Jews and Judaism is often absorbed there, especially – and very importantly – in that part of the Jewish Space which is part of the cultural market. This generally does not provide an adequate basis for understanding Judaism, particularly where the information contains stereotypes and prejudices about Jews. The fashion for the esoteric and the New Age makes things even more problematic when Gentiles, seeking a (for them) new kind of spirituality, develop an interest in Judaism, believing it to be an esoteric cult, even though Judaism is, in fact, an exoteric religion par excellence, and has little to do with New Age practices.[11]

These perceptions of Judaism may unfold before a background of vague guilt feelings towards Jews, and possibly of resentment of those feelings.

German Gentiles are generally not familiar with the intricacies of the difficult relations between Jews and Gentiles in Germany, and they are almost certainly not aware of Jews' perceptions of those intricacies, which are very different from Gentiles' perceptions of them.

This description of some German Gentiles using the Jewish Space as a place to deal with their identity problems is, unfortunately, real. Their fascination with things Jewish may have little to do with Judaism, as manifested by their ignorance about it, but has to do with needs of their own. Jews are little inclined to serve as a quaint ethnic backdrop in the Jewish Space for non-Jews dealing with their own needs, especially when they and Jewry's (historical) suffering are used for such ends. This discussion shows how the Jewish Space serves as both a magnifying glass and a burning glass for the complex relationship between Jews and non-Jews in Germany today.[12]

While the cultural market may seem to give German Gentiles the impression that they can (in the extreme) change identity, be rid of their Germanness and become Jewish – in whatever way, and as if Germanness and Jewishness were mutually exclusive – by joining in activities in the Jewish Space, this is in fact not true. When used in this way, the Jewish Space is not a space within civil society where Jews and non-Jews come together to enhance mutual understanding, much less to further tolerant democratic pluralism or other such values.

Gruber writes, 'it is the low level of contemporary Jewish cultural consciousness – regarding religious as well as secular Jewish traditions – that has made some German and other Jews so sensitive to what they perceive as cultural appropriation or usurpation, not just of music but of other aspects of the Jewish phenomenon' (Gruber 2002: 227). We contend that appropriation or usurpation of Jewish culture by non-Jews in the Jewish Space is a reality, and not merely a misperception on the part of Jews. In addition, we think it is not a *low* level of contemporary Jewish cultural consciousness, but a *very acute* such consciousness, combined with the awareness of the intricacies of Jewish-non-Jewish interaction in Germany that enables Jews in this country to see where non-Jews are overstepping boundaries and are using the Jewish Space for their own ends, sometimes at the expense of Jews. Jewry in Germany has not yet been able to recover from its destruction in the *Shoah* to be collectively strong enough to have a guiding influence on the Jewish Space in Germany. In this situation, it takes an enormous amount of inner strength to build up Jewish life, in private and especially in public settings.

Conclusion

We think that the Jewish Space in Europe is a more complex phenomenon than Pinto posits. The Jewish Space lies partly within civil society, partly within the cultural market. Some issues come up in both areas, for example the issue of respect, the question of being clear about one's identity as a Jew or a non-Jew, or being on the Jewish or non-Jewish side when commemorating the *Shoah*. In addition, tensions may arise in the Jewish Space because of its dual nature as being in both realms: part civil society, part cultural market, part Jewish, part non-Jewish. The cultural market and civil society display different forms and mechanisms of social interaction. Jews and Gentiles enter the Jewish Space with different preconceptions of it, whether or not they are aware of them. Their expectations, their perceptions, their behaviour, their interpretations of discussions and events differ, and this is typical of the difficulties in intercultural communication. Many of these differences are based on Jews' and non-Jews' differing historical experiences, and the complex relationships between Jews and Gentiles that are partly a result of those differing experiences. Of particular importance, of course, is the difference between Jews' and non-Jews' experiences of the *Shoah* and the Second World War, and their ways of dealing with those experiences in their families, communities, and religions.

We think that we are still far away from the time when the *Shoah* can become an '"internal" European issue, a chapter in each country's national history' (Chapter 1), as if it were a historical experience akin to so many others, or even a bridge between Jews and non-Jews. The abyss of the *Shoah* still separates the perpetrators' and the victims' sides, and will continue to do so until both sides have worked through their respective experiences fully. That the perpetrators and their descendants have not yet done so adequately is visible concerning concrete measures, such as compensating victims, concerning societal debates like the Walser-Bubis debate, and when the two sides try to come together in commemoration. The core of the matter is that they still commemorate different things, which is why attempts to commemorate together remain unsatisfactory for both sides.

Where Jews feel uncomfortable with the Jewish Space, we think that it is *because* civil society does not yet acknowledge Jews' entitlement to a distinct place in it, and that appropriate respect is lacking, since the perpetrators' side has not yet come to terms with their deeds. There is even the danger (exemplified in the Walser-Bubis debate) that non-Jews refuse to accord to Jews a special voice at all in the societal discourse about the *Shoah*. The analogous phenomenon in the part of the Jewish Space that is in the cultural market is pseudo-Jewish material provided by non-Jews that reflect their prejudices and stereotypes about Jews and Judaism. The Jewish Space is not yet a neutral meeting place for Jews and Gentiles.

Especially where the Jewish population is small, rebuilding of Jewish life and Jewish institutions (in a manner appropriate to today, not one-to-one rebuilding of what was irrevocably destroyed in the *Shoah*) is still occurring, and needs to continue for many years. The Jewish Space may have the effect of attracting sufficient numbers of Gentiles to make many more events feasible than if the audience were restricted to Jews. But it is above all in places with few Jews that the non-Jewish influence on the Jewish Space may become predominant. Particularly in such a situation, Jewish cultural ownership of the Jewish Space is critical, lest non-Jewish perspectives and stereotypes become integrated (possibly unknowingly) into Jewish life.

We have devoted a large part of this chapter to discussing some of the complexities and difficulties present in the Jewish Space. This should not be misconstrued as a generally negative attitude towards it. The Jewish Space serves important and positive functions, which we mentioned at the outset, but did not think necessary to discuss in detail. Rather, we urge the reader to examine closely what is offered in the Jewish Space, and by whom, how it is used, and by whom, with which preconceptions, and to which ends. We should think carefully about when to focus on interaction (in whichever form) with non-Jews, and when on internal Jewish rebuilding. We should consider where to focus our efforts for rebuilding Judaism in Europe in its entire spectrum, with the full range of religious and secular institutions. A strong Jewish presence is an essential prerequisite for a functioning Jewish Space, a Jewish Space where Jewish voices enrich civil society, where Jewish (not pseudo-Jewish) culture is celebrated, and, yes, a Jewish Space that is 'good for the Jews', too.

Notes

1. The *Historikerstreit* (Historians' Debate) in 1986 between Ernst Nolte and Jürgen Habermas (as well as many others) was largely about whether or not the *Shoah* was unique. Nolte advocated 'normalising' the historical evaluation of the *Shoah* as though it were like any other historical episode, and complained that the debate on Nazi history could not (and would not) be laid to rest.
2. Most of the forced labourers alive today are not Jewish, yet the issue is perceived and discussed by many as one of German industry and other employers versus Jewish forced labourers. The fund is called 'Remembrance, Responsibility, and the Future'.
3. Habermas (1996) analyses legal and factual equality in more depth than is possible here. Particularly interesting is his chapter 8: 'Kampf um Anerkennung im demokratischen Rechtsstaat'.
4. Such a view of Jewish history in Germany is lacking in the Jewish Museum Berlin, for example.
5. The issue of respect is, of course, not unique to the relationship between Jews and Gentiles, but is present in other societies as well, for example in race relations in the U.S.
6. In this context, we think that since non-Jewish Germans have decided to build a Memorial for the Murdered Jews of Europe, then this is praiseworthy, but they should have commissioned a non-Jewish German to design it, not Peter Eisenman, an American Jew. We say this regardless of the merits of Eisenman's design. With a Jew designing it, it becomes possible for non-Jewish Germans to regard the monument as above criticism, and – by association – themselves above criticism as well. This is an example of Jews being considered 'labourers of memory': after designing the Memorial, they must also assume responsibility in case of any criticism, thus exonerating non-Jewish Germans.

7. Our observation that the cultural market profits mainly from the easy-to-sell parts of cultures neither supports a normative statement that the market should provide an entire culture nor excludes the possibility that that could be done.

8. Such dolls are shown in the documentary 'The Secret', by director Ronit Kerstner, 2001.

9. Unfortunately, some Jews, too, use such images, and create such a distance, albeit coming from a different background and angle (see Gruber 2002: 63–8).

10. Gruber discusses this phenomenon of non-Jews active in the Jewish Space (although she does not use the term 'Jewish Space'), calling such people 'virtual Jews' (Gruber 2002: 43–50). Some would like to be perceived as Jews; others would not. In any case, if they do not convert, they are not Jews, so we do not find the label 'virtual Jews' helpful: on the contrary, the label helps blur the lines.

11. Many people unfamiliar with New Age ideology do not seem aware of the anti-Semitic content of some writings basic to the New Age movement, or that some principles propounded by that movement are diametrically opposed to basic tenets of Judaism, e.g., that all humans are created equal (Brearly 1994).

12. See also the section on the Jewish Space in Germany in the Introduction.

Bibliography

Biale, David, Michael Galchinsky, and Susannah Heschel. 1998. *Insider/Outsider: American Jews and Multiculturalism*. Berkeley, University of California Press.

Bodemann, Y. Michal. 1994. 'A Reemergence of German Jewry?'. In *Reemerging Jewish Culture in Germany: Life and Literature Since 1989*, eds. by S. L. Gilman and K. Remmler. New York, New York University Press.

Bodemann, Y. Michal. 1996a. '"How can one stand to live there as a Jew ..."'. In *Jews, Germans, Memory. Reconstructions of Jewish Life in Germany*, ed. Y. M. Bodemann. Ann Arbor, University of Michigan Press.

Bodemann, Y. Michal. 1996b. 'Reconstructions of History: From Jewish Memory to Nationalised Commemoration of Kristallnacht in Germany'. In *Jews, Germans, Memory. Reconstructions of Jewish Life in Germany*, ed. Y. M. Bodemann. Ann Arbor, University of Michigan Press: 179–223.

Bodemann, Y. Michal. 1997. 'Ein böses Possenspiel'. In *Die Tageszeitung* (5/6 July). Berlin: 10.

Brearly, Margaret. 1994. 'Possible Implications of the New Age Movement for the Jewish People'. In *Jewish Identities in the New Europe*, ed. Jonathan Webber. London/Washington, Littman Library of Jewish Civilization: 255–72.

Gruber, Ruth Ellen. 1996. *International Perspectives 35: Filling the Jewish Space in Europe*. New York, American Jewish Committee.

Gruber, Ruth Ellen. 2002. *Virtually Jewish. Reinventing Jewish Culture in Europe*. Berkeley, University of California Press.

Habermas, Jürgen. 1996. *Die Einbeziehung des Anderen. Studien zur politischen Theorie*. Frankfurt am Main, Suhrkamp.

Institute for Jewish Policy Research. 2000. *A Community of Communities, Report of the Commission on Representation of the Interests of the British Jewish Community*. London, Institute for Jewish Policy Research.

Kruyer, Wanya F. 2002. 'Insiders and Outsiders'. In *Bet Debora Journal 2: The Jewish Family – Myth and Reality*, eds. E. Klapheck and L. Dämmig. Berlin, Edition Granat: 67–9.

Waterman, Stanley. 1999. *Cultural politics and European Jewry.* JPR Policy Paper no. 1. London, Institute for Jewish Policy Research.

Wilkomirski, Binjamin. 1995. *Bruchstücke. Aus einer Kindheit 1939–1948.* Frankfurt am Main, Jüdischer Verlag.

Wilkomirski, Binjamin. 1996. *Fragments: Memories of a Wartime Childhood.* New York, Random House.

Chapter 11

'The Germans Will Never Forgive the Jews for Auschwitz'.[1] When Things Go Wrong in the Jewish Space: The Case of the Walser–Bubis Debate

Sandra Lustig

The Jewish Space can be a place for encounters between Jews and non-Jews that enhance mutual understanding about things Jewish. But things can also go terribly wrong in the Jewish Space. It can be like a magnifying glass (where the complexities of Jewish–non-Jewish relationships become visible, or come into focus) and a burning glass (where conflicts in those relationships flare up). In this chapter, just one example – the Walser-Bubis debate of 1998/9 – is analysed in order to illustrate the intricacies of the interactions between Jews and non-Jews in the Jewish Space in post-*Shoah* Europe, which otherwise would go unnoticed by observers unfamiliar with the situation, and in this case, unfamiliar with the German language. Out of the very many such disputes in post-*Shoah* Germany, this example is particularly suitable for analysis because of the wealth of readily available material about it. And outside of public disputes, similar issues come up time and again in everyday situations when Jews and non-Jews interact. This analysis shows some of the perturbations, even the main-stream anti-Semitism, in the Jewish Space in post-*Shoah* Germany. In the debate, the term 'Jewish Space' was not used at all; however, discussions about *Shoah* commemoration certainly fall within its boundaries.

This analysis focuses on the interaction of Jews and non-Jews in the course of the Walser–Bubis debate. First, the content and subtext of Walser's speech are presented, followed by comments on Walser's use of language and a discussion of how he and his supporters interacted with

Jews during the debate, and finally, conclusions are drawn from this analysis. Extensive passages are reproduced here in the original and in translation (by the author) to enable readers to judge for themselves how to interpret what was said and written, and to show in particular how Walser uses language and constructs his argument.[2] Many interesting aspects of this case lie outside the scope of this chapter.[3] They include Walser's writing and reception throughout his literary career, his politics, his use of literary language in this speech, his use of citations,[4] a psycho-analytical reading of the debate, and the clash between Jewish and Christian ethics in terms of dealing with misdeeds and guilt.

In October 1998, the Peace Prize of the German Booksellers' Society, a highly prestigious award, was bestowed on Martin Walser, one of the most prominent post-war writers in Germany. His acceptance speech was received with a standing ovation by practically the entire audience of over a thousand – apart from Ignatz Bubis, then head of the Zentralrat der Juden in Deutschland (Central Council of Jews in Germany), and his wife. Bubis called Walser an incendiary, which sparked a debate that went on for several months with a plethora of articles, columns, and letters to the editor published in newspapers and magazines across the country.[5] Two months after Walser's speech, there was a face-to-face conversation between the two, and Bubis retracted his accusation. Walser did not apologise, nor did he accept Bubis's apology.

On the surface, Walser spoke of the use and abuse of references to the *Shoah* in appropriate and inappropriate contexts,[6] how he resented being reminded of it time and again, and how he felt that the Germans' guilt was being abused.[7] He spoke of the necessity of looking away, and said that one need not atone for everything.[8] He spoke of his conscience,[9] the fetters of language, of not being permitted to speak one's mind,[10] and the suffering of the German people because of the division of the country after the Second World War.

Yet the subtext of Walser's speech was at least as important as the text itself. And it was this as much as the text itself that caused such heated dispute.[11] Walser insisted that he had *not* been misunderstood – and, indeed, people on both sides of the debate understood him the same way. The subtext was that it was in fact the Germans who were the victims of the Second World War, and that it was the Jews, certain intellectuals, and the media who were forcing the Germans into the defensive when it came to talking about the Second World War and the *Shoah*,[12] and were compelling them to commemorate the *Shoah*, which – as a result of this coercion – they did only in a ritualistic manner. Walser and his supporters felt attacked, and resented that. Many of those who wrote to him heaved a sigh of relief: at last, a respected public figure had dared to say out loud what so many had been thinking for a long time, had broken free of the fetters that were keeping them from speaking their minds, in the face of allegedly overpowering control of people's speech. Walser's critics, however, objected to his turning the tables and putting Jews in the position of the perpetrators and non-Jewish Germans in the place of the victims. Walser's particular use of language supports the view that he – whether consciously or not – conveyed a subtext in addition to the statements he made explicitly. Openly anti-Semitic statements are fairly rare in current-day mainstream Germany (although they have become somewhat more frequent since unification of the country, since the political situation in the Middle East has flared up, and since the terrorist attacks of 11 September 2001); anti-Semitic sentiment is expressed in code and by allusion; so, too, by Walser.[13] He did not even use the words 'Jew' or 'Jewish' in his speech, except in one particular context when making a minor point.[14]

Walser used key words in his speech in a sense slightly different from their usual meaning, thus creating ambiguity and opening up space for conveying his subtext. For example, *wegschauen* (literally: 'looking away'), a word with clear connotations: looking away when crimes are committed against minorities today, and also the behaviour of so many Germans that made it possible to discriminate against and kill millions of Jews, in any case behaviour that should be condemned. Yet Walser defended his own *wegschauen* when horrific scenes are presented on television, scenes of the *Shoah* that, he complained, were presented again and again. As Walser used *wegschauen*, it was very close to stating that 'looking away' is ethically acceptable, even ethically necessary, behaviour. In this context, he coined the word *wegdenken* ('thinking away', or turning his thoughts away) to underscore the extent of his behaviour of averting his eyes and his thoughts from the *Shoah*. Walser's acceptance speech for the peace prize, his lecture at Duisburg, and his conversation with Bubis (the three times he spoke in the course of this debate) are riddled with such examples of using language not to express his thoughts clearly and directly, but to carry an anti-Semitic subtext via allusion or implicit redefinition. As Salomon Korn, a member of the Zentralrat der Juden in Deutschland who took part in the conversation between Walser and Bubis, put it, Walser created an enormous background onto which his audience could project associations, and one can infer from Walser's statements in the conversation that he did not disagree (Schirrmacher 1999: 458).

Walser was vague at certain key points. He seemed to believe that he and the Germans were the true victims of the Second World War and were constantly being attacked, yet he did not name those he accused of attacking (see n. 9 below). He also spoke of 'Instrumentalisierung unserer Schande zu gegenwärtigen Zwecken' ('exploitation of our disgrace for current purposes'; op. cit. p. 12). In his speech, he did not say who was behind this alleged 'exploitation', nor did he specify which 'current purposes' he meant. When confronted with the fact that this was widely interpreted as meaning that forced labourers during the Nazi era were exploiting Germans' guilt to extort higher compensation payments, compensation being a contentious topic at the time, Walser denied that he had meant that, professing ignorance of the details of that dispute. (op. cit. p. 445). He said he had alluded to comments that the division of Germany after the Second World War was deserved because of Auschwitz, and he considered that line of argument to be an exploitation of Auschwitz. (op. cit. p. 444) Walser denied any link to current politics, stating that he had been talking about literature and language, and in any case, his speech was directed at Germans, not at the State, and that it was mainly about the media, not 'any foreign problem', which he apparently considered compensation to be.[15] (He did, in fact, refer to politics in discussing the case of an East German spy in prison in reunified Germany, and closed his speech with a plea for clemency towards him.) Still, Walser insisted that he had not been misunderstood.

Rommelspacher thinks that Walser's pattern of turning the tables and using vague language is what makes his speech scandalous:

> He does not encourage analysis of when and why commemoration so often fails, but stirs up vague suspicions. ... What is deeply troubling about the current debate about the peace prize speech is the following: in the production "Bubis versus Walser" exactly the scene is reenacted that has nourished anti-Jewish sentiment for centuries – the vengeful Jew who cannot leave one in peace, and the Christian as victim who seeks redemption in still, lonely suffering. (Rommelspacher 1999)

Walser's way of expressing his ideas made it very difficult to argue with him. If anti-Semitic sentiment is uttered overtly, one can discuss it by simply pointing to explicitly anti-Semitic passages. But if it is uttered in code and by allusion, as by Walser, one must first interpret the statements to uncover their meaning before arguing against their anti-Semitic content, and whoever made such statements can deny that that interpretation is correct.

Walser denied even the possibility that others – in particular, the extreme right, more openly outspoken anti-Semites, and others hostile to minorities – might use his speech for their own ends (op. cit. pp. 450–1). He refused to acknowledge the potential for their using his speech; indeed, he refused to acknowledge their very existence.[16] Yet these groups could and did use his speech. It was widely reprinted and praised in the rightist press, a fact that Walser ignored, as did Schirrmacher, who neglected to include such material in his documentation of the debate or even to mention its existence.[17]

How did Walser and his supporters treat Jews in the debate itself? First of all, his remarks contained not an iota of empathy towards Jews or other victims of Nazi persecution. Nor did the letters to him that he selected for publication in the volume documenting the debate. Many of those letter writers prefaced their remarks by pointing out how much they had read about the Nazi era, how many concentration camp sites they had visited, that they had had personal contacts with Jews, and the like, to give credibility to their stance (sometimes stated outright) that they are not anti-Semitic. But they continued not with empathetic remarks about reaching out to Jews and other victims of the Nazi era, or about defending them in such debates, but with statements about Jewish control of the media, Jewish greed, how Jews manipulate Germans, and other stereotypes.[18]

Walser responded very harshly to criticism coming from Jews. Early on in the debate, he called Bubis's criticism 'nothing else but departing from the dialogue between human beings' ('nichts anderes als das Heraustreten aus dem Dialog zwischen Menschen', op. cit. p. 81). Instead of responding to Bubis's criticism, he accused him of leaving human discourse, essentially making him into a creature not to be considered part of human society. Later, Avi Primor, then the Israeli ambassador to Germany, wrote a column that began with a story from the Talmud, and explained it as a metaphor. 'A person of high standing who tolerates a stain on his coat deserves the death penalty. ... The Talmud tries to emphasise how disastrous it can be if a person regarded as a role model is careless'. (op. cit. p. 381)[19] Walser's response to this was furious:

> I consider what the ambassador says here an outrage. You understand, the image of the death penalty, that was only a metaphor. But why does he begin with a metaphor with the death penalty? Of course he says that this is about a metaphor. And still, the first image that he uses is that he who tolerates a stain on his jacket deserves the death penalty. Where is the stain on my jacket? Where is the carelessness? I tell you, I cannot tolerate this way of dealing with people. And if that fits in with a common way of dealing with people, then you shouldn't be surprised if the people start rebelling. (op. cit. pp. 460–1).[20]

Walser may have meant that he, as a writer, used language with exceeding care, and resented being accused of carelessness on that count; he went on to speak about language. But that would not explain the vehemence of his response to Primor adequately. And indeed, Walser did not respond to the content of Primor's column.

Walser's criticism of Jews did not stop short of direct verbal attacks on Bubis himself: 'And, Mr Bubis, I must tell you that I devoted my attention to this field while you were still concerned with entirely different things. You turned to these problems later, you turned to these problems later than I did' (op. cit. p. 442).[21] One must bear in mind that Walser knowingly said this to the face of a survivor who lost most of his family in the *Shoah*, and who had only narrowly survived himself.[22] The *'ganz andere Dinge'* ('entirely different things', which in German definitely carries a negative connotation in this context) that Walser referred to have been understood as Bubis's real estate dealings. A plausible interpretation is that Walser intended to claim moral superiority concerning commemoration since he believed that he had, after all, been dealing with the issue for a longer period of time than Bubis had, and that Bubis had first spent his time making money – a stereotypically 'Jewish' occupation – before turning to commemoration as a way of making non-Jewish Germans feel guilty. Bubis had stated that he had not been able to come to terms with his experiences in the *Shoah* for a long time, and had only later begun to discuss the issue in public. But rather than respecting Bubis's way of dealing with his emotional pain, Walser used it as a weapon against him in the debate. Walser's stance ignores the fact that victims' not dealing with their suffering in order to survive has a quality entirely different from perpetrators' not dealing with their crimes. This attack, too, shows how Walser created room for interpretation and association rather than using language precisely and clearly to carry his anti-Semitic attack on Bubis: one cannot take his meaning directly from his words, one must infer and interpret to capture any meaning at all.

In other places, Walser exploited Jews' remarks for his own ends. In the conversation with Bubis, he quoted the Jewish philosopher Jakob Taubes to express the idea that Jews should not criticise non-Jewish Germans, whereas Taubes had actually said that Jews were not in a position to do so.[23] In quoting a Jew rather than using his own words, Walser avoided taking responsibility for his own opinion, and attempted to deflect any potential criticism of his taking this position: after all, what can be wrong with such a stance, if it was a Jew who took it (even if the Jew he quoted meant something else)? What is more, he used this quotation by a Jew to exclude Jews from the discourse at all. This position – that Jews should not have a voice in the discourse about commemoration – ties in with Walser's concept of conscience. If and when he commemorates, he wants to do so only on his own terms, without interference from or interaction with others – least of all, the victims.

Walser's stance of not accepting Jews as legitimate participants in the discourse became apparent a second time. Near the end of their conversation, Bubis apologised for calling Walser an incendiary. Walser did not accept Bubis's apology, brushing him off and saying that he did not need one.[24] In doing so, Walser indicated again that he refused to enter into discourse with Bubis at all: had he considered Bubis someone legitimately involved in the dispute, he would not have belittled the meaning of his gesture. What is more, Walser had actually expected Bubis to apologise as a precondition for even speaking with him.[25] This is another example of an attack on Bubis, turning the tables on who had done wrong and is therefore in the position that necessitates an apology. Walser himself did not utter a word of apology. Nor did he question his own words and thoughts as to what might have provoked Bubis so strongly. Interestingly, Bubis did not demand an apology of Walser.

There may well be something to Walser's comments on references to the *Shoah* in inappropriate contexts, which can result in a cheapening or vulgarisation of the *Shoah*. Bubis and other Jews had previously commented on that problem, too, but in a very different way. Walser may also have a point in criticising the ritualistic nature of commemoration, and he repeated again and again that he was concerned about the language used in commemoration. But it is simply not credible that these issues were what Walser was actually talking about. If they were in fact his concerns, he would have expressed them clearly and unambiguously;[26] he would not have spouted anti-Semitic stereotypes (in an oblique manner); he would not have treated Jews so rudely; and he would have discussed his ideas with his critics. He would have analysed the problems he perceives, rather than making accusations; he would have put his finger on why commemoration was ritualistic; he would have teased out what exactly was the nature of the problems he saw in the use of language; and possibly, he would have developed ideas to overcome these problems. But Walser did none of that.

That the Walser-Bubis debate occurred was not an indication of a level playing field for Jews and non-Jews. On the contrary: the fact that Walser gave such a speech, and received a standing ovation, the fact that it was necessary for Bubis to respond to it (since at first nobody else did), and much that Walser and other members of Germany's elites said in the ensuing debate, showed that the cultural mindset of empathy with and respect for the other as a matter of course – a prerequisite for discourse in civil society – is simply not yet prevalent. It is important to remember that many of those supporting Walser's point of view are not members of the extreme right: on the contrary, they represent part of Germany's elites and educated middle class. They include such pillars of society as Rudolf Augstein (editor of *Der Spiegel* until his death in 2002), Klaus von Dohnanyi (former mayor of Hamburg), and Frank Schirrmacher (one of the publishers of the *Frankfurter Allgemeine Zeitung*), who gave the address in praise of Walser as peace prize recipient, organised the conversation between Walser and Bubis, and wrote a column more supportive of Walser as a commentary on that conversation.

Even though the Walser-Bubis debate of 1998/9 is over, the topic itself is still alive. For example, the German Social Democratic Party staged an election-year event titled '*Nation. Patriotismus. Demokratische Kultur.*' ('Nation. Patriotism. Democratic Culture.') on the symbolic date of 8 May 2002, the anniversary of the end of the Second World War in Germany. The event featured two speakers: Chancellor Gerhard Schröder, who spoke on the theme of the event, and none other than Martin Walser, on '*Über ein Geschichtsgefühl*' ('On a Feeling about History'). His speech echoed many themes of his 1998 peace prize speech. The choice of speaker shows, at the very least, that Walser's ideas are still of interest, and not only to the extreme right wing: the Social Democratic Party (SPD) is, after all, a centre-left party. In giving Walser such a prominent platform, the SPD legitimised his views, even endorsing them by inviting him rather than someone else. The response to Walser's speech at the SPD event was more critical than the response to his peace prize speech, yet Schröder, for example, did not distance himself from Walser.[27]

Jews have little to gain from participating in such debates. The best outcome that Jews can hope for in such disputes is that more people realise that anti-Semitism does in fact still exist. These debates are about defending Jews' basic civil liberties: their recognition as equals in society whose voices deserve to be heard, and even that does not always succeed. Jews come out of such debates feeling less secure in their status in society as Jews, indeed bruised. Bubis himself commented shortly before his death, 'I have achieved nothing or almost nothing' and 'A large part of the population thinks like Martin Walser' (*Stern* interview, 1999). Also, given the small number of Jews in many post-*Shoah* societies, Jews' scarce resources (including intellectual manpower) are bound up in such debates. This makes it more difficult for Jews to devote their time and resources to rebuilding Jewish life and developing positions on issues of more intrinsic value to them. These debates can reinforce the stereotype of Jews as perpetual victims even when the non-Jewish side denies that anti-Semitism is even an issue, as in the Walser-Bubis debate: then, they perceive Jews as people claiming falsely to be victims, which reinforces yet another anti-Semitic stereotype: that Jews cannot be trusted since they do not reliably speak the truth. On the other hand, of course, it is essential for Jews to protest against unacceptable anti-Semitic speech and deeds, especially in a situation where non-Jews may not necessarily be relied upon to do so.

What makes this type of debate so difficult is the emotional situation on both sides. Jews, living with the losses and the continuing impact of the *Shoah*, are of course sensitive even to traces of anti-Semitism, and tend to be aware of this. Non-Jews, too, are emotionally bound by their role in the *Shoah* and by the responsibility it placed on following generations, but seem less aware of their emotional scars. They also seem less aware of the vestiges of anti-Semitism that are often present in their own attitudes and upbringing.[28] When Jews and non-Jews debate face to face like this, these emotional issues stand in the way of mutually respectful discourse. To oversimplify, Jews feel, 'there they go again, those anti-Semites, hurting us yet again; what will they do next?' and non-Jews feel, 'there they go again, those Jews, trying to make us feel bad, even though we younger people didn't do anything wrong'. Jews – by their very existence – seem to be seen as a living reproach, a constant reminder of the *Shoah*, regardless of what they say or do. In addition, Jews need to argue against the belief held by many non-Jews that anti-Semitism has been overcome and that, in any case, they themselves (the non-Jews) are not anti-Semitic. (Walser doubtless does not consider himself anti-Semitic, and he defended those who wrote to him against the idea that some of them might be anti-Semitic; op. cit. p. 449). Indeed, anti-Semitism seems to have been silently redefined as a phenomenon of the past or of a few fringe lunatics, as an attitude held only by those who actually killed Jews in concentration camps in the *Shoah*. So when non-Jews today are accused of anti-Semitism, they respond viciously, as though they had been accused of murder. The confrontation of these emotional situations on both sides helps to explain why these conflicts evoke such sharp and vitriolic responses. Emotions and emotional responses must certainly be a legitimate part of any discourse (humans are intensely emotional creatures, after all); awareness of the emotions on both sides, and respect and empathy for them, must form the foundation of discourse if it is to be successful.

If there was a lasting effect of the Walser-Bubis debate, it was certainly not to strengthen Jews' role in civil society; on the contrary, it enhanced Walser's status. After all, it was Bubis, not Walser, who retracted his statement. Bubis lost face, not Walser. Bubis admitted he had been wrong, not Walser, and in taking the role of the guilty party, Bubis was seen to have absolved Walser of any wrongdoing or guilt. In that sense, Walser won the debate, and Bubis lost. Without the debate, Walser might not have been called upon for a high-profile event with the Chancellor. Like many debates about Jews and anti-Semitism in Germany before and since, the Walser–Bubis debate did not show mutual respect and empathy between Jews and non-Jews, but an atmosphere which permitted anti-Semitic sentiment to be expressed, discussed, and defended for months on end without an immediate, strong, and unequivocal response by mainstream society. To be sure, there was also support for Bubis; but only after he alone had protested Walser's speech. It is the lack of an unequivocal public response that is problematic, much more than the views of one particular writer.

Notes

The author expresses her gratitude to Dr Steven Less for his careful reading and thoughtful comments on this piece. It was originally a comment of Less's on 'Caught Between Civil Society and the Cultural Market: Jewry and the Jewish Space in Europe. A Response to Diana Pinto' (Chapter 10 in this volume) that encouraged me to write this chapter. Special thanks also to Arne Behrensen for calling the existence of the documentation by Dietzsch et al. to my attention.

1. This quip has been attributed at least to Austrian-Jewish writer Jean Amery, German-Jewish publicist Henryk Broder, German journalist Eike Geisel, and Israeli psycho-analyst Zvi Rex, whose name is given most frequently. Apologies if its true author is not mentioned.
2. The chapter can be read without referring to the notes for an understanding and interpretation of the debate. The notes provide evidence to document exactly what Walser and his supporters actually said, and give more background and depth.
3. For a more general discussion of the debate which sets it in the contexts of politics and of discourse about the *Shoah*, but does not analyse the intricacies of Walser's argument, his anti-Semitism, and his language, see Riemer.
4. Walser was accused of misinterpreting the quotations he used in this speech: see, e.g., Klaus Georg Koch on his use of Hegel, Heidegger, and Kleist (Schirrmacher 1999: 209–12), Maya Rauch on his interpretation of Kleist (op. cit. p. 588–9), and Dieter Borchmeyer on his use of Thomas Mann (esp. op. cit. p. 610–11).

5. Schirrmacher (1999) documents much of the debate between Walser and Bubis and includes contributions to the public debate, as well as dozens of letters written directly to Walser or Bubis which each selected from the hundreds he received. A number of letter-writers, including prominent ones, refused permission to reprint their letters in this volume (op. cit. p. 681), their names are not recorded.

    A second volume documenting the debate is *Endlich ein normales Volk? Vom rechten Verständnis der Friedenspreis-Rede Martin Walsers – Eine Dokumentation* (*A Normal People at Last? On the Right-Wing* [or: *Correct*] *Understanding of Martin Walser's Peace Prize Speech. A Documentation*) (Dietzsch 1999). The play on words in the title is intended, as explained in the introduction (op. cit. p. 6). The collection includes articles and columns from different categories of the press: the opinion leaders of the extreme right-wing press; a 'grey area' of the press located between the extreme right wing and staunch conservatism; the press of the *Vertriebene* (Germans forced to leave previously German areas after the Second World War, e.g., Pomerania and Silesia); the press of *Shoah* deniers; other anti-Semitic ideologues and militant Neonazis; and a few items from a category called 'the extremism of the centre'. This final category includes material from the mainstream press: an interview with Horst Mahler (a previously leftist lawyer who had been a member of the terrorist organisation *Rote Armee Fraktion*, now with the extreme right-wing National Democratic Party) in *Focus*, one of the two leading weekly news magazines; a commentary by Rudolf Augstein, editor until his death in 2002 of *Der Spiegel*, the other leading weekly news magazine; a contribution by Kathi-Gesa Klafke, a German university student, in *Der Spiegel*; and four letters to the editor published in the *Frankfurter Allgemeine Zeitung*. Without exception, all the material documented supports Walser and/or attacks Bubis or other Jewish positions in the debate.

    With just one exception (the piece by Klafke in *Der Spiegel*), none of the more than eighty items documented in *Endlich ein normales Volk?* is included in Schirrmacher's volume, not even the material from the mainstream press. In his epilogue, he writes that he 'documents the most important texts' (Schirrmacher 1999: 681). If the reader were therefore to assume that Schirrmacher gives an accurate representation of the debate, albeit one which did not perhaps include every last piece published, he or she would miss entirely the extreme right-wing contributions, whose existence Schirrmacher does not even mention. This is disturbing for three reasons: the content of the right-wing publications themselves, the proximity of the mainstream debate to them, and the denial both of their existence and of the proximity of the mainstream debate to the extreme right wing. Schirrmacher may have decided to exclude right-wing material to avoid giving its authors additional exposure or credibility; however, he did not say that he had done so. His volume also omits the article by Rommelspacher quoted in this chapter.

6. For example, quoting from a speech he gave in 1977, Walser said:

    "Wir dürften, sage ich vor Kühnheit zitternd, die BRD so wenig anerkennen wie die DDR. Wir müssen die Wunde namens Deutschland offenhalten." Das fällt mir ein, weil ich jetzt wieder vor Kühnheit zittere, wenn ich sage: Auschwitz eignet sich nicht dafür, Drohroutine zu werden, jederzeit einsetzbares Einschüchterungsmittel oder Moralkeule oder auch nur Pflichtübung. Was durch solche Ritualisierung zustande kommt, ist von der Qualität Lippengebet (Schirrmacher 1999: 13).

    "Trembling with audacity, I say that we should not recognise the Federal Republic of Germany, just as we do not recognise the German Democratic Republic. We must keep the wound called Germany open." That occurs to me because now again, I am trembling with audacity when I say: Auschwitz is not suitable as a routine way of threatening, an always available means of intimidation or a moral cudgel or even just a compulsory exercise. That which comes out of such ritualisation has the quality of a muttered prayer.

7.   Walser did not deny the historical fact of the *Shoah*:

'Kein ernstzunehmender Mensch leugnet Auschwitz; kein noch zurechnungsfähiger Mensch deutelt an der Grauenhaftigkeit von Auschwitz herum; wenn mir aber jeden Tag in den Medien diese Vergangenheit vorgehalten wird, merke ich, daß sich in mir etwas gegen diese Dauerpräsentation unserer Schande wehrt. Anstatt dankbar zu sein für die unaufhörliche Präsentation unserer Schande, fange ich an wegzuschauen. Ich möchte verstehen, warum in diesem Jahrzehnt die Vergangenheit präsentiert wird wie noch nie zuvor. Wenn ich merke, daß sich in mir etwas dagegen wehrt, versuche ich, die Vorhaltung unserer Schande auf Motive hin abzuhören, und bin fast froh, wenn ich glaube, entdecken zu können, daß öfter nicht mehr das Gedenken, das Nichtvergessendürfen das Motiv ist, sondern die Instrumentalisierung unserer Schande zu gegenwärtigen Zwecken (op. cit. pp. 11–2).'

'No person to be taken seriously denies Auschwitz; no sane person quibbles about the horrors of Auschwitz; but if I am reproached for this past every day in the media, I notice that something in me rebels against this constant presentation of our disgrace. Instead of being thankful for the unceasing presentation of our disgrace, I begin to look away. I want to understand why the past is presented in this decade as never before. When I notice that something in me rebels, I try to analyse the reproach of our disgrace for motives, and I am almost pleased when I believe I can discover that often the motive is no longer commemoration, not being permitted to forget, but the exploitation of our disgrace for current purposes.'

8.   Speaking about how he would have had to defend speaking about beautiful things in this speech if he had decided to do so, whereas people expected a critical lecture of him:

'Daß ich mein Potpourri des Schönen hätte rechtfertigen müssen, war mir schon klar. Am besten mit solchen Geständnissen: Ich verschließe mich Übeln, an deren Behebung ich nicht mitwirken kann. Ich habe lernen müssen wegzuschauen. Ich habe mehrere Zufluchtwinkel, in die sich mein Blick sofort flüchtet, wenn mir der Bildschirm die Welt als eine unerträgliche vorführt. Ich finde, meine Reaktion sei verhältnismäßig. Unerträgliches muß ich nicht ertragen können. Auch im Wegdenken bin ich geübt. An der Disqualifizierung des Verdrängens kann ich mich nicht beteiligen. Freud rät, Verdrängen durch Verurteilung zu ersetzen. Aber soweit ich sehe, gilt seine Aufklärungsarbeit nicht dem Verhalten des Menschen als Zeitgenossen, sondern dem vom eigenen Triebschicksal Geschüttelten. Ich käme ohne Wegschauen und Wegdenken nicht durch den Tag und schon gar nicht durch die Nacht. Ich bin auch nicht der Ansicht, daß alles gesühnt werden muß. In einer Welt, in der alles gesühnt werden müßte, könnte ich nicht leben' (op. cit. p. 8).

'It was clear to me that I would have had to justify my potpourri of beautiful things. The best way to do so would be with such confessions: I shut myself off from evils that I cannot help to rectify. I have had to learn to look away. I have several corners of refuge into which my eye flees immediately when the [television] screen presents me the world as an unbearable one. I think my response is proportionate. I need not be able to bear the unbearable. I am also practised in thinking away [a term Walser coins, as in 'looking away' – SL]. I cannot participate in declaring repression inappropriate. Freud advises one to replace repression with condemnation. But as far as I can tell, his labour of enlightenment applies not to the behaviour of man as a contemporary, but to him who is rattled by his own destiny of drives. Without looking away and thinking away, I would not make it through the day, much less through the night. I am also not of the opinion that everything must be atoned for. I could not live in a world in which everything would have to be atoned for'.

9.   The conscience is central to Walser's argument. In his view, the individual develops a conscience by himself, on his own terms, independent of interaction with his fellow

human beings; in other words, the conscience needs no direction from any moral authority. After quoting Heidegger and Hegel, he summarises:

'Ein gutes Gewissen ist keins. Mit seinem Gewissen ist jeder allein. Öffentliche Gewissensakte sind deshalb in der Gefahr, symbolisch zu werden. Und nichts ist dem Gewissen fremder als Symbolik, wie gut sie auch gemeint sei. Diese "durchgängige Zurückgezogenheit in sich selbst" ist nicht repräsentierbar. Sie muß "innerliche Einsamkeit" bleiben. Es kann keiner vom anderen verlangen, was er gern hätte, der aber nicht geben will' (op. cit. p. 14).'

'A clean conscience is no conscience at all. Each person is alone with his conscience. Public acts of conscience are there in danger of becoming symbolic. And nothing is more alien to the conscience than symbolism, even though it may have been meant well. This "constant withdrawal into one's self" [Hegel] cannot be represented. It must remain "inner solitude" [Hegel]. No one can demand of another what he would like, but what the other does not want to give'.

Walser goes on to interpret a quotation from a play by Heinrich von Kleist:

'Also, es wird ganz vom Gefühl des Verurteilten abhängig gemacht, ob das Todesurteil vollzogen wird. Wenn der Verurteilte das Urteil für ungerecht halten kann, ist er frei. Das ist Gewissensfreiheit, die ich meine' (op. cit. p. 14).

'So, it depends entirely on the convicted person's feeling whether or not the death penalty is executed. If the convicted can consider the verdict unfair, then he is free. That is the freedom of the conscience that I mean'.

Walser expanded on his concept of conscience in his conversation with Bubis.

'Herr Bubis, das sage ich Ihnen: Ich will meinen Seelenfrieden, verstehen Sie? Und wie ich ihn kriege, das ist in mir, das ist mein Gewissenshaushalt. Und da lasse ich mir von niemandem, auch nicht von Ihnen, dreinreden. Mein Gewissen bleibt mein Gewissen'. (op. cit. p. 449).

'Mr. Bubis, let me tell you this: I want my peace of mind, do you understand? And how I get it is my business, that is the balance sheet of my conscience. And I do not let anyone, including you, interfere with that. My conscience remains my conscience'.

And:

'Ich habe vom Gewissen gesprochen, das man nur für sich hat, und mit dem man allein ist, und das sich keine Vorschriften machen lassen darf' (op. cit. p. 459).

'I spoke about one's conscience which one has only for oneself, with which one is alone, and which must not permit itself to be dictated to'.

10.   'Aber in welchen Verdacht gerät man, wenn man sagt, die Deutschen seien jetzt ein normales Volk, eine gewöhnliche Gesellschaft?' (op. cit. p. 13).

'But what does one get suspected of if one says that the Germans are now a normal people, an ordinary society?'

11.   Whether or not Walser intentionally used a subtext to convey his message is a question only he himself could answer, were he so inclined.

12.   Walser placed himself firmly on '*die Seite der Beschuldigten*' ('the side of the accused'; op. cit. p. 11). Not using the term 'the side of the perpetrators' or 'the side of the guilty' indicates that he did not acknowledge the Germans' guilt or responsibility for the crimes of the *Shoah*, nor felt shame because of them; on the contrary. In using the term 'the accused', he shifted attention to the accuser (whom he did not name) and placed the perpetrators and himself in the place of victims of accusation. This leaves open the possibility that 'the accused' are innocent, thereby potentially even victims of false accusation. Such a situation would mean that the accusers were in fact the guilty party, in effect turning the tables on historical reality. In addition, in this view, it is the accusers who are causing the problem, so it is they who have the power to end it: if they shut up

and went away, the problem would be over – a shifting of responsibility. When it comes to commemoration, Walser again saw himself as the victim. He seemed to feel the need to defend himself, but did not specify who he felt was attacking him: 'intellectual(s)' (op. cit. p. 11, twice on p. 12), 'the media' (p. 11, twice), 'thinkers' and 'writers' (each on pp. 10 and 14), 'a name worthy of admiration in the intellectually authoritative weekly newspaper' (p. 10), 'someone' (p. 12), 'people … who feel responsible for other people's consciences' (p. 13), and finally, 'soldiers of opinion … when they coerce the writer into opinion service at moral gunpoint' ('Meinungssoldaten … wenn sie, mit vorgehaltener Moralpistole, den Schriftsteller in den Meinungsdienst nötigen') (p. 15). Walser also used the passive voice, e.g., on pp. 11 and 12, to accuse without naming the accused. These characterisations are typical anti-Semitic stereotypes of Jews: as know-it-all intellectuals, as controllers of the media, and as morally superior people.

13. An example from Walser's speech may illustrate this. Near the beginning of his speech, when talking about his thoughts and feelings while selecting a topic for it, he said he felt that people expected the following of him:

> 'Er wird fünfundzwanzig oder gar dreißig Minuten lang nur Schönes sagen, das heißt Wohltuendes, Belebendes, Friedenspreismäßiges. Zum Beispiel Bäume rühmen, die er durch absichtsloses Anschauen seit langem kennt. Und gleich der Rechtfertigungszwang: Über Bäume zu reden ist kein Verbrechen mehr, weil inzwischen so viele von ihnen krank sind' (op. cit. p. 7).

> 'He [Walser] will say only beautiful things for twenty-five or even thirty minutes, that is, pleasant things, invigorating things, things fitting for the peace prize. For example, praising trees which he has known for a long time by looking at them without intention. And immediately be forced to defend himself. Talking about trees is no longer a crime, since so many of them are sick'.

This passage cannot be understood in a literary context without reference to an often quoted excerpt from Bertolt Brecht's poem 'An die Nachgeborenen' ('To Future Generations'):

> Was sind das für Zeiten, wo
> Ein Gespräch über Bäume fast ein Verbrechen ist
> Weil es ein Schweigen über so viele Untaten einschließt!
> What times are these, where
> A conversation about trees is almost a crime
> Because it includes silence about so many atrocities!

Beginning with Brecht: to talk about trees, a symbol of life, means not to talk about atrocities, and not to talk about atrocities is in itself almost a crime. When Brecht wrote this poem, he was in exile, and he clearly meant the atrocities committed by the Nazis. What might Walser mean? One may plausibly interpret him as suggesting that he might like to talk about trees. But if he did so, he would be attacked for not talking about atrocities. Yet, according to Walser, to talk about trees is no longer a crime. The reason it is no longer a crime is not because the atrocities have been atoned for and the perpetrators have made amends – Walser does not mention this possible reason – , but because so many of the trees are sick. (One might continue this interpretation with the allusion to *Waldsterben*, the dying of the forest, that near-holy symbol of Germanness, but I leave that for another place and time.)

Walser saw himself forced into the defensive if he were to choose to talk about trees, not atrocities, but he did not say by whom. His defence for choosing to ignore speaking about atrocities was that so many trees are sick, i.e., are victims of sickness. So Walser's victims were no longer the victims of atrocities, but the trees as victims of sickness, and he himself also the victim of a potential attack by an unnamed attacker. In this way, he – not explicitly, but by widely understood allusion – switched the roles of victims and perpetrators: Brecht's perpetrators are clearly the Nazis, the victims are victims of the Nazis; Walser's perpetrators are unnamed attackers (at this point; more on this issue becomes visible later on), his victims are the trees, in a symbolic sense, and above all, Walser himself. It is unlikely that Walser was not aware of Brecht's poem and his own abuse of the quotation.

In reality, the recipient of the peace prize is free to speak on a topic of his or her choice. If Walser feels compelled to raise the issue of the *Shoah* (in whatever way: as the explicit theme of his talk, or named as a subject he chose not to talk about), the need to do so must come from Walser himself.

14. Walser mentioned a book he had written that traced a Jewish family's process of assimilation, and criticised a critic's reproach that it did not mention Auschwitz (op. cit. p. 12).

15. 'Nun stellen Sie sich vor, in einer Rede in der Paulskirche, die ausschließlich an ein deutsches Publikum und nicht an den Staat gerichtet ist, die sich hauptsächlich in ihrem Kritikbestand an die Medien wendet, da werde ich über die Ansprüche von Zwangsarbeitern oder überhaupt für irgendein ausländisches Problem sprechen – das liegt mir so fern' (op. cit. p. 444).

'Now imagine, in a speech in St Paul's church [the venue of the peace prize award ceremony – SL] that is directed exclusively at a German audience and not at the state, whose criticism is directed mainly at the media, in such a speech, I would speak about the claims of forced labourers or for any foreign problem whatsoever – nothing is further from my thoughts'.

16. In his speech:

'Warum werde ich von der Empörung, die dem Denker den folgenden Satzanfang gebietet, nicht mobilisiert: "Wenn die sympathisierende Bevölkerung vor brennenden Asylantenheimen Würstchenbuden aufstellt ..." Das muß man sich vorstellen: Die Bevölkerung sympathisiert mit denen, die Asylantenheime angezündet haben, und stellt deshalb Würstchenbuden vor die brennenden Asylantenheime, um auch noch Geschäfte zu machen. Und ich muß zugeben, daß ich mir das, wenn ich es nicht in der intellektuell maßgeblichen Wochenzeitung und unter einem verehrungswürdigen Namen läse, nicht vorstellen könnte. ... Ich kann solche Aussagen nicht bestreiten; dazu sind sowohl der Denker als auch der Dichter zu seriöse Größen. Aber – und das ist offenbar meine moralisch-politische Schwäche – genausowenig kann ich ihnen zustimmen. Meine nichts als triviale Reaktion auf solche schmerzhaften Sätze: Hoffentlich stimmt's nicht, was uns da so kraß gesagt wird. Und um mich vollends zu entblößen: Ich kann diese Schmerz erzeugenden Sätze, die ich weder unterstützen noch bestreiten kann, einfach nicht glauben. Es geht sozusagen über meine moralisch-politische Phantasie hinaus, das, was da gesagt wird, für wahr zu halten. Bei mir stellt sich eine unbeweisbare Ahnung ein: Die, die mit solchen Sätzen auftreten, wollen uns weh tun, weil sie finden, wir haben das verdient. Wahrscheinlich wollen sie auch sich selber verletzen. Aber uns auch. Alle. Eine Einschränkung: alle Deutschen. Denn das ist schon klar: In keiner anderen Sprache könnte im letzten Viertel des 20. Jahrhunderts so von einem Volk, von einer Bevölkerung, einer Gesellschaft gesprochen werden. Das kann man nur von Deutschen sagen. Allenfalls noch, soweit ich sehe, von Österreichern' (op. cit. pp. 10–11).

'Why am I not mobilised by the indignation that compels the thinker to write the following beginning of a sentence: "When the sympathising population sets up hot dog stands in front of burning residences of asylum seekers ...". Imagine: the population sympathises with those who have set fire to asylum seekers' residences, and because of that, sets up hot dog stands in front of the burning asylum seekers' residences to make money to boot. And I must admit that I could not imagine it if I were not to read it in the intellectually authoritative weekly under a commendable name. ... I cannot deny such statements; both the thinker and the writer are too respectable to do that. But – and that seems to be my moral-political weakness – I can agree with them just as little. My nothing other than trivial reaction to such painful sentences: hopefully, what is told us so crassly isn't true. And to expose myself altogether: I can simply not believe these sentences that cause pain, that I can neither support nor deny. So to speak, it goes beyond my moral-political imagination to consider what is said there to be true. An unprovable intuitive feeling comes to mind: those who come out with such sentences want to hurt us, because they feel that we deserve it. They probably want to hurt themselves, too. But us, too. All of us. One qualification: all Germans. Because that is already clear: in no other language could one speak like that of a people, a population, a society in the last quarter of the twentieth century. One can say that only of Germans. At the most, as far as I can tell, of Austrians, too.'

First of all, this quotation shows Walser's disregard of the reality of popular sentiment against foreigners: he simply refuses to believe it, although he claims he trusts his source. The quotation is also another example of how he turns the tables: rather than acknowledging that the asylum seekers whose residences are firebombed are the victims in the situation he discusses, and that those who committed arson and those who supported them are the perpetrators of these egregious crimes, and rather than condemning them, he accuses those who criticise those crimes and their perpetrators and sympathisers of doing so with the intent of hurting him – Walser – and, indeed, all Germans.

In the discussion with Bubis, he said,

'Für mich existiert die Nationalzeitung nicht' (op. cit. p. 460). 'From my point of view, the *Nationalzeitung* [an extreme right wing newspaper] does not exist'.

17. See n. 4.
18. For example, Volker Fieber writes in a letter to Walser:

'Ihre Frankfurter Rede war wirklich nicht mißverständlich. Wir, die "normalen deutschen Bürger", haben Sie schon richtig verstanden und empfinden Ihre Worte tatsächlich befreiend. … Warum lassen Sie sich auf Diskussionen mit Ignatz Bubis ein? Herr Bubis meint und will etwas völlig anderes als Sie. Seine Ziele unterscheiden sich grundsätzlich von Ihren Gedanken, denen Macht und finanzieller oder politischer Einfluß nicht als Antrieb gelten. Sie werden mit Herrn Bubis immer aneinander vorbeireden. Erschreckend aus den zahlreichen Beiträgen ist auch die Erkenntnis, wie jüdische Kreise unser Denken und Äußern manipulieren und "allen Deutschen" ein Nationalzeitungsdenken verordnen wollen. … Erinnerungen wach zu halten heißt nicht, instrumentierte [*sic*! He must mean 'instrumentalisierte' – SL] Aussagen ständig in Medien zu wiederholen, monströse, unsinnige Denkmäler zu bauen und der Welt ein ganzes Volk zeitlos in Sippenhaftschande und als Täter vorzuführen, verbunden mit immer neuen finanziellen Forderungen. … Nur durch Lernen und Ändern falschen Verhaltens kann ein gutes Zusammenleben von Deutschen und Juden in Deutschland entstehen. Aktivitäten von Juden um Ignatz Bubis und Michel Friedman oder ehemals Werner Nachmann und Heinz Galinski fördern nicht unser friedvolles Miteinander. … Ich bin übrigens kein Antisemit. Im Gegenteil. Meine Frau erhält zu Weihnachten ein Buch von Michael Wolffsohn und nächstes Jahr wollen wir Israel besuchen, um Land und Leute ohne Vorurteile kennenzulernen. Also, lassen Sie weiter von sich hören, verehrter Herr Walser, oder besser noch–im Fernsehen etwas von sich sehen. Wir, die "normalen Bürger" – einschließlich der Juden in Deutschland – werden es Ihnen danken (op. cit. pp. 468–9).

'Your speech in Frankfurt was really not to be misunderstood. We, the "normal German citizens", understood you correctly and indeed feel your words to be liberating. … Why do you get involved in discussions with Ignatz Bubis? Mr. Bubis means and wants something entirely different from you. His goals are fundamentally different from your thoughts which are not driven by power and financial or political influence. You and Mr. Bubis will always talk past each other. The insight from the many contributions is frightening: how Jewish circles manipulate our thinking and expression and want to classify "all Germans'" thinking as though it were from the *Nationalzeitung* [an extremist right-wing newspaper]. ... Keeping memories awake does not mean constantly repeating exploited statements in the media, building monstrous, senseless monuments [a reference to the Memorial for the Murdered Jews of Europe in Berlin], and presenting to the world an entire people in the disgrace of collective detention and as perpetrators for all time, combined with new financial demands again and again. ... Only through learning and changing wrong behaviour can Germans and Jews live together well in Germany. Activities of Jews around Ignatz Bubis and Michel Friedman, or formerly Werner Nachmann and Heinz Galinski, do not promote our peaceful cooperation. ... I am, by the way, not an anti-Semite. On the contrary. My wife will receive a book by Michael Wolffsohn [a contemporary German-Jewish historian – SL] for Christmas, and next year we want to visit Israel to get to know the country and the people without prejudice. So, Mr Walser, let us hear more from you, or, better still – see you on television. We, the "normal citizens" – including the Jews in Germany – will thank you for it.'

19. 'Ein geistig Hochstehender, der auf seinem Rock einen Fleck duldet, hat die Todesstrafe verdient. ... Der Talmud versucht zu betonen, wie verhängnisvoll eine Nachlässigkeit eines Menschen, der als Vorbild gilt, sein kann'.

20. '[W]as der Botschafter hier sagt, halte ich für eine Unverschämtheit. Verstehen Sie, das Bild mit der Todesstrafe, das war nur eine Metapher. Aber warum fängt er mit einer Metapher mit der Todesstrafe an? Er sagt natürlich, es gehe hier um eine Metapher. Und trotzdem ist das erste Bild, das er einführt, daß der eine Todesstrafe verdient hat, der einen Fleck auf seinem Rock duldet. Wo ist der Fleck auf meinem Rock? Wo ist die Nachlässigkeit? Ich sage Ihnen, diesen Umgang mit Menschen ertrage ich nicht. Und wenn das einer bisher eingeführten Umgangsart entspricht, dann müssen Sie sich nicht wundern, wenn die Leute sich wehren'.

21. 'Und, Herr Bubis, da muß ich Ihnen sagen, ich war in diesem Feld beschäftigt, da waren Sie noch mit ganz anderen Dingen beschäftigt. Sie haben sich diesen Problemen später zugewendet; Sie haben sich diesen Problemen später zugewendet als ich'.

22. Ellen Presser, quoting Anita Kaminski, wrote,
'Bubis und Walser sind beide 1927 geboren. Bei Kriegsende waren sie 17 Jahre jung: "Ignatz Bubis ist ohne Zweifel Opfer gewesen, Walser aber kein Täter"' (op. cit. p. 509).
'Bubis and Walser were both born in 1927. At the end of the war they were 17 years young: "Ignatz Bubis was doubtless a victim, but Walser was not a perpetrator."' Walser joined the *Wehrmacht* as a volunteer aged sixteen, but he probably did not commit atrocities himself.

23. 'Es ist kein Geheimnis, daß ich Jude bin, und zwar bewußt und Erzjude als solcher, und das bringt für mich einige Probleme mit sich, überhaupt in deutschen Landen. Konträr zu dem, was viele tun, bringt mich das in die Lage, mich des Urteils zu enthalten. Über viele Dinge zögere ich, den Stab zu brechen, weil wir als Juden in all dem unaussprechlichen Grauen, das geschehen ist, vor einem bewahrt geblieben sind, nämlich mitzumachen. Wir hatten keine Wahl. Und wer keine Wahl hat, das heißt, ich war gar nicht gegen Hitler, sondern Hitler war gegen mich. Wer keine Wahl hat, ist auch im Urteil eingeschränkt. Das heißt, er kann nicht beurteilen, was die Faszination anderer ist, die stolpern, die rutschen, die wollen, die fasziniert sind. Jedenfalls wird es für ihn ein Problem der Faszination' (op. cit. p. 452).

'It is no secret that I am a Jew, in fact consciously so and an arch-Jew as such, and I believe that is problematic, in any case in Germany. Contrary to what many do, it puts me in a position to abstain from judgement. There are many things that I hesitate to condemn, because in all the unspeakable horrors that happened, we as Jews were spared one thing, and that is participating. We had no choice. And he who has no choice, that means, I wasn't against Hitler, but Hitler was against me. He who has no choice is also restricted in his judgement. That means, he cannot judge what others' fascination is, those who stumble, who slip, who desire, who are fascinated. In any case it becomes a problem of fascination for him.'

24. Towards the end of the conversation between Walser and Bubis, there was the following exchange:

> **Bubis:** ... Aber ich möchte jetzt versuchen, zu einer Klärung zu kommen: Wie verbleiben wir?
>
> **Schirrmacher:** Also, was ist jetzt der Stand der Dinge?
>
> **Walser:** Also ich finde, wir haben ein zumindest sehr lebendiges Gespräch gehabt. Und wir sind dabei nicht ...
>
> **Bubis:** Und ein wichtiges.
>
> **Walser:** ... ein wichtiges, und wir müssen nicht davon ausgehen, wie sehr der eine den anderen überzeugt hat. Das, was wir miteinander gesprochen haben, das darf auch einmal in deutscher Öffentlichkeit friedlich gesagt werden. Und wenn es gesagt werden kann, dann ist das schon etwas.
>
> **Bubis:** Ich darf Ihnen mein Fazit sagen. Ich kann so viel sagen: Nachdem Sie in diesem Gespräch Ihren Standpunkt erläutert haben, nehme ich den Ausdruck geistiger Brandstifter zurück.
>
> **Walser:** Das brauchen Sie nicht. Ich bin keine Instanz, vor der man was zurücknimmt. Ich bin kein Offizier aus dem Casino. Ich brauche das nicht. ... (op. cit. pp. 463–4)

> **Bubis:** ... But I would like to try to achieve a clarification now: what shall we agree on?
>
> **Schirrmacher:** Well, how do things stand now?
>
> **Walser:** Well, I think that we have had a conversation that was at the least very lively. And during it, we did not ...
>
> **Bubis:** And an important one.
>
> **Walser:** ... an important one, and we need not assume how much one of us convinced the other. That which we have said to each other, that can be said peacefully in public in Germany. And if it can be said, then that is something already.
>
> **Bubis:** Let me tell you my conclusion. I can say this much: after you explained your position in this conversation, I retract the expression incendiary.
>
> **Walser:** You need not do that. I am not an authority before which one takes things back. I am not an officer from an officers' club. I do not need that. ...

25. In their conversation, Walser said:

> 'Herr Bubis, ich will Ihnen jetzt etwas sagen. Man hat mir gelegentlich öffentlich wie privat gesagt, daß ich mich doch endlich mit Herrn Bubis treffen müsse. Das hat man Ihnen umgekehrt auch gesagt. Und dann hat man Ihnen gesagt, solange Sie den Vorwurf des Brandstifters erheben, könne es kein Treffen geben. Und dann haben Sie gesagt, daß sich erst in einem Gespräch klären kann, ob man den Vorwurf zurücknehmen könne. Und da, das sage ich Ihnen, daraufhin hätte ich eigentlich nie mit Ihnen ein Gespräch führen dürfen. Wissen Sie warum? Sie hätten mich schon wieder auf Bewährung empfangen. Deutsche müssen beweisen, daß sie human sind, eo ipso sind sie es nicht. Ich soll mich im Gespräch mit Ignatz Bubis bewähren' (op. cit. p. 462).

'Mr Bubis, let me tell you something now. People told me on occasion in public and in private that I should finally meet with Mr Bubis. Conversely, people told you that, too. And then one told you that there could not be a meeting as long as you accuse me of being an incendiary. And then you said that one could only clarify in a conversation whether it is possible to retract the accusation. And then, I tell you this, then I should actually never have had a conversation with you. Do you know why? You would have received me on probation again. Germans must prove that they are humane, *eo ipso* they are not. I am supposed to prove myself in a conversation with Ignatz Bubis'.

26. Walser's linguistic capabilities are undisputed, as in Friedrich Hitzer's characterisation in his letter to Bubis:

    'barocken Meisterstilisten der Formel I des Literaturbetriebs' ('baroque master stylist of the Formula I of the literature business'); (op. cit. p. 39).

27. This was not the last time Walser made headlines. His novel *Tod eines Kritikers* (*Death of a Critic*) (Walser 2002), which immediately topped the bestseller lists, triggered a controversy about whether or not it was anti-Semitic even before it was published in the summer of 2002.

28. A recent study (Welzer 2002) explores the emotional side of 'normal' non-Jewish Germans' consciousness of the Nazi era and the *Shoah* based on interviews with three generations of family members. The mental images gained from family situations have the quality of certitude, as against the book-learning from history classes at school. In the family narrative, the persecution of the Jews is marginalised, and none of the family members' actions are perceived as part of the *Shoah*. The certitude that one's own family members were heroes (at times even despite stories told to the contrary) clashes with the book-learning about the persecution of the Jews.

Bibliography

Dietzsch, Martin, Siegfried Jäger, and Alfred Schobert, eds. 1999. *Endlich ein normales Volk? Vom rechten Verständnis der Friedenspreis-Rede Martin Walsers – Eine Dokumentation.* [*A Normal People at Last? On the Right-Wing (or: Correct) Understanding of Martin Walser's Peace Prize Speech. A Documentation.*] Duisburg, Duisburger Institut für Sprach- und Sozialforschung (see also http://members.aol.com/dissdui).

Riemer, Jeremiah M. 'Germany Reaches a Crossroad'. *Dimensions* 13(1): 3–8.

Rommelspacher, Birgit. 1999. 'Öffentliches Reden, privates Schweigen' ['Public speaking, private silence']. *Christ und Sozialist/Christin und Sozialistin* 1–2.

Schirrmacher, Frank, ed. 1999. *Die Walser-Bubis-Debatte. Eine Dokumentation.* [*The Walser-Bubis Debate. A Documentation.*] Frankfurt am Main, Suhrkamp.

Walser, Martin. 2002. *Tod eines Kritikers.* [*Death of a Critic.*] Frankfurt am Main, Suhrkamp.

Welzer, Harald, Sabine Moller, Karoline Tschuggnall. 2002. *'Opa war kein Nazi'. Nationalsozialismus und Holocaust im Familiengedächtnis.* [*'Grandpa was no Nazi.' National Socialism and the Holocaust in family memory.*] Frankfurt am Main, Fischer.

'Herr Bubis, was haben Sie bewirkt?' ['Mr Bubis, what have you achieved?']. Interview with Ignatz Bubis, *Stern* 31 (1999).

NOTES ON CONTRIBUTORS

Editors

Sandra Lustig (Berlin) was instrumental in organising the *Galut 2000* conference where many of the papers in *Turning the Kaleidoscope* were presented. The daughter of German-Jewish refugees, she was born in the United States and has lived in Germany since her family moved there in 1973. Her Jewish activities include founding and running a Jewish *Stammtisch*, an informal monthly gathering of Jews in Berlin, and leading sessions at the Bet Debora conferences, Limmud, and elsewhere. She is a free-lance consultant and translator, and a Senior Policy Advisor with Ecologic – Institute for International and European Environmental Policy, a not-for-profit think tank she co-founded. She has also taught environmental planning as an Assistant Professor at the Technische Universität Berlin. She holds a *Diplom* in Urban and Regional Planning from the Technische Universität Berlin and a Master's in Public Affairs from the Woodrow Wilson School of Public and International Affairs, Princeton University.

Ian Leveson (Berlin) is a Network Services Manager in IT Services at Deutsche Welle TV in Berlin, where he has lived since 1988. He is co-chair of 'Starbug', the European Users Group for users of Avid Broadcasting and Newsroom Systems. He has been involved in grass-roots Jewish activities in Berlin, including the Jewish Group Berlin (*Jüdische Gruppe Berlin*), the Jewish Cultural Society (*Jüdischer Kulturverein*), the Friends of the Jewish Museum in Berlin, and Meshulash Berlin. He was a founding member of the Egalitarian Synagogue in the Oranienburger Straße, Berlin, and of *Gesher – Forum für Diasporakultur*, and co-initiator of the *Galut 2000* conference. He is currently contributing to *Kol Dor*, examining futures for the Jewish People globally. His research interest is Jewry's adjustment to European integration, economic liberalisation, globalisation and to no longer being Western Europe's only non-Christian minority. One focus is on the Jewish-Muslim relationship in Western societies, on which he has led workshops at the annual British Jewish conference, Limmud, and elsewhere. Born and bred in Scotland, he holds an M.A. (Social Science) in Economic Geography from the University of Edinburgh.

Contributors

Y. Michal Bodemann (Toronto/Berlin) is Professor of Sociology at the University of Toronto and has been a Visiting Professor of Sociology and Anthropology at the Freie Universität Berlin and at the Humboldt-Universität zu Berlin, as well as at Tel Aviv University. He was also a Visiting Fellow at the Moses Mendelssohn Zentrum, University of Potsdam, Germany. Numerous publications on German-Jewish relations and on classical German sociological theory. Among his books are *Jews, Germans, Memory: Reconstructions of Jewish Life in Germany* (Ann Arbor: University of Michigan Press, 1996), *Gedächtnistheater. Die jüdische Gemeinschaft und ihre deutsche Erfindung* (Hamburg: Rotbuch Verlag, 1996), *In den Wogen der Erinnerung. Jüdische Existenz in Deutschland* (Munich: DTV, 2002), and *A Jewish Family in Germany Today. An Intimate Portrait* (Durham, NC: Duke University Press, 2005).

Lara Dämmig (Berlin) studied library science in Berlin and later edited a library science journal. Today she works for a Jewish organisation in Berlin. She was an active member of the East Berlin Jewish Community. In the early 1990s she was instrumental in organising a Rosh Chodesh group and an egalitarian minyan which was a predecessor of the Synagogue Oranienburger Straße. She is a frequent contributor to the magazine *Jüdisches Berlin*, is involved in research on Jewish women's lives in Berlin, and is engaged in interreligious dialogue. She is one of the founders of Bet Debora and was an organiser of the conferences in 1999, 2001, and 2003 as well as co-editor of the *Bet Debora Journals* which document the conferences. She and Elisa Klapheck edited *Bertha Pappenheim – Gebete/ Prayers* (Teetz: Verlag Hentrich & Hentrich, 2003, in German and English).

Lars Dencik (Stockholm), born of Jewish parents from Czechoslovakia who escaped the *Shoah* by finding refuge in Sweden, is Professor of Social Psychology and directs the research program *Social Psychology in a Radicalised Modernity* and the *Centre for Childhood- & Family Research* at Roskilde University, Denmark. He has conducted studies on Jewish life in modern Sweden, Finland and Norway, and is part of an international network of researchers and intellectuals dealing with contemporary European Jewry. He is also a member of the Academic Committee of *Paideia – the European Institute for Jewish Studies* in Stockholm. Among his recent publications are 'Transformation of Identities in Rapidly Changing Societies', in M. Carleheden & M. Jacobsen (eds), '*The Transformation of Modernity*' (London: Ashgate, 2001), and 'Jewishness in Postmodernity: The Case of Sweden', in Z. Gitelman et al. (eds), *New Jewish Identities: Contemporary Europe and Beyond* (Budapest: Central European University Press, 2003).

Michael Galchinsky (Atlanta, GA) is Director of the Program in Jewish Studies and Associate Professor of English at Georgia State University. He is the author of *The Origin of the Modern Jewish Woman Writer* (Detroit: Wayne State University Press, 1996) and editor of *Grace Aguilar: Selected Writings* (Peterborough, CA: Broadview Press, 2003). Along with David Biale and Susannah Heschel, he co-edited *Insider/Outsider: American Jews and Multiculturalism* (Berkeley: University of California Press, 1998). His current project is 'To Dance at Three Weddings: Jews and International Human Rights,' a legal and social history of Jewish human rights activism.

Elisa Klapheck (Berlin) was ordained as a rabbi by the Aleph Rabbinic Program in 2004 and has been rabbi of the community "Beit ha'Chidush" (House of Renewal) in Amsterdam since 2005. Previously, she was editor-in-chief of the magazine *Jüdisches Berlin*. She grew up in Düsseldorf, Germany, and studied political science in Nijmegen (Netherlands) and Hamburg. While working as a journalist for *Der Tagesspiegel*, *Die Tageszeitung*, and a variety of radio and television stations, she studied Jewish Studies in Berlin and was active in renewing Jewish life in Berlin. She was instrumental in founding Bet Debora and was co-director of the Bet Debora conferences. In 1999 she edited a biography and the works of Regina Jonas, the first woman rabbi in the world *Fräulein Rabbiner Jonas. Kann die Frau das rabbinische Amt bekleiden?*, edited and with comments and an introduction by Elisa Klapheck (Teetz: Verlag Hentrich & Hentrich, 1999; in English translation: *Fräulein Rabbiner Jonas. The Story of the First Female Rabbi* [San Francisco: Jossey Bass, 2000]). She and Lara Dämmig edited *Bertha Pappenheim – Gebete/Prayers* (Teetz: Verlag Hentrich & Hentrich, 2003, in German and English). Her newest book is *So bin ich Rabbinerin geworden, Jüdische Herausforderungen hier und jetzt*, [How I became a (Woman) Rabbi, Jewish Challenges Here and Now] (Freiburg: Herder, 2005).

Clive A. Lawton (London) is co-founder and Executive Director of Limmud. He is Chair of Tzedek, the Jewish Third World Aid charity, as well as Chair of North Middlesex University Hospital. He writes for the *London Jewish News*, and is on the faculty of the European Centre for Jewish Leadership – Le'atid, the Melton programme and the School of Oriental and African Studies (SOAS) of London University. He is a Magistrate and advises the Home Office (Interior Ministry) and the police on race equality and diversity matters.

Diana Pinto (Paris) is an intellectual historian and writer. She is a summa cum laude graduate of Harvard University, where she also obtained a Ph.D. in Contemporary European History. Dr Pinto was for many years a Consultant to the Political Directorate of the Council of Europe for its civil society programmes in Eastern Europe and the former Soviet Union. Her interest in the renewal of Jewish life in Europe stems from her interest in pluralist transnational civil societies. She has lectured and written extensively on contemporary Jewish life both in academic and institutional Jewish settings.

Göran Rosenberg (Stockholm) is a Swedish writer and journalist, born in 1948 to Polish-Jewish survivors of the Holocaust. In 1990 he founded the Swedish monthly magazine of essays and opinions *Moderna Tider*, of which he was the editor until 1999. He is a regular columnist and essayist for the Swedish daily newspaper *Dagens Nyheter* and a frequent contributor to Swedish Television. Among his books are *Friare kan ingen vara, an essay on the American idea* (Stockholm: Norstedts, 1991) and *Det förlorade landet, Israel en personlig historia* (Stockholm: Bonniers, 1996), also in Norwegian, Danish, Dutch, German (*Das verlorene Land, Israel eine persönliche Geschichte*, Frankfurt: Suhrkamp Verlag, 1998), and French (*L'utopie perdue, Israël une histoire personelle*, Paris: Denoël, 2002). His most recent book is *Plikten, profiten och konsten att vara människa* (*Duty, Profit and the Art of Being Human*, Stockholm: Bonniers, 2003). His essays have been translated and published in, among others, *Neue Zürcher Zeitung, Lettre International, Daedalus, The New York Times* and *New Perspectives Quarterly*. Göran Rosenberg holds a Ph.D. (hc) from the University of Gothenburg.

INDEX